Journey into Romanesque

Endpapers: Detail from the Romanesque west porch of St Stephen's Cathedral, Vienna.

Frontispiece: Central portion of the tympanum at Moissac depicting the Last Judgement, *c.* 1115.

George Nebolsine

Journey into Romanesque

A Traveller's Guide to Romanesque Monuments in Europe

Edited by Robyn Cooper

Weidenfeld and Nicolson
5 Winsley Street London W1

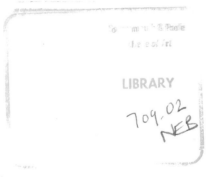

Designed by John Wallis for
George Weidenfeld and Nicolson Ltd, London

SBN 297 17882 2

Phototypeset by BAS Printers Limited, Wallop, Hampshire
Printed and bound by Jarrold and Sons Ltd, Norwich

Contents

I The sources and development of Romanesque Art

II Romanesque Europe

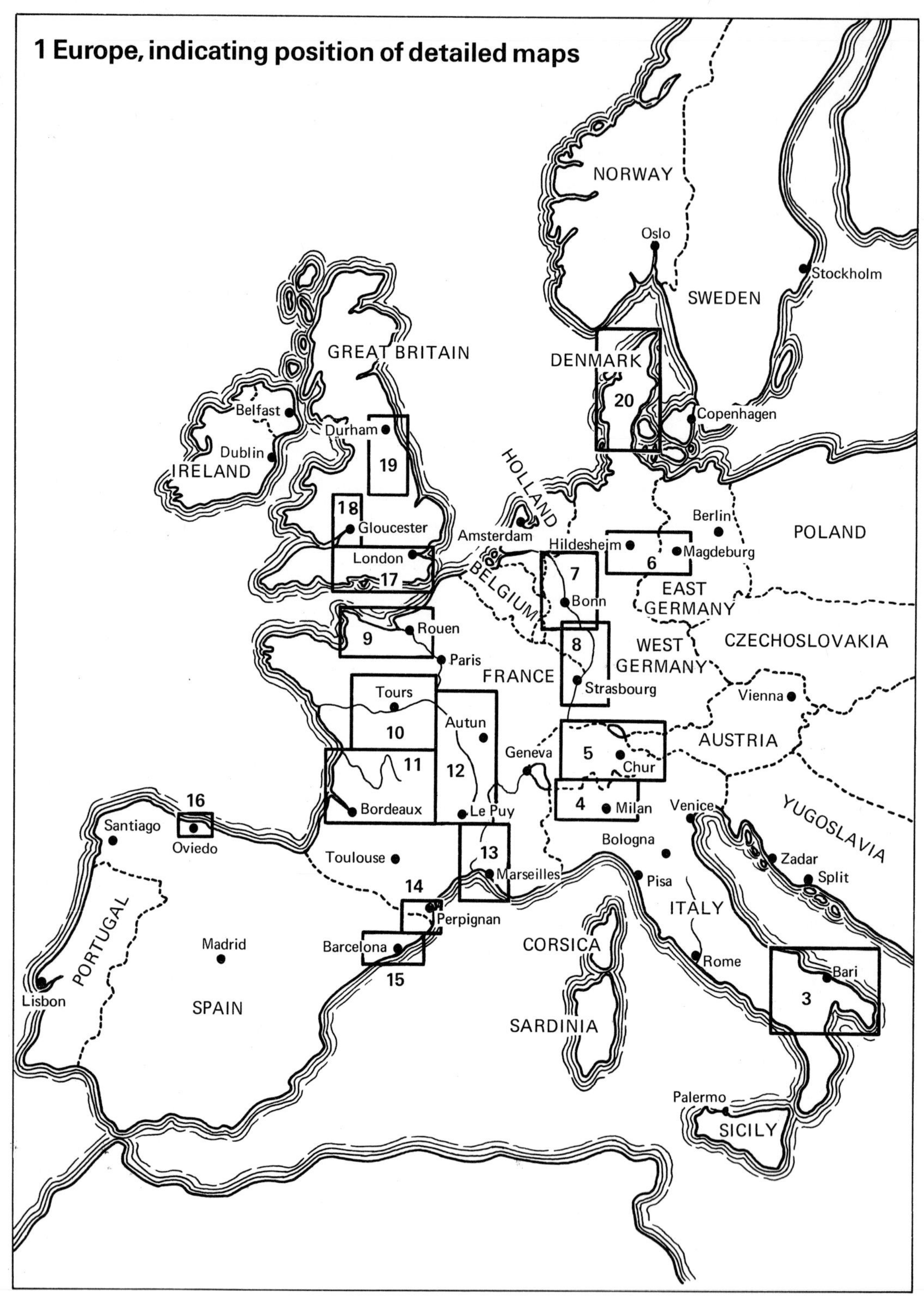

1 Europe, indicating position of detailed maps

Maps

KEY

Motorway

Main road

Secondary road

Photographic Acknowledgements

The author and publishers wish to thank the authorities of the following museums, institutions and libraries for the illustrations on the pages listed below: the Ashmolean Museum, Oxford, 86, 90 (*margin*), 91, 93, 113 (*top*); the British Museum, London, 31, 33, 38, 52; The British Travel Association, London, 235; The Courtauld Institute, London, 24 (*bottom*), 34 (*right*), 41, 45 (*top*), 83, 97, 101, 103 (*top*), 108, 112, 127, 134, 142, 148, 155, 160, 162, 176 (*top*), 192, 197, 216, 219, 221, 223, 224, 228, 237, 239, 241, 242, 243, 245, 252, 256, 258, 260; The Spanish National Tourist Office, London, 227; The Swedish Travel Association, London, 265; Utrecht University Library, 45 (*bottom*); the Victoria and Albert Museum, London, 18, 20, 21, 26, 27, 34 (*left*).

The illustrations on the pages listed below were obtained from the following sources: Alinari-Giraudon, 95; Ampliaciones y Reproduciones Mas, Barcelona, 169, 222; Anderson-Giraudon, 91; Archives Photographiques, Paris, 173 (*left*); Bildarchiv, Marburg, 136, 138, 144; Bildarchiv, Rheinisches Museum, Cologne, 50; Foto Lala Aufsberg, Sonthofen, 151; Mansell Collection, London, 251; Picture Point Limited, London, 35, 80, 81, 92; Reportage Photographique Yan, Toulouse, 200.

The illustrations on the pages listed below were photographed by: James Austin, 88–9; T. Benton, 83; F. H. Crossley, 239; Jean Dieuzaide, 195; Kerry Dundas, 233; André Held, 128, 165, 211, 212, 213, 263; Charles Manning, 87, 90, 98, 100; Ursula Pariser, 127; Jean Roubier, 94; Edwin Smith, 246, 247; C. G. Zarnecki, 241, 242.

All other illustrations are from the private collection of the author.

Preface

Romanesque art is the art of the epic age of our civilization, of the period of the formation of the European languages, literature and poetry, and the setting down in writing of the legends of King Arthur, Parcival, Tristan and Isolde, Lohengrin, Galahad, Charlemagne, Roland, Barbarossa and El Cid. It is the art of the age of faith and the great Crusades. The first martial architecture since Rome was Romanesque. The finest abbeys and the first great cathedrals, with their lavish, ecstatic compositions in stone, paint and glass, are Romanesque.

The name 'Romanesque' is in some ways a misnomer. It was wished upon the style by those who despised it and wanted to demean it. In England it was called 'Norman', but this regional characterization is scarcely more flattering. For a long time 'Lombard' was the standard word for Romanesque, again a regional name. Each of the regions of France – Burgundy, Languedoc, Poitou – has given its name to a 'school' of Romanesque sculpture and architecture, and French scholars delight in finding distinctions amongst them.

Although these differences are real, the significant factor of Romanesque, with all deference to great authorities, lies not in its infinite diversity but in its essential unity. The unity of Romanesque is of the spirit and its inner meaning and significance. The external expression varies with time and with place, but it never loses this essential unity. Indeed, the style gave Europe an aesthetic unity to match the spiritual unity, the oneness under God which came near to being realized in the 11th century. Romanesque created a common language of art from Yugoslavia to Portugal, from the coasts of the Mediterranean to the fiords of Scandinavia. It was carried to the remotest hamlets of Europe and to the Holy Land.

In this extraordinary development no single artist or architect stands out. Moreover no single structure, sculpture or painting symbolizes the style. It is subtle; it has great flexibility and vitality, constantly producing fresh effects and attempting daring experiments.

The language of Romanesque art is basically different from that of classical art. It sought to portray not the outer man but the inner spirit. The spirit is its guiding light and human form is subordinate to this. To gesture and emotion it is kin, to perspective, proportion and symmetry almost a stranger. Because of its peculiarities Romanesque art had many detractors. Only a little over a hundred years ago, Romanesque sculpture was destroyed to be used as building blocks.

Romanesque architecture represents the evolution of early Christian building. In the south of Europe the process was one of continuation, in the north, recovery. It was out of the fusion of these two traditions that Romanesque architecture was born. It entered a period of brilliant development in the Rhineland in the first half of the 11th century, and in Normandy and Burgundy in the second half, from there spreading throughout Europe.

In the plastic arts there emerged around 1000 a number of 'schools' or ateliers of metalworkers. It was not until a century later, particularly in France, that large-scale stone sculpture was used in decorating the great doorways and column capitals of churches. Manuscript painting, having earlier reached its zenith of quality, inspired both sculptors and mural painters. Mural art developed parallel with large-scale sculpture. The goldsmith's art, even before 1000, reached the highest standards of perfection in Hildesheim and spread thence to the area of Cologne and the River Meuse. Shortly after 1100, stained glass, some of the best ever made, was first produced for Chartres. European literature, poetry and music has its birth at the height of this artistic activity and coincides with the close of pre-national Europe and the beginning of nationalism in art as well as politics.

To understand Romanesque it is necessary to study its forerunners, to find the derivations of the style and compare it with the styles it superseded. There is no doubt that three styles, or rather, points of view were intermingled – the Roman, Byzantine and Barbarian. Scholars have also found a number of other influences: Syrian, Armenian, Coptic, Sassanian, the ancient Eastern cultures of the Euphrates valley, and of even India. The family tree of Romanesque has grown appallingly complex. Coupled with the paucity of art products and analysable data from such remote times, speculation and conjecture have taken the place of clearly established fact. Without becoming too involved in the resulting sharp differences of opinion between scholars, we shall attempt to convey something of the intensely interesting nature of the search for the sources of Romanesque art.

Therefore to appreciate Romanesque one should know its forerunners and origins, one should see many examples of it in many lands, study photographs and plans of buildings as well as reproductions of murals and miniatures, church treasures, details of buildings, and even fragments of stone decorations. Romanesque requires also a contribution from its audience. Without this contribution and an internal adjustment to the art's language, one cannot know it. It is in a spirit of eager enquiry and sympathy that this work of personal, rather than scientific, evaluation is written.

Editor's note. It was unfortunate that George Nebolsine died before the completion of his manuscript. My task has been to prepare it for publication. In so doing I have tried to finish the work in the spirit in which it was conceived. The book has been divided into two parts. The first is a general introduction to the origin and development of Romanesque. The second is in the nature of a practical guide to the most interesting of surviving monuments and works of art.

Part I

The sources and development of Romanesque Art

1 Early Christian Art in the West, and the Antique Tradition

Christianity was born in an eastern province of the Roman Empire, it spread rapidly to the West along the great sea and land routes, and in 313 won official recognition when Constantine, for reasons of state rather than promptings of conscience, published his Edicts of Toleration from Milan. At a later date, Christianity was elevated to the status of religion of the Empire. Its early history is thus integrally bound up with late Imperial history and its art is part of the larger whole of late antique art. This was an art which, though decaying, was far from decadent. It was also far from homogeneous reflecting, as it did, the tastes and traditions of the diverse races within the borders of the Empire. At the same time Roman culture preserved a certain unity through the interaction of the different styles.

In this section we shall concentrate on the early Christian art of the Latin West, leaving aside for the moment Byzantium (as the Roman Empire in the East, officially established in 395, came to be known) and the eastern provinces, such as Syria and Egypt. But it should be emphasized that this division is fairly artificial, and it was not until the end of the 5th century, when the death certificate of the old Roman Empire was finally signed and sealed, that the various artistic tendencies crystallized into separate styles – 'Byzantine', 'Coptic', 'Syrian'. The last two came to a sudden end with the Arab invasion of the 7th century, but the first flourished throughout the whole of the Middle Ages. It is worth noting that Arab civilization was also indebted to Rome.

Another important fact needs emphasizing, and that is that the decline of the Graeco-Roman aesthetic had begun before the official recognition of Christianity, which only hastened a tendency already apparent. The movement away from a purely representational art towards one which was more stylized, abstract and expressionistic was the result of the influence of the art of the provinces over that of the metropolis. This art shows qualities which are found in provincial art of any time and in any place; preference for flat, bright colours; disregard of space and the modelling of figures; frontal poses; and the concentration on expressive gesture. But in the eastern provinces this approach reflected also the cultural legacy of ancient Mesopotamia as well as the influence of the sophisticated art of Sassanian Persia.

This popular art began invading art at official levels in about the 3rd century, at a time when provincials were playing an increasingly important role in the administration of the Empire. The taste for it was part of a reaction against the physical world and a search for a supra-terrestial meaning to life. The rise of Christianity, only one of the many mystical religions which flourished towards the close of the antique world, was symptomatic of this same reaction. Not surprisingly, the new style suited most effectively the transcendentalism of the Christian faith and had a decisive influence on the formation of the Christian aesthetic.

At the same time the Graeco-Roman tradition survived in other late antique styles – the revivalist 'Neo-Attic', the impressionistic and picturesque 'Alexandrian' with its interest in architectural and landscape settings, and the more prosaic, narrative style associated with Rome – and these, too, had an influence on Christian art in its formative stage.

Before the Peace of the Church, Christian art was naturally limited in its expression by the discrimination against the new religion, punctuated by outbursts of persecution. It was therefore a discreet art. It was also a humble art, since most of the first Christians came from the poorer classes. The earliest places of worship were simply rooms set aside in a private house or, occasionally, a whole house.* These were decorated with frescoes, such as those from the house-church at Dura-Europos, on the Euphrates (now in the Yale University Gallery). The most important and extensive fresco remains, however, are in the Roman catacombs, which were the subterranean burial grounds of the early Christians.

Stylistically these paintings reflect the diverse traditions of late antique art. Their general theme is Redemption usually represented symbolically, partly because of the need for discretion, partly because of the profound sense of the mysteries of the faith. Many images which became part of the common symbolic vocabulary of Christian art originate at this time, such as the Chi-Ro monogram, the peacock and the vine-scroll.

The resources of pagan art were freely drawn upon and so close is this early dependence that it is not always easy to determine whether a work is pagan or indeed Christian. Many Christian 'types' were established at this time, though some were not particularized until the 4th century. Thus winged Victories became angels, the seated philosopher became standard for an Apostle. The pose of 'orants' with arms outspread in the Roman attitude of prayer was later very common in the depiction of saints. On the other hand the various representations of Christ, as the Good Shepherd, Orpheus, Apollo

* There is also documentary evidence that more ambitious, though still unpretentious, structures were built, but nothing remains of these.

and Dionysius – always beardless and youthful – did not survive the early Christian period. The range of biblical scenes is limited and most of these are from the Old Testament, perhaps because the actual circumstances of Christ's life did not lend themselves to symbolic representation.

Apart from the Good Shepherd statues, of which a number have survived, pre-Constantinian sculpture was confined to sarchophagi reliefs. Like paintings they show a close dependence on pagan motifs, while the biblical subjects illustrated are even more limited. These first expressions of Christian art in fresco and marble, though humble, restricted and seldom of high artistic quality, are of great importance for they established the patterns which religious art was to follow for centuries to come.

The recognition and legalization of Christianity brought the power and wealth of the Empire into the service of its art. The result was most sudden and dramatic in architecture. It became necessary to erect large and imposing churches to house congregations and commemorate holy sites and tombs. The pagan temple was not a suitable model since it was designed to contain the sacred image, not a host of people. A prototype was found in basilicas, large meeting halls of many uses. The Christian basilica did not derive from any specific type but was a new creation within a traditional framework. The 4th century was a time of experimentation and it was not until the 5th century that the standard basilica of the Latin West developed. This consisted of an oblong wooden-roofed hall divided into nave and side aisles by two, sometimes four, rows of columns surmounted by an arcade. Light came through clerestory windows above the nave. At the eastern end was an apse covered by a semi-circular dome, at the west an atrium which later lost popularity and gave way to a single portico. In contrast to the richly-worked interior, the exterior was very plain.

A second church type was centralized with a square, circular or polygonal plan covered by a vault or tent-shaped wooden roof. This functioned as a martyrium, housing the relics of saints or commemorating the sites especially associated with Christ and His Apostles, and as a baptistery, since the baptism by full immersion practised at the time required special facilities. The origin of these buildings lay in pre-Constantinian architecture in Italy (such as the *heroa* and tombs along the Appian Way) and the Aegean coastlands. The most famous of all martyria was the Holy Sepulchre in Jerusalem, a Constantinian foundation rebuilt in the 7th and 11th centuries. In the Middle Ages it inspired a number of smaller 'Holy Sepulchres' scattered all over Europe from Brindisi in Italy to London. The octagonal-shaped standard Latin baptistery appeared in the 5th century, but though the type continued to be built in Italy throughout the Middle Ages, it fell into disuse in northern Europe.

In addition to these types, a group of churches built in the 4th century during the period of experimentation must also be considered. Although they had little immediate influence they played an important part in the develop-

ment of the architecture of the West. These churches attempted to combine the functions of basilica and martyrium under one roof. The earliest solution to this problem was St Peter's, Rome (replaced in the 16th century by Michelangelo's Renaissance structure). It was a five-aisled basilica with a continuous transept to provide a suitable setting for the tomb of the Saint and facilitate the movement of the faithful around the shrine. Its only immediate successor was S. Paolo fuori le mura. The Church of the Nativity at Bethlehem, another Constantinian foundation, was a basilica with an attached octagon, replaced by a trefoil sanctuary in the 6th century. At Milan an important political and religious centre in the 4th century, S. Simpliciano used a cross-plan (derived from the Apostoleion in Constantinople) – yet another solution to the problem. It is one of the five early basilicas of this city which still survives, incorporated into a Romanesque church. North of the Alps the Imperial cities of Trier and Cologne were also well-endowed with churches, and another example of the composite martyrium-basilica was the Imperial basilica of Trier which copied S. Simpliciano.

The effect of the Peace of the Church on the decorative and pictorial arts was less sudden and startling than on architecture. But there were changes. The scope of church art was considerably widened by new needs and the new wealth at its disposal. The interiors were decorated with wall paintings and mosaics. The floors were paved with stone flags or marble and inlaid mosaic work, known as *Opus Alexandrinum* (from which Roman 12th- and 13th-century Cosmatesque work derived). The art of manuscript illumination, secular and religious, developed in about the 5th century, although none of the earliest works survive except in later copies. Another important field for the artist was carved ivory work, used for reliquary boxes, private devotional panels and consular diptyches.

On the other hand, one notable disappearance from Christian art was sculpture in the round. The reasons for this are not clear. Perhaps it was because of the association of statuary with pagan image worship, particularly the Emperor cult, in defiance of which so many of the first Christians had suffered martyrdom. It was succeeded by relief work in stone, ivory and wood. An important survival of the last are the 5th-century wooden doors of S. Sabina, Rome.

Another change was the expansion of iconographical themes, particularly of scenes illustrating the New Testament. To a large extent symbolic representation yielded to narrative, and events which were once referred to indirectly were now explicitly described, the most important being the Crucifixion. The system of placing Old and New Testament scenes side by side in a complementary fashion developed, as we see with the mosaics in the nave of S. Maria Maggiore, the doors of S. Sabina, and on sarcophagi in superimposed zones. This theme of the mystical correspondence of the two Testaments was revived in the Middle Ages.

The early Church functioned as a school as well as a place of worship. The

Opposite
Consular diptych of Rufus Gennadius Probus Orestes, Consul at Rome, 530. London, Victoria and Albert Museum.

Leaf of an ivory diptych. Roman, late 4th century. London, Victoria and Albert Museum.

Leaf of the consular diptych of Flavius Anastasius. Constantinople, 517. London, Victoria and Albert Museum.

Adam and Eve from the sarcophagus of Junius Bassus.
4th century. Rome, The Vatican.

illiterates were taught bible lessons through story-telling paintings. Graeco-Roman painting offered no didactic precedents. However this characteristic form of visual education has an affinity with the propagandist story-telling reliefs on Imperial monuments, like Trajan's Column and the Arch of Constantine.

Christian art at this time owed a good deal to Imperial art, particularly for the themes of triumph which emerged. Christ in Majesty and ceremonies of coronation were the translation into a Christian context of Imperial iconography. The new monumental expression which Christian art developed, also largely derived from Imperial traditions. The most obvious example of this development was the appearance of the mature, bearded Christ, who gradually replaced the earlier youthful type.

The early Christian period in the West came to an end with the final collapse of the Roman Empire in 476. The political power of the Italian peninsula declined catastrophically and Rome became a provincial backwater. Yet its traditions were maintained in Italy, albeit in a weakened and decayed form, and the cultural history of the peninsula was one of continuous, uninterrupted development.

Beyond Italy, antique influences remained strongest in lands where Roman domination had a long history – Spain and southern France. Elsewhere Rome faded to a memory kept alive by the vast monuments which survived and by pilgrimages to the Eternal City. But the memory was strong, as shown by the Carolingian and Ottonian revivals in the 8th and 10th centuries, when the Empire of the West and its cultural traditions were resurrected.

Roman building methods were not entirely lost and mediaeval architecture evolved out of the early Christian building experiments. The mediaeval church was descended from the Roman basilica. But this statement, once made, must be qualified if, by basilica, we mean the standard 5th-century basilica of the Latin West. In the first place Western architecture in the 6th century was invaded by building types native to the eastern provinces. In the second place, some of the most influential of early Christian churches, such as St Peter's, were not typical. They attracted mediaeval builders, not only because of their obvious religious associations, but also because they pointed the way to the solution of the problem of housing relics and worshippers under one roof. It was the scale, as much as anything else, of Imperial secular and religious monuments, which caught the imagination of the mediaeval architect and inspired him to emulate and surpass the grandeur of these earlier achievements.

Mediaeval art was also indebted to late antiquity. It borrowed its decorative motifs and forms, like the Corinthian capital, rosettes, the inhabited vine scroll (of eastern provenance but adopted in the West in the 4th century), the acanthus leaf and the perspective zig-zag. Mediaeval religious iconography developed from early Christian, though by the Romanesque period the range of subjects treated had expanded considerably. It also adopted many of those pagan types which had been christianized. Various forms of artistic expression in the Middle Ages, such as ivory carvings, cast bronze reliefs, or manuscript and mural paintings stem from late antiquity, whether as part of a continuous progress, or the result of efforts of recovery. The revival of sculpture in the 12th century was assisted by the rediscovery of the drill, a late antique innovation, and by the study of sarcophagi reliefs and the carvings on triumphal arches. Lastly, both the Carolingian and Ottonian styles were influenced by the early Christian and through this they absorbed a certain amount of the Graeco-Roman tradition. The dynamic energy of Romanesque art, on the other hand, is a long way from the serenity of the classical aesthetic, although there are a few works which show classicizing tendencies, like the bronze font of Rainier of Huy at Liège, or the sculptured portals at Arles and St-Gilles-du-Gard in Provence.

Corinthian capital in the porch of St-Benoît-sur-Loire, France.

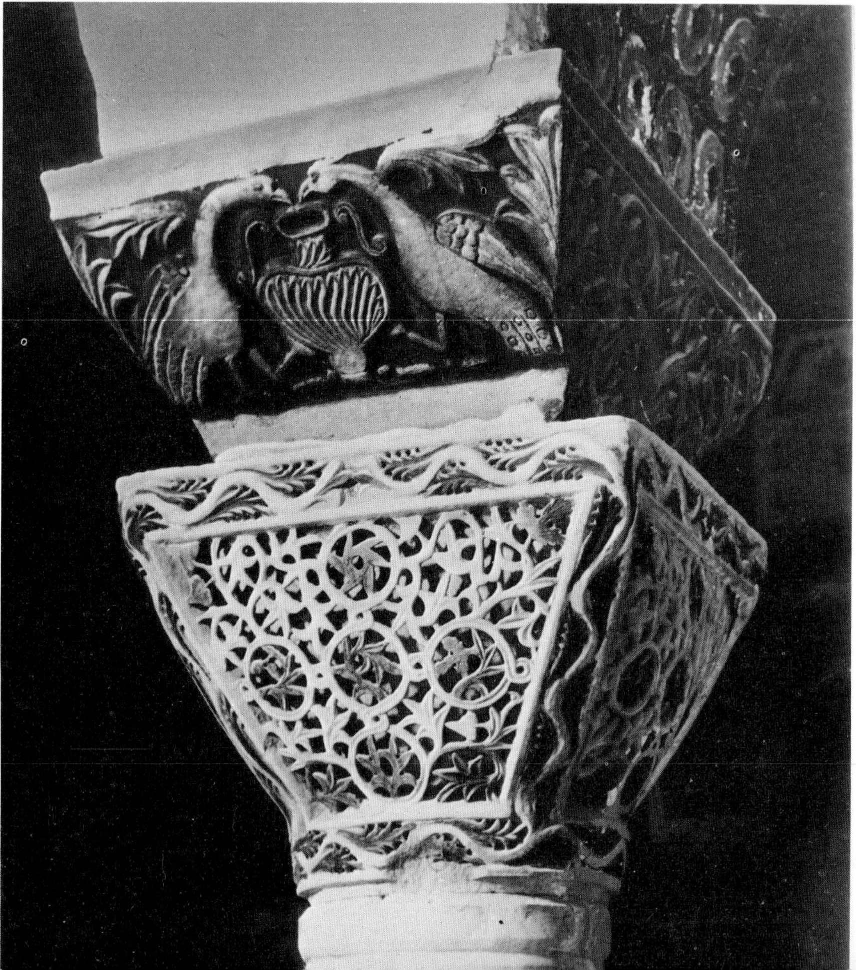

Capital from S. Vitale, *c.* 530. Ravenna, Italy.

2 Byzantium and the West

In 330 Constantine, for strategic, political and religious reasons, transferred the capital of the Empire to the shores of the Bosphorus and founded a 'New Rome' which came to be known as Constantinople. Of Constantine's city nothing remains, the most ancient surviving monuments being the great walls built between 413 and 447, which protected the city for a thousand years. At first only one, though politically the most important, of the many Imperial cities, Constantinople became the great metropolis of the Christian world. Barbarian invasions reduced the cities of the West to the status of provincial towns while the cities of the eastern Mediterranean were lost to Islam.

In 395 the Roman Empire, for purposes of administration, was split into two. The split developed into a schism. The Empire in the West broke up into a number of separate barbarian kingdoms, but the Empire in the East managed to preserve its existence for over a thousand years. Although it inherited the legal and administrative traditions of the old Empire and called itself the 'Roman Empire', Byzantium was Roman in name only. Its culture was rooted in late antiquity but it evolved in a way very different from that of western Europe, and its art represents the fusion of Hellenism and the Orient.

The former bequeathed its technical skills, ornamental types, and above all its humanistic values and elegant tastes. At no time was a Byzantine artist not capable of imitating the classical antique and at certain times, as in the West, there were antique revivals. The beginnings of the incursion of the expressionist, abstract style of the eastern provinces go back to the late Imperial period, as we have seen, and its influence on Byzantine art is simply a continuation of this tendency. But Constantinople was nearer the source and the penetration was deeper. It was also open to direct influences emanating from states beyond the eastern frontiers of the old Empire: Sassanian Persia and (with serious reservations) Armenia. After the Arab conquests in Asia Minor, Byzantine art reflected some degree of influence from this quarter as well.

Textile fragment (silk) showing the combat of a hero and a lion. Byzantine or Near Eastern, 8th–9th century. London, Victoria and Albert Museum.

It was not until the 'golden age' of Justinian in the 6th century that an art which can be properly distinguished as 'Byzantine' emerged. Its architecture was distinguished by the use of the dome. The exact source of dome construction is shrouded in mystery. It is clear that it was in use throughout the Mediterranean world but it was probably in the East that the solution to the crucial problem of building a dome over a square was found, with squinches or pendentives effecting the transition. The dome was used in many forms – the single dome, as at Sts Sergius and Bacchus, the multiple domes, as in the now destroyed church of the Holy Apostles, and the buttressed compound dome as at St Sophia. This central feature was accompanied by a symmetrical, round, polygonal or cruciform plan. Strangely enough Justinian's St Sophia, most marvellous and beautiful of all Byzantine structures and one of the great monuments of Christian architecture, did not inspire copies. The standard Byzantine church had a Greek cross or cross-in-square plan.

The sumptuousness of Byzantine art was most superbly expressed in the brilliantly coloured mosaics, with their glittering gold background, which

Ivory panel, probably from a book cover, showing the Ascension.
Byzantine, first half of 11th century. London, Victoria and Albert Museum.

covered the walls of churches. The individual tesserae are placed with great subtlety and the scenes as a whole are cleverly related to their architectural framework. Frescoes and manuscript paintings were also brilliantly coloured. Illuminations were often painted onto pages of purple-tinted vellum, as in the late 5th- or early 6th-century Sinopensis, the Codex Rossano and the Codex of Genesis. Carving on capitals and cornices was deeply undercut and the effect is like fine lace-work. Magnificent textiles with highly orientalized patterns such as confronted animals were woven in Imperial workshops. Metalwork was covered with bright enamels and precious stones. Byzantine artists maintained the tradition of ivory carving, lost for a time in the West.

The history of Byzantine contact with the West begins with Justinian's conquests in Italy in the 6th century. He might have seen himself as restoring to the Empire territory lost to the barbarians, but to the population of the peninsula the deliverers were invaders – a measure of the gulf that had already grown up between the Greek and Latin worlds. Rome came under the tutelage of Greek and Syrian governors and Popes and Greek monasteries were established. The 6th-century mosaics in Roman churches were in the Byzantine manner. Ravenna, conquered in 539 and the seat of the Byzantine exarchs until the Longobard invasion, was thoroughly Byzantine in its art and a source of Byzantine influence in the West. It is possible, for example, that the immediate origin of the blind arcading which decorated the exterior walls of early and mature Romanesque churches was Ravennate building – the Mausoleum of Galla Placidia and S. Apollinare in Classe have this feature. Although Byzantine political domination did not last much beyond the 7th century, the Italian peninsula remained an important centre for the dissemination of Byzantine culture right through the Middle Ages.

Over the next two centuries, sometimes referred to as the 'Dark Ages', Byzantium exercized a political and cultural power far greater than that of any European kingdom. To the West it presented an image of political stability, greatly to be envied, of a sophistication and refinement to be imitated, and a level of culture to be emulated. Visitors to the capital, a centre of pilgrimage since the transference of the True Cross from the Holy Land, which had fallen to the Arabs, brought back treasures to be copied and translated into other media in monasteries as far distant as England. Diplomats bore away with them elaborate Imperial presents to their rulers. The naïve wonder of the Western visitor is apparent in the reaction of one pilgrim who said of St Sophia: 'The human mind can neither tell it nor make description of it.'

There was also movement in the other direction. Greek and Syrian traders maintained a steady traffic between the Mediterranean and central as well as northern Europe. Their trade across the Rhône into Merovingian France and across the Alps to central Europe, the Low Countries and Saxon England brought articles of luxury – textiles, jewellery, ivories and probably manuscripts to remote areas. The Near Eastern coins and small objects found all over Europe indicate that the traffic was considerable.

There is also evidence of the emigration of Greek craftsmen to the West at certain times. During the Iconoclast period (725–843), when the pictorial arts were severely limited by the ban on the use of religious images, artists came in search of work, particularly to nearby Italy.

The Emperor Charlemagne also appears to have had Greek artists working for him. Certainly architecture, ivory carving, manuscript and mural painting, and mosaics (of which only one tiny example in the Oratory of Theodulf at Germigny-des-Prés survives) from the period reflect Byzantine as well as influences, from late Antiquity.

In the 10th century the impact of Byzantium reached a climax in western Europe when Otto II of Germany married the Byzantine princess Theophano in 972. The Imperial court eagerly emulated the legendary refinement and luxury of Byzantium.* From the Carolingian Empire and its Ottonian successor these influences spread through northern Europe. The angel reliefs

* The Ottonian period coincided with the Macedonian Renaissance, the finest flowering of Byzantine culture.

of the 10th century in the church at Bradford-on-Avon, for example, derive from this source.

The latter part of the 11th and the 12th centuries saw yet another wave of Byzantine culture in the West. This was the age of great Crusades. One of the routes to the Holy Land passed through Constantinople, and in the wake of the liberating soldiers came pilgrims. The Crusades were also largely responsible for the rise of the Italian commercial cities which were ports of embarkation. Venice, Pisa and Lucca maintained close trading relations with Byzantium and these contacts affected their art and architecture. Venice on the Adriatic coast was most profoundly influenced. The church of S. Marco was modelled on the 6th-century church of the Holy Apostles in Constantinople, and was decorated with mosaics. In the Romanesque period only those areas directly influenced by Byzantium, such as Venice, Rome and Sicily, used this technique for wall decoration.

The Popes in Rome drew upon Byzantine religious and political art in the cultural rehabilitation of the centre of Western Christendom. Further to the south, Abbot Desiderius of the Benedictine monastery of Monte Cassino, employed Greek craftsmen in the embellishment of his church. Apulia has a group of domed churches of a Byzantine type, while art and architecture in Sicily shows many Byzantine features.

It was in the field of monumental painting that these influences were most important. Late Byzantine mosaics and paintings are permeated with humanistic and naturalistic qualities. The fusion of this art with the dynamic, though crude, traditions of native Italian painting opened the way to the early Renaissance.

From Italy Byzantine influences spread north of the Alps meeting up with and reinforcing characteristics emanating from Ottonian Germany. This is apparent in a number of the surviving mural paintings in northern European churches, particularly those associated with the Order of Cluny. In manuscript painting Byzantine influence is most apparent in the works coming from Winchester, particularly the Winchester Bible of the mid-12th century. The dynamic fervour of Romanesque was modified by the serene elegance of Byzantine art which had a decisive influence on the formation of the Gothic style.

In the south-west of France are a group of domed churches of Eastern inspiration. St-Front at Périgueux appears to have been copied from S. Marco, Venice. In Romanesque sculpture one occasionally finds carved lace-like capitals of Byzantine origin, such as the eagle capitals from Cluny or the capitals in the cloister of the cathedral of Le Puy. The rich harvest of Byzantine influence can also be seen in the stylized elongated statues of Chartres, the sculpture of Burgundy and southern France, and the marvellous bronze and enamel work of the Meuse. All these works adopted the Byzantine conventions and costumes in depicting Christ, the Virgin Mary, the Evangelists, the great scene of Christ in Glory, the Last Judgement and many other religious scenes.

3 Eastern Influences

Scholarly controversies have raged in the past about the question of Eastern influences on Christian art. A short while ago, even the influence of Byzantium was discounted and the influence of other Eastern regions virtually ignored. Then, under the influence of writings by such scholars as de Vogue, and Strzygowski, the Eastern question was posed in its extreme form: was not virtually all of Romanesque art an importation from Armenia, Syria and Coptic Egypt?

In support of the Easterners there are some unanswerable facts. Asia Minor, notably Armenia and Syria, were Christian before Rome. Not only the Greek cities of the coastal area, but also the rural interior, were converted and organized into bishoprics before the conversion of Constantine. There were Christians in Armenia in the 2nd century and as early as 300 Christianity was adopted as the state religion of the Armenian kingdom. Georgia in the Caucasus was Christianized in the 4th century.

The churches built at this early time, and their decoration, were strongly influenced by preceding Eastern cultures: Persian art, Buddhist art, and the art of the Euphrates and Nile valleys all played a part.

The controversy has died down somewhat in recent years. The recognition of the overall unity of the world of late antiquity has rendered somewhat specious the idea of an East-West division, while mere superficial resemblance between buildings perhaps a thousand miles apart is no longer considered proof of influence, whether direct or indirect. These observations apply especially to architecture. This does not mean that particular features characteristic of Eastern building did not penetrate the West. But the East can no longer be considered as the fountain-head of Romanesque architecture.

The arguments for the orientalization of Western culture are much more valid when applied to the decorative arts and Christian iconography. As we have already stated, the breakdown of the Graeco-Roman aesthetic was in

Opposite
Panel from the centre of a large composite Nativity, showing the adoration of the Nativity. Probably Syrian, 6th century. London, British Museum.

part due to the increasing influence of the ideas and art of the eastern provinces, which at the time were themselves being 'orientalized' by a reversion to their own native cultural traditions under the impact of Sassanian Persia.

In the early formative years of Christian art, Sassanian culture was at its height. Under the Sassanian dynasty in Persia, Nestorian Christianity, which was suppressed in Byzantium as a heresy, enjoyed a large measure of tolerance. Nestorians sent missionaries into Turkestan and China. Monuments have been found, dated in the 8th century, showing Christian penetration.

Surviving monuments of Sassanian culture resemble Romanesque architecture and decoration. Ruins of three palaces in the Euphrates valley at Sarvistan (350), Firuzabad (450) and Ctesiphon (550) show the three-fold arched entrance, as in the mediaeval cathedral, and employ multiple domes, as at S. Marco, Venice and St Front, Périgueux. They also use barrel vaults and have blank arcading as a decorative motif. But since barrel vaulting was a technique extensively used by the Romans, and blank arcading appears also on Roman buildings, it is highly unlikely that Sassanian architecture exerted any influence on Western mediaeval building. On the other hand it appears that the use of the squinch to support the dome was a Sassanian invention. This was adopted by the Arabs and from them entered the West.

Much more important are the Persian textiles which reached the West via Byzantium, either direct or copied, or via copies made in Coptic Egypt. The motifs include confronted beasts, fantastic animals and horsemen in pairs. The textiles were easily transportable and these Persian motifs reappear in European painting and carving.

The church building of the eastern provinces of the Empire was more varied than in the West. From the 6th century, and increasingly during the 7th and 8th centuries, Europe was invaded by church types native to these regions, particularly the Aegean coastlands and the hinterlands of Asia Minor, Anatolia and Syria. Thus we find basilicas with galleries over the aisles, basilicas with three apses, small cross churches often with 'dwarf' transepts and aisleless churches with barrel vaults. The use of towers, singly or in pairs, may also derive from these sources.

The exteriors of early Syrian churches had articulated architectural decorations. The apses are decorated with round arched windows, purely decorative blank arcading is used in combination with decorative pilasters on external walls, the apses have decorated columns on each side. We find these features on the exterior of Romanesque churches, although this does not necessarily mean that their origin was solely Syrian. The rosette, to be seen frequently in Romanesque, is extensively used here.

The Syrians, who were the most highly endowed of the Semitic people of the time, were also great traders and spread their Christian art and symbolism to remote parts of Europe, particularly to the Rhône valley where there were Syrian settlements.

Limestone lintel or architrave, showing St Pakene and St Victor on horseback.
From Sohag, Egypt. 8th–9th century. London, British Museum.

They were the chief inheritors of the old Assyrian and Babylonian traditions. It is readily noted in Syrian art that Christ is no longer the carpenter's son of Nazareth or the Good Shepherd, but the Lord of All, in accordance with the ancient Semitic idea of the divine as something awesome and awe-inspiring. Perhaps the most copied of all Syrian scenes is the formula for Christ's Ascension, which represents Christ seated in an oval borne by four angels. This is repeated frequently in Romanesque tympana. Another scene of Syrian origin is that of the Nativity with the Virgin reclining after her ordeal. A very interesting ancient Babylonian iconographical type which entered Christian art was Gilgamesh, revered as a Chaldean Hercules, strangling two lions. In classical art this became Hercules, and entered Christian art in the guise of Daniel in the lions' den. Certain decorative features are also transmitted to the West: the vine-scroll enclosing beasts and birds, so common in Romanesque manuscripts and sculpture, the Tree of Life symbol, double-headed eagles, winged sphinxes, beasts devouring each other, and birds with interlacing necks.

The art of the early Christians in Egypt is called 'Coptic'. This art spread to the West with monasticism. Through this contact many Coptic traits were brought into Western art. According to some scholars this art is inspired by superstition, obsessed by sex, and infantile. This harsh judgement is not shared by many other students of the subject. There is a kinship between Coptic and Syrian art. Their painting and decoration were emulated in Western Europe. Taken from illuminations of manuscripts, they were reproduced in all manner of art media: sculpture, mural painting, stained glass, goldsmith work and general decorative design.

One important contribution of Syria and Coptic Egypt to the West, which should be mentioned, is monasticism which originated there. Monasteries existed before the Christian era in the Near East and Egypt, where the

Left : Coptic textile fragment (linen-wool) showing a winged victory. 5th century. London, Victoria and Albert Museum.
Right : Exterior view of the Cathedral of Ani, Turkey. 10th century.

institution had probably been introduced from Buddhist India. Monastic life was first introduced to Europe in the 4th century, but found its permanent establishment at Monte Cassino in the 6th century. However, Western monasticism differed from its Eastern predecessor in an important respect. The latter followed the eremetic system, that is, hermit settlements sometimes loosely connected. This was adopted in Ireland, but elsewhere the cenobotic system, that is groups bound by common laws, was followed.

As well as Sassanian Persia, Syria and Coptic Egypt, Armenia on the eastern borders of the Empire often comes into discussions on the Eastern sources of Western mediaeval art. Its architectural genius is undeniable, surviving buildings and numerous ruins demonstrate the amazing grasp of building techniques by the Armenians. Armenian buildings of the 10th and 11th centuries resemble Romanesque churches in the use of blind arcades and the lavish sculptural decoration. But the resemblance is probably due to the parallel development of the two civilizations rather than direct Armenian influence. On the other hand it would be foolish to deny that Armenian architecture could occasionally exert an impact on Western and, above all, Byzantine building.

Opposite
The Dome on the Rock, Jerusalem. Built in 691 and constantly undergoing reconstruction.

The quest for Eastern sources has taken enthusiasts to China and India. The silk trade was the basis of the West's contact throughout the early centuries of our era with these distant lands. Records at Sinai show a visit there by a monk from India. But it could only be in 'translation' by Copts, Syrians and Byzantine craftsmen that Oriental art reached and took effect in

Ireland, France and Italy. We know of no direct contact of the Orient with the West.

One possible example of this 'translation' is the decorated tympanum which became universal in France and Spain from the beginning of the 12th century. Previously this form of decoration was unknown in Europe. The immediate precedents are sometimes found in Egypt and Armenia and date from between the 5th and 7th centuries. Preceding these are the sculptured tympana of India, such as Buddhist sculpture showing Buddha surrounded by smaller figures carved in a semicircular decorated frame, dating from 100 BC

Not only may the whole idea of a sculptured doorway with a sculptured tympanum have come from the Near East, but the themes that are carved in the semicircle have been traced to the manuscript illuminations of Coptic origin. It has been argued that the decoration of abbeys in the 12th century underwent a profound 'orientalization', which was the conscious borrowing of sophisticated decorative motifs from the East for the embellishment of new abbeys and churches under construction on the pilgrimage routes to Compostela.

Finally a few words must be said about the influence of early Arab art. Islamic influence dates from the conquests of North Africa, Palestine and a large area of Asia Minor in the 7th century; Spain and Armenia in the 8th century; the south coast of France, Corsica, Sardinia, Sicily and portions of southern Italy in the 9th century. A large part of these lands was held until the 11th century when the tidal wave was turned back from the European extremities.

The earliest Moslem architecture dates from the 7th century and is located in Asia Minor and Egypt. Its indebtedness to other civilizations is apparent in buildings like the Dome of the Rock (688) in Jerusalem, ultimately inspired by the Holy Sepulchre, and the Great Mosque, Cordoba. Early Arabic art took over wholesale Byzantine, Syrian, Persian and Graeco-Roman methods, motifs and forms and out of this amalgam an individual culture of the highest sophistication and refinement was forged. Its architecture was distinguished by the use of the dome on squinches, and pointed and horseshoe arches. The latter was of Visigothic origin, but was developed by the Arabs. According to some authorities the pointed Gothic arch came from Sicily where Norman rulers embarked on extensive building campaigns in the 11th century, using Arab masons.

Islamic influences were strongest in Sicily and Spain. In Spain there developed a style, known as 'Mozarabic', which was the art of Christians in the Arab-dominated areas. It is a remarkable adaptation of Islamic art to Christian requirements. It spread north to the non-Arab part of Spain. From Spain Islamic influences, along with its silks, ivories, jewellery and other works of art, spread into France where it played a role in the formation of the Romanesque style.

4 The Influence of the Art of the Invasions

The main reason for the collapse of the Roman Empire in the West was not so much internal weakness as the pressure of the 'barbarians' within and without its frontiers. The most important of the barbarian peoples were the Germanic tribes: the Visigoths who invaded Italy but finally settled in Spain, the Longobards who followed the Visigoths into Italy, the Franks in France and western Germany, the Burgundians in the south of France, and the Angles and Saxons in England.

The ultimate source of the migrations was southern Russia and here too lay the roots of Barbarian culture. It derived from the art of an oriental race, the Sarmatians, who invaded the south of Russia, then occupied by the Scythians, and imposed their art on the area in the 3rd century BC. This art depicted highly stylized animals together with geometric designs.

How did Barbaric art influence Western art? To have asked such a question a century ago would have exposed the questioner to ridicule. Did not the Invasions uproot the Graeco-Roman tradition and reduce the Roman Empire to barbarism? Was not the barbarian influence purely destructive? Witness the sorrowful, child-like imitations of sculpture that have survived. What could be more puerile or lacking in artistic skill or taste?

But Barbarian art did exert its influence. The reappraisal of this art that has followed the study of all forms of primitive art during recent decades has come to recognize its profound influence upon aesthetics. Through this awareness we are able to approach with new appreciation the Germanic antecedents of Romanesque art.

To discover Barbarian art we must go to museums, for there is no architecture above ground and the barbarian tombs themselves are of little interest from the artistic point of view. The scraps and pieces of weapons, jewellery, pottery, coins and house utensils are of much interest to art historians, but little to the amateur.

The Influence of the Art of the Invasions

Three points are worth making. In the first place the objects of the various tribes who penetrated into every corner of Western Europe and as far as Iceland and Greenland have much in common and in many cases are indistinguishable one from the other.

Secondly until it came into contact with the Mediterranean world, this was a non-representational art. It is geometric or zoomorphic, that is, using animal forms. These are highly stylized as in Mesopotamian and Siberian art of an earlier age.

Thirdly, gold ornaments were in widespread use, and these ornaments are very finely worked using precious stones and cloisonné of complex workmanship. The rubies used on some objects are said to be traceable to the Far East. The cloisonné techniques are of great strength and beauty as evidenced by the objects in the Sutton Hoo Treasure in the British Museum. The Childeric sword hilt in the Bibliothèque Nationale, Paris, reveals the barbarian love of cloisonné. As in the Treasure of Sutton Hoo the designs are abstract and are rather like the patterns on oriental carpets. In the Cabinet des Médailles in the Bibliothèque Nationale, are a collection of jewels and ornaments discovered at Tournai in the tomb of Childeric, father of Clovis, traditionally regarded as the first king of France. Clovis, chief of the Franks, was converted to Christianity by St Remigius at Reims in 498.

Once these nomadic peoples had settled, their cultural traditions were quickly modified by contacts with the superior civilization of the old Roman Empire and Byzantium. Theodoric, the 5th-century king of the Ostrogoths, and the most romanized of the Goth conquerors of Italy, made a notable effort to harmonize both Roman and Goth cultures. The stone carvings of the Longobards of the 7th and 8th centuries are an interesting mixture of Barbarian, Byzantine and Roman motifs, These works were once condemned as marking the lowest ebb in the long history of Italian culture. Today, however, such an evaluation seems quite mistaken. The sculpture shows an expressive boldness that cannot be written off as purely grotesque or lacking in artistic taste.

The Germanic tradition was weakest during the Carolingian and Ottonian periods when Western culture was saturated with late antique and Byzantine influences. But it did not disappear entirely. In the 11th and 12th centuries there was something like a revival of Barbarian motifs and the stylization and abstraction of Romanesque art and its taste for pattern-making is in part due to their influence. Barbarian influence is particularly strong in England in the Romanesque period because of the penetration of Scandinavian art which accompanied the Viking invasions of the 9th and 10th centuries.

Left: Gold belt buckle with interlacing animal patterns, from the Treasure of Sutton Hoo. 654–5. London, British Museum.
Opposite: Two examples of Barbaric carving.

5 Celtic and Anglo-Saxon Art to 850

Long after the conversion of Ireland and northern England to Christianity, and the arrival of Roman bishops to rule over the church and advise the kings of these lands, pagan Celtic art not only persisted, but was also the sole style for metalwork for church use, for the great stone Tall Crosses, and above all, the illumination of manuscripts – the supreme achievement of pre-Carolingian Western art. Celtic art invaded the Continent through the newly formed monasteries established by Irish missionaries. This art flourished until the Carolingian Renaissance when in England and on the Continent it yielded to a large extent to the revival of Byzantine and Carolingian forms. In Ireland it persisted until the monasteries themselves suffered obliteration at the hands of Norman and Danish marauders. It reappears briefly in the 12th century in Ireland in stone sculpture.

The mysterious origins of this style, its superb manifestation in the 7th and 8th century, when it represented the most vital and accomplished of European arts, has caused it to be profoundly studied by scholars of many lands. Unfortunately for those who would have certainty and clarity in such matters, there is a good deal of dispute as to where and by whom the masterpieces of Celtic illumination were produced.

First, let us examine the subject matter of the disputes. These are primarily the three great illuminated manuscripts, the Books of Durrow and Kells, and the Lindisfarne Gospels. Their names, being somewhat arbitrary, do not necessarily indicate their place of origin. There are many other manuscripts in the same general style, most of which, however, being of subsequent date, would scarcely clarify the first question of origin.

Opposite
Page from the Lindisfarne Gospels. *c.* 698. London, British Museum.

The style is distinguished by the intricacy of its abstract ornament. Interlacing is predominant and appears in endless variations. The designs recall engraved or inlaid metalwork, and point to the influence of the Barbarian metalwork of the Invasions. Human and animal forms are secondary

and very stylized. This has been regarded by art historians as pointing to oriental or Coptic inspiration. No clear evidence exists of the time and means by which such inspiration may have been transmitted and blended with primitive Celtic art forms dating from pre-history, which have much in common with the ultimate products of Celtic art of the 7th century. Mediterranean influences are apparent in the Lindisfarne Gospel and its portraits of the Evangelists. This is not surprising since it probably originated in Northumbria, in the north of England, which had been in direct contact with Rome since the beginning of the 7th century. Benedict Biscop, for example, travelled to Rome from Northumbria no less than five times, bringing back with him illuminated manuscripts and other artistic treasures to enrich and embellish his newly founded monasteries.

The mystery of Celtic art does not stop with the obscurity of its distant origins. The meaning of the symbolism is also unknown. Scholars have noted a passage in *The Golden Ass* of Apuleius written in the 2nd century AD in North Africa. In this passage the author describes a religious ceremony seen by him in Africa, which gives a verbal description of what might be a progenitor of the Book of Kells.

> The High Priest drew from the sacred recess of the shrine certain books written in unknown characters, partly represented in compendious form, the words expressive of their meaning by figures of animals of every kind, and partly fortified against the inquisitive perusal of the profane by characters wreathed like knots and twisting round the shape of a wheel, and with extremities twining with one another, like the tendrils of a vine.

The immediate provenance of the three great 7th-century masterpieces of illumination already referred to, is also subject to dispute.

One view is that the centre of Celtic art was in Ireland; that Celtic art followed the Irish missionaries into Iona in Scotland, to Lindisfarne in Northumbria, and later to establishments at St Gall, Bobbio and Luxeuil on the Continent; and that the great illuminations were the product of Irish monasteries. The other view holds that, while the Irish monks founded the great cultural centres of Northumbria and the Continent, this happened long before the masterly illuminations were produced; that by the middle of the 7th century the centre of insular culture had shifted from Ireland to Northumbria where an extraordinary upsurge was in progress, and that the finest works were the product of this upsurge and were carried to the Continent by Anglo-Saxon monks in the next century and were then carried back to Ireland.

The wondrous thing is that in the 7th century, a period of very limited cultural activity on the Continent, the Irish and Northumbrian monasteries poured out a stream of art products, missionaries and brilliant men, a stream that culminated in the great Alcuin, chief adviser to Charlemagne. Then at the height of their productivity in the 9th century all these monasteries succumbed in fire and pillage to the bloody onslaught of the Normans and Danes, and the culture they represented never recovered its strength.

6 The Carolingian Revival

The first large-scale revival of antique art did not occur till around 800 AD. Called Carolingian after its sponsor, Charlemagne, the style proclaimed the emergence of a fresh culture north of the Alps, which drew its inspiration from late Imperial Rome and Byzantium rather than from Celtic and Germanic traditions. The historical circumstances of this cultural revolution can be briefly stated, its psychological basis would require much deeper analysis as would its effects, which extend into all subsequent European art history until the Renaissance.

Charlemagne's conquests in Europe led him inevitably into papal politics. He restored a fugitive Pope to the papal throne and was rewarded by the grateful Pontiff, not only with the Imperial title, but also with the gift of the city of Ravenna. This was ransacked for art works to decorate his northern palaces. It was Charlemagne's ambition to create, or rather re-create, the Roman Empire in the West and rival the culture and political power of the Empire in the East. He surrounded himself with a brains trust of brilliant men, like the Anglo-Saxon Alcuin and the Visigoth Theodulf, who set about bringing education and civilization to the vast Empire. Everything was changed: the script, the arts of painting, sculpture and architecture. Charlemagne took from Italy what he had found there and this meant embracing Byzantine as well as Romano-Christian art. The two chief contributions of the Carolingian period to the development of mediaeval art were the revival of monumentality in building and the renaissance of the human figure in the pictorial arts.

Of the great Imperial Palace at the royal seat, Aachen, only the Chapel survives, a galleried octagon. The prototype most often cited for this building is S. Vitale at Ravenna (itself deriving from the 6th-century church of SS. Sergius and Bacchus and the 7th-century Chrysotriclinion in the palace of Justinian II, in Constantinople). But Roman origins have also been found, for example, in the 5th-century baptistery near the old Lateran basilica. However the precise model does not really matter. What counts is that Aachen was inspired by one type of centralized building of the early Christian era.

The major Carolingian churches have disappeared: the abbey of St-Denis (begun in *c.*754), the church of St-Riquier, Centula and the convent church of Fulda. But something must be said about them because they were of crucial significance for the development of Romanesque. All were basilican, reviving this Roman type which had disappeared in the preceding two centuries. Fulda was actually a conscious imitation of St Peter's at Rome, although it had three aisles, not five. St-Riquier was the most complex and accomplished of the Carolingian churches. It was of cruciform plan with a second transept at the west end and a tower above each crossing. The west end of the church was highly developed. The origin of this so-called 'westwork', which became a distinctive feature of German Romanesque, is complex and its function much disputed. A further innovation was the addition of a western apse, which we see on the 9th-century plan of the monastery of St Gall. Large crypts, first adopted in Rome, also came into use in the North at this time. This innovation reflected the pressure of the growing cult of relics – unlike Byzantium, the West preferred to worship the saint through his fibula rather than his image – and the need to house them in a manner befitting their sanctity. The elaboration of the east and west ends of churches may also reflect this same impulse.

The adoption of the antique outlook on art, the glorification and idealization of the human form, and the greater realism in the depiction of nature meant, to some extent, the ousting of the abstract art of the Celtic, Merovingian and Longobardian styles. Nonetheless many of the Carolingian miniatures combine naturalistic figures with elaborate, insistent Celtic decoration. The naturalistic school at Reims developed the purest examples of the new art marking the Carolingian revolution. The carvings in ivory of the 'Ada' school achieve impressive results in the finest antique tradition.

The earliest illuminations appear to have clung closely to their antique models – usually Italian works of the 5th and 6th centuries. Later on however the increasing assurance of artists, combined with the limited number of manuscripts available to them, resulted in original creations in the antique manner. The productions of Carolingian workshops and the different styles they displayed are too numerous to be dealt with here. It should be pointed out though, that antique sources provided no single style. There is a good deal of difference between the painterly technique of the Codex Aureus (in the Munich Library), the plasticity and full modelling of the Ada manuscripts, and the nervous and energetic linear treatment of the Utrecht Psalter. The above remarks are equally true of Carolingian metalwork and ivory carving. Yet Carolingian art is no mere pale imitation, despite the return to antique styles and the influence of Byzantium. These influences are transformed by the enthusiasm with which they were grasped and by a modifying Northern

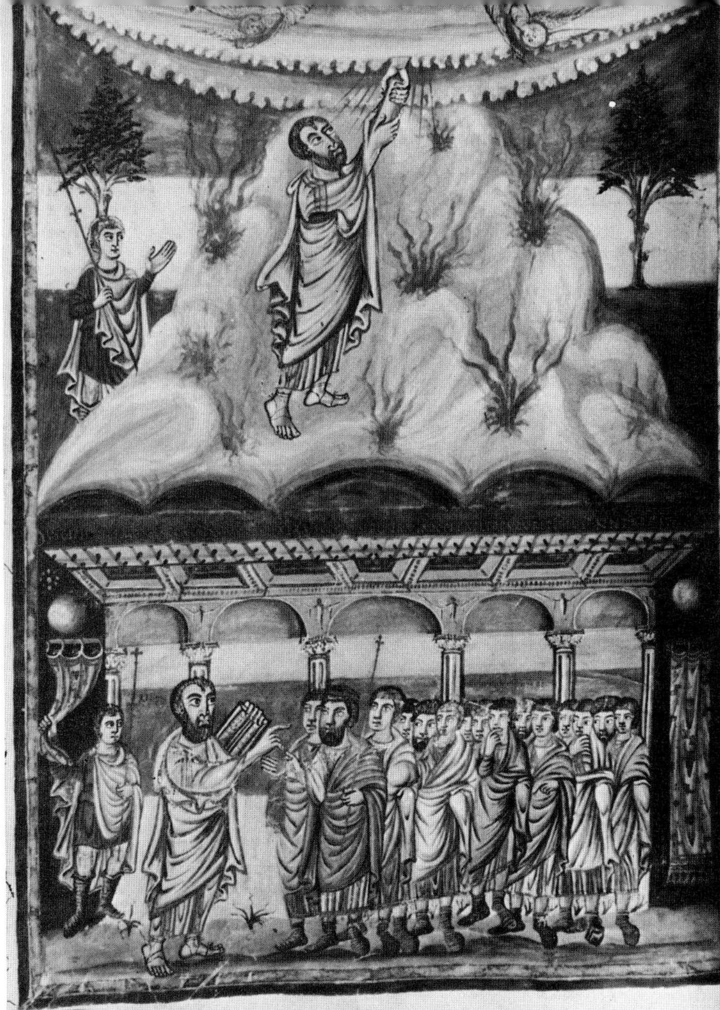

Moses receiving the Tables of the Law, and Moses expounding the Law to the Israelites, from the Moutier-Grandval Bible. Carolingian, Tours. 834–43. London, British Museum.

Utrecht Psalter, Reims. *c.* 832. Utrecht, University Library.

dynamism. In Carolingian wall paintings the effect of the revival of antique models is less apparent and their appearance is more strongly mediaeval. One tradition the Carolingian age failed to revive was that of large-scale sculpture and relief.

Unlike Romanesque art which spread all over Europe, Carolingian art stayed close to the Frankish lands which were the heart of Charlemagne's short-lived 'United Europe'. With Charlemagne's death and the division of his Empire, came a grim revival of a different kind which brought art and architecture almost to a standstill. This was the revival of sheer terror throughout Europe by the merciless lust of the new pagan raids of Magyars and Normans. Entire communities, deep in the heart of the Carolingian lands, were pillaged. What could not be carried off was burned. Men and women were killed or taken into slavery. Monasteries and their inhabitants knew no mercy from these scourges. Northern France, England and Ireland fell, other parts of France and Germany were despoiled.

Meanwhile the Arabs gained domination of the Mediterranean, pillaged its coasts and regained Sicily and almost all of Spain and southern Italy. Western civilization, faltered, and almost disappeared. In these dark days of terror and destruction, the Carolingian revival of the arts persisted in producing masterpieces in isolated localities, at Reims, Reichenau and Winchester, leaving us precious examples of the developing art of the new Europe. Reanimated by monastic artists of great skill the Carolingian revolution broadened into the Ottonian style, the direct precursor of Romanesque art.

The Carolingian age made the great contribution of linking the cultural and political destinies of Italy and the North. The curious and long-lived alliance between Italy and Germany sprang from the independence and strength of the Carolingian and Ottonian dynasties and the weakness of Italy. The Germans were invaders and conquerors who stayed to admire and emulate Mediterranean art. But they always converted this art into a north European formula. It was in the post-Carolingian centuries that Western civilization gradually found itself.

Opposite: Gold cover, with pearls and precious stones, of the Codex Aureus of St Emmeran. Carolingian, *c.* 870. Munich, Staatsbibliothek.

7 Europe at the Millennium

A special and grim importance had been attached in the Middle Ages to the year 1000. There was a tradition that the world would come to an end at this time with the second coming of Christ, and that the dead would rise from their graves. Comparable to the atom bomb, this threat appears to have had little impact on the people. Their troubles were far more immediate. The Carolingian Empire had fallen first into discordant parts and later into squabbling fragments. There was no political leadership above that of the local duke. The Papacy had become a football of politics among the Roman nobility. A constant state of war existed between feudal lords, who would do battle for a village, a church or a parish, periodically burning each other's castles and abbeys.

The remarkable thing is that European cultural life did not come to a halt. At this time Europe stood at the very threshold of one of its most glorious periods of artistic production. The tremendous drive to build and decorate new churches of cut stone, which were, in the words of the monk, Glaber, to cover the earth with a white mantle, the sophisticated goldsmith work, ivory carving and illuminations did not spring out of a void. Indeed there is abundant evidence, if we look for it, of high quality art and architecture in the 10th century which was certainly no 'Dark Age'.

Evidence of cultural activity is not lacking in other fields, as the careers of Gerbert, later Pope Sylvester II, and his contemporary, Otto the Great, reveal.

Of humble parentage, Gerbert learned Latin in an abbey school. This was the key to advancement and influence. He was picked out for his intelligence on the occasion of a visit to the abbey by the count of Barcelona and sent to serve the bishop of Vich in the Spanish March. Here Gerbert was exposed to Arab culture which trickled through the 'iron curtain' separating the Christian and Arab worlds in Spain. He developed a keen interest in mathematics and astrology, adding these to his love of the Roman classics.

After three years in Spain he was sent on urgent monastery business to Rome and there appeared before the Pope and the Emperor Otto I. Both were impressed by him and offered to keep him in their respective entourages, but he next appears as a scholar conducting one of the great schools of the time, that of Reims. One of his pupils was the future king of France, Robert, son of Hugh Capet.

Gerbert became involved in an intellectual dispute with a German scholar, Othric of Magdeburg, which reached the ear of Emperor Otto II, who ordered that the controversy be tried in a debate before him at Ravenna. Gerbert won and shortly after was appointed abbot of Bobbio, the monastery in northern Italy which traces its origin to St Columban. This post was not to his liking and he soon returned to France to become secretary to Hugh Capet. He travelled widely in Germany and Italy, engaging in the complex politics of this feudal age. Emperor Otto III called him to aid the cultural elevation of his Empire, granted him a private domain in Alsace and made him archbishop of Ravenna. The next and fully logical step was the Papacy which he received in 999. This brilliant career as a scholar, diplomat and churchman is proof that the year 1000 could scarcely be called a 'Dark Age'.

The most dynamic force in 10th-century Europe was that of Otto the Great. Succeeding to the dukedom of Saxony at twenty-four, he started his reign by subduing rival feudal lords, rescuing and marrying Adelaide, the young widow of the Lombard king, and mounting a long and bloody struggle against the ever menacing Magyars. The great victory at Lech in 955 ended this scourge. This opened a new era of prosperity in the Teutonic lands. Otto restored the Roman Empire in the West in 962, and with this restoration came a revival of Carolingian cultural traditions.

The continuity of European artistic development in the Middle Ages is seen in the architecture of the 10th and the first years of the 11th centuries. Two styles appear which, though distinct, have a number of features in common, particularly in exterior decoration. This is not surprising since ultimately they derived from the same early Christian sources. Ottonian architects working with their Carolingian inheritance, looking again at early Christian building, and deriving fresh ideas from Byzantium, particularly its provinces, built imposing structures which expressed a development towards a new conception of space and mass. One example of this is St Cyriakus, Gernrode which used galleries over the aisles and alternating supports (probably derived from Byzantine provincial churches like Hagios Demetrios at Salonika). These features are seen in the abbey church of St Michael, Hildesheim, though here the galleries are confined to the eastern and western transepts. They help to break up the simple pattern of the standard basilica thus creating a more complex rhythm. The exteriors of Ottonian churches are decorated with blind arcades and eaves niches. However, in contrast with Romanesque churches, the innovations we have just described are used for colouristic effect rather than articulation.

SC GEREON
VICTOR

The second style which emerged around the year 1000 is known as 'first Romanesque' because, until quite recently, it was considered the immediate mainspring of Romanesque architecture. In fact it was the continuation of what has been called the 'international provincial' architecture which was influenced by the early Christian buildings of the east Mediterranean. It flourished in southern Europe from the 5th until the 11th centuries. The best known of the 'first Romanesque' churches are in Lombardy and northern Spain. They are small, substantially built vaulted structures, their exteriors distinguished by those decorative features we have just described in Ottonian architecture. They usually have small dwarf transepts and a crossing tower.

A third contribution came from France, where two complex systems for the treatment of the plan of the east end developed. The first was the ambulatory with radiating chapels, which, as far as we know, first appeared in the crypt of St-Martin, Tours. The second was the staggered plan with chapels laid step-wise, which was used in the second abbey church of Cluny in 981. It was out of the fusion of these various trends that Romanesque architecture was born.

When we turn to the figural and decorative arts we find again no hiatus in the development from Carolingian to Romanesque art. The continuity can be clearly traced in goldsmith work, bronzes, ivories and illuminations. The great centre of cultural activity was, of course, Ottonian Germany, for here there were the patrons and economic resources.

Despite the fact that Ottonian art is impregnated with Byzantine and antique forms, we can discern hints of the approaching Romanesque style. Thus in manuscript illumination, particularly that coming from Reichenau, we find a tendency to eliminate the background, a new emphasis on line and a new expressiveness. The elongation and agitated drapery of the fresco figures in the church of St George, Reichenau, is another indication. A more interesting example is the famous bronze doors of Bernward at St Michael's, Hildesheim. The inspiration may have been the doors of S. Sabina, Rome, but stylistically the little figures are a long way from early Christian prototypes. A final example is the deeply moving carved crucifixes, such as the Gero Cross. Ottonian art reflects the beginnings of the influence of the great religious revival which was to have such a decisive influence on the Romanesque style.

Before passing to Romanesque and somewhat by way of a digression it would be well to summarize the significance of the misnamed 'minor' arts of the early Middle Ages – the small works of metal, ivory, and miniature painting. They were truly the major arts during this period. And they were in large measure responsible for the design of the great murals, sculptured doorways and stained glass that embellished Romanesque architecture. Being portable, small objects could be viewed, admired and copied in many places. The treasures of art dating between 600 and 1000 that have survived destruction are almost entirely small objects of the type mentioned.

Opposite
Ivory relief, showing Christ in Majesty blessing St Victor and St Gereon. Ottonian, *c.* 1000. Cologne, Schnütgen-Museum.

8 Romanesque

Romanesque may be considered the first European style. Like all art-historical terms 'Romanesque' eludes easy definition, both as a period and as a style. The conventional time span is from the last quarter of the 11th century to the end of the 12th century, with a Gothic overlap beginning with Abbot Suger's rebuilding of the abbey of St-Denis in about 1145. However in the Holy Roman Empire the transition from Ottonian to Romanesque early in the 11th century is almost imperceptible, while in Spain and Italy Romanesque continues well into the 13th century.

From the point of view of style the initial impression is one of bewildering variety. Certainly the influence of local traditions and the tastes of individual patrons are factors to be taken into consideration. But despite the diversity of expression, Romanesque architecture and art has an overall unity. Close contacts were maintained at the highest social level, even if masons and craftsmen were less mobile. And shared traditions, problems and aims combined to give Romanesque all over Europe a broad common denominator.

The 11th and 12th centuries were times of economic recovery after the terrible devastations of the previous century and a half. The population grew, the lands under cultivation were extended, and commerce and industry revived in the cities and towns. The rise of the cities was accompanied by the appearance of a displaced urban proletariat which put pressure on the agrarian based feudal system, but as yet its decline was barely apparent. In theory, and to a large extent in practice also, feudalism with its clearly defined order for society and ideals of mutual dependence and responsibility was at the basis of mediaeval life. The tensions generated by social change found an outlet in the Crusades and thousands of the poor and disaffected flocked behind its banners, and went off to liberate Spain and the Holy Land. The Crusades were also a way of postponing, or at least mitigating, conflicts at a higher level, so that though it would be a mistake to underestimate the tensions and pressures (and

Opposite
Tree of Jesse from the Psalter of Henry of Blois. Winchester, *c.* 1140–60. London, British Museum.

a reflection of these appears in Romanesque art), they remained somewhat below the surface. Comparative peace and stability, as well as prosperity, reigned.

The Crusades were one expression of the great religious upsurge of the 11th and 12th centuries. Another is the monastic revival which began in the 10th century at Cluny in France. Although it inspired a number of similar and independent reform movements Cluny remained the dominant Order. It was given the extraordinary privilege of being responsible only to the Pope, which freed it from any local interference, and it was fortunate in having a series of abbots of unusual longevity, and outstanding ability and piety. In time, reformed houses dependent on Cluny, grew up and the influence of the Order spread all over Europe, reaching its point of culmination during the abbacy of St Hugh (1049–1109). Under his long administration the authority of Cluny extended to over a thousand branch houses. The Order acquired great political and spiritual power in Europe. These developments were accompanied by a cultural pre-eminence.

Its international structure cut across all feudal boundaries, enabling the Order to work as a unit in remotely scattered regions and to serve as a cosmopolitan vehicle for all manner of enterprises – in diplomacy, the planning of Crusades, the spread of learning, the creation of international routes and networks of abbeys to service the great pilgrimage traffic, and the transmission of its art to every corner of Europe.

In the 12th century there came a second monastic revival, also originating in Burgundy. The Cistercian movement began at Cîteaux and Clairvaux and from there spread throughout Europe. It began as a protest against the worldliness and decadence into which Cluny had fallen. The Cistercians were distinguished by the simplicity of their lives, which was echoed in their buildings.

A third important manifestation of religious fervour was the cult of the relics and the popularity of pilgrimages. The relic cult which offered to the devout a form of contact with holy and indeed divine personages reached its height in the Middle Ages. Monasteries vied with each other to obtain and exhibit holy remains. The naïvité, if not outright fraud, involved in this strange rivalry, is hard for us to comprehend. It would seem that Mary Magdalene, the Virgin and many of the Apostles had fled Palestine and left their bones all over Europe: Mary Magdalene at Marseilles and eventually Vézelay, St James at Compostela in Spain.

The remote location of some of the most sacred places only added to their glamour. The popularity of the Holy Land naturally increased after its liberation from Islam. But even before this, pilgrims made the dangerous journey. The chronicler Glaber wrote in the 10th century:

At this time a crowd of countless people started to come from the whole world towards the Sepulchre of the Saviour at Jerusalem. Nobody had ever seen such an affluence. There were first of all simple people, then people of the middle classes,

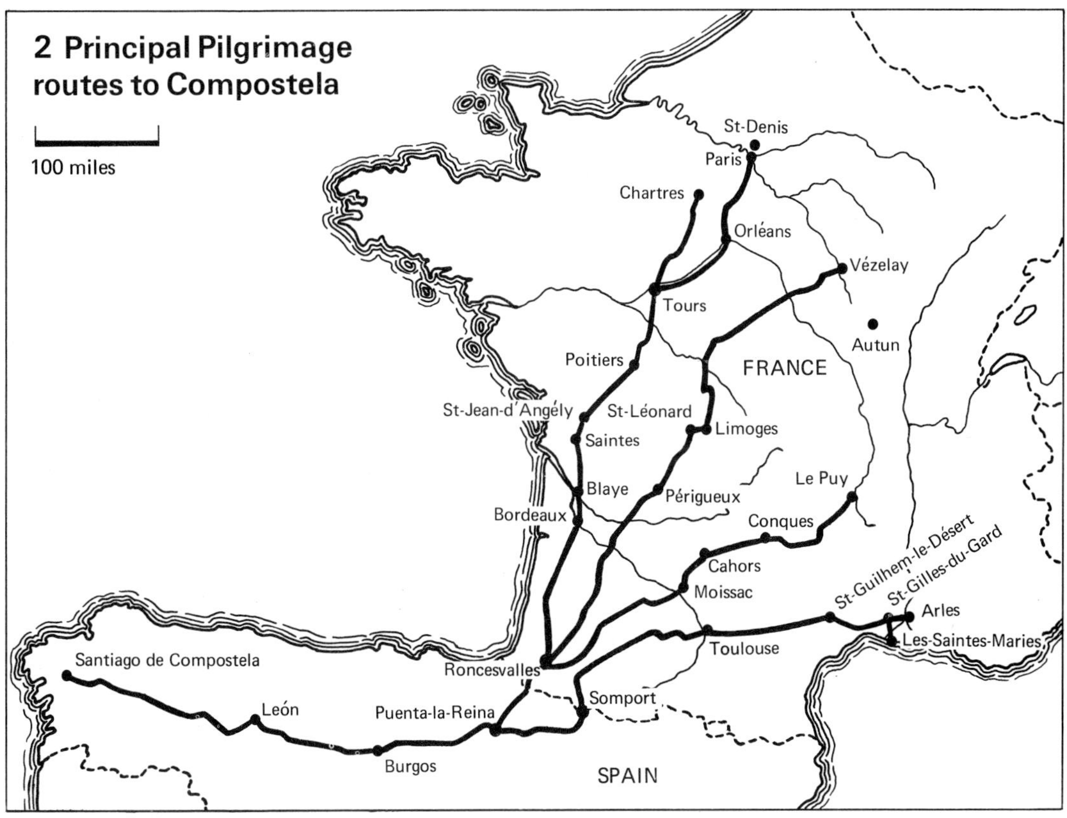

then the greatest kings, marquises, prelates, and then something that had never been before; one saw the women of the high nobility make the route to this place in company with the most miserable and poor people.

The two great European pilgrimage centres were Rome and Compostela.

Something of the joyous atmosphere of the pilgrimage is conveyed in Chaucer's *Canterbury Tales*. It was a social as well as an individual experience, a little like a contemporary holiday cruise or guided tour. The hardships and deadly dangers of the voyage in mediaeval times were mitigated by the company of people from all walks of life, the sight of sacred places of legendary beauty, the promised absolution of sins to be earned, and no doubt the hope of the fulfilment of some secret wish by the interposition of the Holy Personage as a reward for all dangers and hardships. To the younger men there was also the opportunity of joining with the knights in Spain or in the Holy Land waging war against the Infidel. This carried with it the chance of great material rewards in the spoils of war. Clearly the experience of a pilgrimage was the event of a lifetime, sometimes tragic, but certainly exciting and always a break from the humdrum of ordinary life.

No voluntary movement of this importance occurred in the history of Western civilization until the recent cult of tourism. Pilgrims in the 12th century were probably as numerous, relatively, as tourists are today. Their long journeys took them hundreds of miles from their homes, seven hundred miles to Compostela from the centre of France, and much farther by land or sea to the Holy Land.

The pilgrimages had as an important by-product the erection of innumerable abbeys, not only to house the relics and the brothers of the Order in proper surroundings, but also to service the pilgrims on the long routes. This was particularly true of the route to Compostela. Since early times this was the special, though not the exclusive, care of Cluny. The Order had helped to organize the pilgrimage to the tomb of St James in every possible way. At the turn of the 10th century, under the lash of the competitive appeals of Jerusalem and Rome for the pilgrims' favour, it went to extreme lengths to restore and maintain Compostela's popularity. Four converging highways through France led to Compostela. The route was one of the best equipped in Europe. Tolls were removed, monasteries and hostels operated as 'way stations'. These elaborate 'way stations' afforded not only security but also spiritual inspiration in their remarkable collections of relics, their decorated doorways and cloisters of exquisite beauty and the utmost perfection of workmanship.

There survives a travel guide written in 1120, describing the landmarks of these journeys. It is known as the Calixtus Codex, and contains all sorts of helpful details for the pilgrim. The author, a Cluniac monk named Almery Picaud de Parthenay-le-Vieux, shows a keen appreciation of good food and wine, an abhorrence of the 'barbarian' customs of the Spaniards, and of the sorry quality of their food, and a wholesome distrust of the quality of the water met with on his travels.

The book gives many details of the wonderful shrines on the way. We learn of the Golden Shrine of St-Gilles-du-Gard at Arles (still one of the great Romanesque abbeys, though now without the shrine). We learn also of the great cemetery called Aliscamps at Arles (still exhibiting the early Christian sarcophagi admired by Aimery). The church of St-Honorat at Lerin with its Carolingian walls is mentioned as harbouring the relics of its founder.

'Burgundionibus et Theutonicis' (Burgundians and Teutons) travelling to Santiago de Compostela are urged to visit Conques (still one of the finest abbeys in France) containing the relics of St Foy (the reliquary is still there). Those coming from further north should visit Vézelay, the repository of the relics of Mary Magdalene.

At Limoges the guide mentions St-Léonard's shrine, at Périgueux, that of St-Front, sent by St Peter to convert the town. At Angély in Poitou the relic head of St John the Baptist is preserved, at Blaye the 'tomb' of the mythical 'Roland'.

On the route from Tours a visit to Orléans is recommended, to see the wood of the True Cross and the great church of St-Martin, now destroyed.

Another interesting association of Cluny with the Santiago pilgrimage and Spanish Crusades is its sponsorship of the *Chanson de Roland*. Cluniac abbots apparently enrolled not only the knighthood of France in the war with the Saracens but also the mythical past. They were responsible for the re-writing of the history of Charlemagne, to make him the prototype that was needed for the Crusades.

The *Chanson de Roland*, first French literary masterpiece, dates from around 1100 and has as its theme the heroic death of Roland and Oliver, two warriors associated with Charlemagne in his war against the Moors. The tale of treachery, bravery and sentiment treats Charlemagne almost as a demi-god. The scene of the poem's tragedy is the pass across the Pyrenees at Roncevalles, which lies on the route to Compostela. The story of the epic is based on slimmest historical foundation. The worldly wise abbots of Cluny stimulated the incessant presentation of this epic song by the 'jongleurs' along the pilgrimage route as one of its main attractions. Perhaps they are responsible for its composition. If so, they were the original patrons of French literature.

In a rare and very early manuscript reference to the presentation of artistic performances the *Roman de Flamenca* tells of the 'jongleurs':

> ... one plays the harp, the other the viole, another the flute, another a fife ... one speaks, the other accompanies him ... those who would hear the history of kings, marquises and counts could satisfy their desire ... one speaks of the Round Table where valiance was honoured ... another tells of Charlemagne ruling France ...

A fascinating theory has been postulated, that the great upsurge of song, folk legend and sculpture after 1100 on the route to Compostela was the result of an effort of Cluny to resurrect interest in Santiago's relics in order to compete with Jerusalem, following its liberation in the First Crusade.

So much for the background to Romanesque. The great religious revival, combined with the destruction of so many churches during the last 'barbarian' wave posed problems, while the increase in prosperity created the initial condition for their solution, namely that more churches could be built and on a larger scale to accommodate the greater numbers of the faithful. Thus it was, in the words of the chronicler, Glaber, that as

> the third year which followed the year 1000 approached, one saw in almost the whole world, but mainly in Italy and Gaul, the rebuilding of churches, although the majority being well-built had no need of it. A veritable contest drove each Christian community to have a more sumptuous church than its neighbours. One would have said that the world itself was removing its vestments and replacing them with a white mantle of churches, the episcopal seats and monasteries consecrated to all sorts of saints, and even the little chapels in the villages were reconstructed by the faithful more beautiful than before.

The 'white mantle' has been interpreted as referring to building in stone and not in timber, which was so very common throughout the early Middle Ages.

Romanesque

Two main problems confronted Romanesque architects. The first was the need to devise complex yet workable plans to cope with the multiplied functions of churches. The custom of daily worship by priests created the necessity for more chapels. Secondly a way of housing relics in a manner befitting their sanctity and of allowing the easy flow of pilgrims around the shrine had to be devised. The difficulties became more complicated when it was a question of not one, but many relics. The relic problem was not particularly new since the cult had been growing since the 8th century. However the scale had increased and the solutions were more involved.

The French innovations in ground plans to which we have already referred – the ambulatory with radiating chapels and staggered apses provided one solution of the problem. The Carolingian-Ottonian two transept, two apse and two choir system was another. Additional apses were also often added to the north side of transepts. Other solutions were adopted in the Romanesque period, for instance, the trefoil plan of St Maria in Capitol at Cologne.

The second practical problem was concerned with stone vaulting. The technique of building vaults on a small scale had not been lost in the early Middle Ages and its survival is seen in the churches of the 'first Romanesque'. What Romanesque architects rediscovered were the principles of large-scale vaulting, and thus they were able to make their churches more fire-proof. The first type adopted was the tunnel vault, to which was added reinforcing transverse arches. The groin vault was also used, initially restricted to crypts and aisles, later covering the nave. The idea of strengthening ribs was then adopted, first appearing at Speyer Cathedral and S. Ambrogio Milan (where the vaults resemble domes), and at Durham Cathedral around the turn of the 11th century. It was out of these experiments that the Gothic system of ribbed vaulting, where the ribs were built first and not added afterwards, developed.

We have emphasized these practical questions, because Romanesque was so very much the art of the builder and engineer. Architecture dominated and the other arts were subordinate to it. What was sought was the articulation of space and wall surface, and the clear definition of the function of the individual structural members and the establishment of their relationship with the whole. At the same time, the different liturgical functions of the church were clearly stated and interrelated. And perhaps it is not too far-fetched to see in this ordering of a Romanesque church a reflection of the established order of feudal Europe. At the same time there is a certain uncompromising quality in its mass and solidity and we are very much conscious of the Church Militant.

How did the Romanesque architect achieve articulation and clarification? In ground plans the individual elements are clearly stated: the nave, aisles, transepts, choir and dependent chapels. The arrangement is complex, but not confused. The use of ribs and transverse arches on vaulted roofs and diaphragm arches on wooden roofs was a means of articulation. So also are the alternating pier and column supports of the nave and the clustered columns

'First Romanesque' church, near Chiasso, Italy.

with engaged shafts rising to its full height. The result is that the interior of churches is broken up into bays which are related to each other by repetition. Another feature was the insertion of a gallery below the clerestory. Sometimes the functional value of the gallery was entirely eliminated by the substitution of a 'blind' triforium which opened straight onto the aisle wall.

Similar spatial and surface articulation was sought for the exteriors of churches. Wall decoration – blind arcades, dwarf galleries, niche friezes, patterned wall-work – was not applied as haphazard ornamentation but used to emphasize architectural function. When we come to discuss sculpture, we shall find it serving the same purpose.

Tower systems varied. In northern and central Italy the tower was usually detached. North of the Alps they were incorporated into the church structure. Rhineland churches were designed for a maximum complement of six. Usually churches had a crossing-tower, either on its own or combined with a single- or twin-towered façade, the latter developed in Normandy from Carolingian-Ottonian antecedents.

Romanesque

In the next section we shall describe the various Romanesque monuments. However it would be useful at this point to mention the key churches and styles of the period. First among these are the great Imperial Rhineland cathedrals of which Speyer was the most important and ambitious undertaking. Consecrated in 1061 it was rebuilt during the reign of Henry IV between 1092 and 1106. It is one of the largest churches in the West, and in terms of size alone it was a challenge to mediaeval builders. Imperial influences spread down into Lombardy, no longer considered the fountain-head of the Romanesque style, and westward to Normandy. Norman builders contributed important features to Romanesque. As well as the two-towered façade they developed the use of the 'blind' triforium and engaged shafts.

The third monastery church at Cluny was built in open rivalry to Speyer. If Speyer symbolized the Imperial conception of the interdependent relationship between church and state, Cluny represented papal independence and freedom from secular interference. The church was destroyed in the French Revolution. The small fragment that remains gives us the barest hint of the vast structure started in 1085 with funds given by Alfonso VI, king of Spain, as a token of thanks for the capture of Toledo from the Moors. It was the finest creation of the Cluniac Order and probably represented the epitome of Romanesque architecture. The church was immense, exceeded only slightly by the 16th-century St Peter's in Rome. It had four side aisles, two transepts with apses attached, and fifteen bays with altars. At the east end was an ambulatory with five radiating chapels. The arches in the nave were pointed, as was the barrel vault. One reason why the Cluniacs preferred the stone vault was to provide better acoustics for the beautiful Gregorian chants of the monks.

Cluny's magnificence is now known only through old prints and the lesser versions of its architecture and decorations in other surviving Burgundian churches. Its outward mass, with the hexagonal towers, resembled the Imperial cathedrals of the Rhine in weight and magnificence. Indeed it was compared to the Imperial cathedrals by the Cluniac monk Gilo in 1113 and is believed to have owed a considerable debt to Rhineland architecture.

The influence of Cluny was felt in Burgundy and neighbouring regions and spread further afield. Related to Cluny are the pilgrimage churches on the route to Compostela, which are also barrel vaulted (though round and not pointed) and have the same type of eastern arrangement.

As far as secular building is concerned, very little survives in the way of houses. On the other hand Europe is strewn with castles in every state of decay. There are some dating to the 10th, 11th and 12th centuries. These are the oldest European castles, since stone construction, known to the Romans and other ancient civilizations, fell into disuse until around 1070, and the really heavily fortified walled castle only came into frequent use in the 12th century. The rebuilding of castles in stone was hastened when the Europeans witnessed the fine quality of equipment used by the Saracens. The great improvement in siege machinery derived from the experience of the First Crusade.

A particularly interesting group of castles is in Germany: Wimpfen, Gelnhausen, Münzenberg and Büdingen. Here we find a new and wonderful architectural style reflecting the influence of Frederick Barbarossa. In the history of Europe Barbarossa cut a considerable and very bellicose figure during his reign of almost forty years. Like his predecessors he invaded Italy many times, but distinguished himself further by pillaging and burning Milan, deposing a Pope and backing his own candidate as anti-pope. He had to abandon his attempt to control the papacy. He arranged the marriage of his son to Constance of Sicily, assuring to that distant isle the Hohenstaufen rule of his grandson, Frederick II. He outmanoeuvred, and finally caused the downfall and banishment of his great rival for the Imperial crown, Henry the Lion of Saxony-Bavaria. Finally, he undertook the leadership of the Christians to recapture Jerusalem from the great Saladin and lost his life in the Third Crusade in 1190.

The Hohenstaufen palace style shows strong Italian influence in its decorative features. It marked a revolutionary change from the dark, airless keeps that passed for royal dwellings in the preceding ages. The palaces have open arcades, not only inside the protective wall but even on the outer wall itself, where the height of the wall permitted this fancy. Such open arcades may be observed in all four castles.

This opening-up of the mediaeval castle to light and air indicates a greater confidence in their defensive power than subsequent history justified. The well-proportioned openings with their carved columns give a cheerful and civilized air to the grim fortresses in which they are found. The originality of the carvings, which differ from castle to castle and from arcade to arcade, suggest the employment of skilled craftsmen.

Wimpfen and Münzenberg were also equipped with strong towers of a more formidable and forbidding construction than the palaces. These great towers, reminiscent of the Italian fortified towers of Bologna and S. Gimignano, have thick walls able to withstand all but very heavy siege machines. Their entrances were some twenty feet above the ground level, accessible only by ladders which the occupants could withdraw into the tower in times of danger. They had no windows, but only narrow slits permitting arrows to be shot out of the tower and air and light to enter. It is believed that some of these fortified towers also had underground passages leading beyond the outer walls of the castle, to permit the replenishment of food supplies or flight in case of imminent danger or capture.

One of the most important developments in the Romanesque period was the revival of sculpture towards the end of the 11th century. This did not spring out of nothing. Traditions of decorative carving had been maintained, and though the decline in figural sculpture after the collapse of the Roman Empire remained unaffected by the Carolingian revival, the traditions were

Animal relief on the exterior of the Cathedral of Modena, Italy. 1099–1106.

not completely lost – witness the remarkable sculptured crosses in England and Ireland, or the reliefs of the Longobard Pemmo altarpiece at Cividale. And if there was little in the way of large-scale stone sculpture a good deal was achieved on a small scale in ivory and metalwork.

The disputes as to whether the revival had its source in Germany, France or Italy need not be gone into here. However it is certainly true that some remarkable capitals survive from Cluny dating from 1095. The lost tympanum was carved between 1115 and 1118. This dating first suggested by the American archaeologist and now generally accepted, puts Cluny sculpture and composition at the beginning of the great wave of Romanesque sculpture, at least in France.*

Romanesque sculpture is confined almost solely to relief work, and it was, in theory at any rate, subordinate to architecture, one of its functions being the emphasis and definition of the elements to which it was applied. It was applied to capitals, around arches and windows, and on doorways. The same principles applied to sculptured reliefs of fonts, altar frontals and pulpits.

Decorative ornament could be geometric or foliated, the first predominating in Anglo-Norman churches, the latter in other parts of Europe. The Corinthian capital was revived and once successful imitations had been accomplished, artists went on to a free interpretation of this type. The acanthus leaf capital was also used, both the Roman form and the spinier type preferred by Arabs and Byzantines. Other foliage ornament included the

* A very elegant piece of research demonstrated the early dating of the capitals. It was found that the columns were raised in 1095, that the capitals must have been sculptured before this date because the tops of the capitals show strokes of the sculpture that could not have been made after the impost was placed. Kenneth John Conant of Harvard, who devoted years to the excavation of Cluny, is author of this demonstration.

Relief of Samson and the lion. *c.* 1220. Museo Civico, Lucca, Italy.

Byzantine palmette, rosettes, and the vine scroll – inhabited or otherwise. The tendency was always towards the stylization of these forms, in contrast with the naturalistic treatment of the Gothic style.

Animal sculpture was very important. The 'best seller' of the Middle Ages, apart from the Bible, was the Bestiary, a natural history based on myths. This book was filled with incredible tales of the characteristics of real and mythical beasts.* From the illustrations in these Bestiaries stems much of the sculpture in the abbeys and cathedrals of France, Spain, England and Italy.

We do not know exactly why wild beasts invaded the column capitals and exterior decorations of Romanesque churches, why they stand guard over the entrances and support the altars, pulpits and tombs. In the 10th century

* The leading Bestiary of the 12th century, written in Lincolnshire, has been translated from the Latin by T. H. White.

Left : Detail of the trumeau of the south portal of the abbey church of Moissac, France, *c.* 1115.
Right : Figure of 'Lust' from the south portal of Moissac. *c.* 1115.

St Nilus stated: 'You ask whether it would be wise to decorate the walls (of churches) on the right and on the left with animal figures so that we may see hares and goats and every kind of beast flying away while men and dogs follow them', and he answered, 'Yes'.

No doubt the attraction of real and imaginary creatures was very great. They played leading roles in the folk tales known to every child and adult. They were the subject of moral lessons in fables. Apart from panthers, dragons, wolves, elephants and hyenas there were mythical beasts like griffins, sirens, chimera, manticores, basilisks, centaurs, Ethiops, skiapods, hippopods, Scythis and, last but not least, the cynephalus which Isidore described in his *Etymologies* as 'more beast than man'. Some of these creatures are used symbolically. The siren represents the debauched woman; monkeys symbolize devils. Temptations and sin are pictured as demons,

Capital from the Cathedral of Autun, France, showing the suicide of Judas. 1125–35.

fierce beasts or monsters of semi-human form either disporting themselves or attacking men. The representation of this weird menagerie might also have had a magical function – the evil thing was banished when it was 'named'.

The reappearance of lions (which scarcely anyone in this age had ever seen alive) in the decorative treatment of churches is itself a problem. Porch columns are set on lions, guarding the entrance way; the rings on great bronze doors are in lions' mouths. They appear in manuscript paintings, initial letters, textiles, and capital sculptures. There are lions affronted and lions addorsed, lions contorted and above all lions splendid. These lions undoubtedly stem from the fine Eastern lions used decoratively since remote antiquity in Persia and traceable to Assyria and Egypt. The motif arrives in Europe well stylized by oriental craftsmen and assumes an honoured place in the marvellous iconography of the Middle Ages.

Capital from Coulombs showing the sleep of the Magi.
Paris, the Louvre.

The practice of animal sculpture was brought sharply into question by the denunciation of St Bernard of Clairvaux, founder of the Cistercian Order. Animal sculpture disappeared in Cistercian architecture.

As well as illustrations from the Bible, figural sculpture depicted scenes from daily life illustrating the Labours of the Months, episodes from the *Chanson de Roland* and the Arthurian cycle, the acrobatic feats of 'jongleurs', Virtues and Vices and the battle between them which derived from the *Psychomachia* of the Roman, Prudentius.

The iconographical sources are as rich and diverse as the subjects treated. The manuscript painting of an ealier age is very important. The best known example of this influence is the Beatus *Commentary on the Apocalypse*, from which the great apocalyptic tympanum at Moissac derived. The *Commentary* was written in 784 at Liebana in Spain. Somewhat later in the 10th century it was illustrated, and copy after copy followed until the 13th century. Twenty of these are still extant. Small ivories were another important source. In fact artists were influenced by all the small portable treasures which came into their hands.

It was in France that the great masterpieces of Romanesque sculpture were accomplished. Here three distinct styles developed, in Burgundy, Provence and in the south-west. The last two styles, especially that of Provence, were penetrated with antique influence from the study of the reliefs on sarcophagi and triumphal arches which still remained. The climax of French sculpture were the great tympana of Autun, Vézelay, Moissac and Toulouse. French influence spread from France to Italy, England and Spain where the imported style was merged with local traditions.

Romanesque sculpture is obedient to laws. The first is dictated by its architectural environment. Figures are distorted in order to fit into their setting. The marvellous thing is that within the confined space allotted to them they achieve a kind of freedom. At the same time they obey some spirit which transcends natural law and natural forms. Human and animal forms are at once stylized and expressionistic. There is a good deal of variety in the different styles, in, for example, the ecstatic frenzy of the Vézelay figures and the calm formality of the Miègeville tympanum at Toulouse.

The Romanesque sculptor also masters a wide range of expression. He is capable of conveying great tenderness, as in the Burgundian sculpture which Autun, Vézelay and Saulieu exemplify. In the lives of the saints, the Bible episodes and not least of all the depiction of ordinary mortals there are scenes revealing humour and tragedy, pain and joy. There is a direct naïve treatment of themes. The simple works carry much dignity and power and leave an unforgettable impression of humility and warmth on the onlooker. In striking contrast is the stern implacability and majesty of the representation of Christ in the tympanum.

Romanesque churches were richly embellished. Cluny, whose decorations reflected the cosmopolitan contacts of the Order, must have been especially brilliant. For example Matilda, the wife of Henry I of England, presented the church with a copper gilt candlestick eighteen feet high. Of this church St Bernard, the purist, wrote:

> ... the church is adorned with gemmes, crowns of light, nay, with lustres like cart wheels, girt all around with lamps, but no less brilliant with precious stones that stud them. Moreover, we see candelabra standing like trees of massive bronze, fashioned with marvellous subtlety of art, and glistening no less brightly with gemmes than with the lights they carry ... O vanity of vanities, yet no more vain than insane.

Of the rich decorations of churches and monasteries, their tapestries, thrones, pulpit ornaments, gold, silver and enamelled crosses, fine bronze doors, fonts and candelabra, carved and jewelled chalices and statues, reliquaries and golden altars, but a small number have escaped thieves and predatory governments. They are not assembled, but are found scattered in individual pieces in museums, cathedral and abbey treasures and in private collections. Looking at individual examples it is hard to visualize and feel the effect of the interior of a church with its painted walls, sculptures, the regalia vestments of the clergy and the beautiful treasures used in the Service. In this lack we are much the poorer, and the faithful of 1100, including the weary pilgrim, much the richer.

Capital from the Cathedral of Autun, showing the flight into Egypt. 1125–35.

Part II

Romanesque Europe

9 Italy and Dalmatia

Rome

By the 5th century the political power of the Empire had passed to the new capital in the East, Constantinople. Rome dwindled, decayed and endured the sackings of successive waves of barbarian invaders. Gregory the Great writes of the conquest of Rome by Genseric the Vandal in 455 when forty-six churches were destroyed:

> Everywhere we see mourning; we hear laments; cities, fortresses and villages are devastated; the earth is a desert; there is no end to the scourging of God's judgement. Behold Rome, once the Queen of the World, to what she is reduced! Rome is empty and has barely escaped the flames; her buildings are thrown down; the fate of Nineveh is upon her.

But the Pope's gloom is rather too pessimistic. The home of the successors to St Peter, the repository of the remains of the Apostle, of St Paul, and other early Christian saints and martyrs, Rome grew in spiritual stature as the head and centre of Latin Christendom. Emperor, monk and humble pilgrim came to the Eternal City, and it is here that we shall begin our journey, not to discover Romanesque, which had little impact in this city, but to uncover its early Christian and antique sources.

The tremendous building activity of the first two centuries after the legalization of Christianity was followed by a decline and stagnation in creative energy. The conservatism of Roman builders throughout the Middle Ages cannot be overstressed. The Byzantine reconquest, which quickly followed the Vandal desolation of 455, had no influence on architecture, and reconstruction was in the old style. This is typical. The Romans were content to restore, rebuild and add. The only mediaeval innovations were the detached campanili*

Opposite
The cloister of Monreale in Sicily. The slender columns show fine examples of Cosmati work.

* There are thirty-six of these still standing.

(supposedly derived from the 8th-century bell-tower of Old St Peter's) and the long porches or galilees added to the entrances of early basilicas.

In sculpture, the appropriation of pagan forms and motifs to Christian purposes can be seen in the sarcophagi preserved in the crypt of *St Peter's*. Here one finds rare examples of a clean-shaven shepherd symbolizing Christ, a classical philosopher representing St Peter, and many other examples of earliest Romano-Christian sculpture. There are fine collections also at the *Vatican*, the *Lateran Museum* and the *Museo delle Terme*. In spite of this wealth of early Christian, not to mention antique, sculpture upon which to draw, Rome played little part in the revival of the 12th century. Mention should be made, however, of the work of the Roman Cosmati family and their followers, known as Cosmatesque. This was a particular kind of geometric ornament of inlaid marble and mosaic, derived from the antique *Opus Alexandrinum*.

Quite a number of frescoes and mosaics have survived, and these are of the greatest significance, for Rome was the only city of western Europe where the art of figure painting was practised without a break from the 4th to the 11th centuries. Thus it is possible here to trace the evolution of painting throughout the Middle Ages, and see the intermingling of pagan, early Christian, Byzantine and Eastern influences. The earliest surviving Christian painting is in the *Catacombs*. Three catacombs are of outstanding interest: *Priscilla*, *Domitilla* and *Calixtus*. The first houses the Cappella Greca, the earliest three-aisled rectangular chapel, which contains the first representation of the Virgin Mary – an early 3rd-century wall painting. Also of interest are the paintings in the catacomb of the *Via Latina*, discovered in 1955, since they include the first representation of narrative scenes of biblical subjects used didactically rather than symbolically.

In the Vatican there are rare early secular and religious manuscripts, great illuminated Bibles, reliquary crosses, and oriental textiles.

Of the great Constantinian basilicas in Rome, the Lateran basilica, Old St Peter's, S. Lorenzo fuori le mura, nothing remains. The only church of this period to survive more or less intact is the rotunda, *S.Costanza*. Traditionally identified as the mausoleum of Constantine's daughter, it was converted into a baptistery in the 5th century.* It contains 4th-century mosaics. The five-aisled basilica of *S.Paolo fuori le mura* (385), rebuilt after a fire in 1823, shows the enormous scale and magnificence of Imperial basilicas, and suggests the vast splendour of the original St Peter's, which it resembles in size and plan. The apse and triumphal arch are original, and 5th-century mosaics are still preserved in this old portion. The church has the largest of all Romanesque Paschal candlesticks, a Cosmatesque work of *c.*1180. The sculptured base reflects the influence of Sassanian art. The adjoining cloister (*c.*1200) decorated with mosaic inlay, is a rare specimen of Romanesque art in Rome.

Two much altered early basilicas are *S.Pudenziana* (4th C.) and *S.Maria*

* At the gates of Rome are the remains of another mausoleum erected by Constantine for his mother, Helena. It is called the Tor Pignatarra.

Maggiore (5th C.). In the apse of the former is a notable 5th-century mosaic with (repaired) large figures of Christ, St Paul and St Peter (original) and many other figures. These mosaics are clearly in the classical pre-Byzantine style. The background shows Jerusalem, and the sky contains symbols of the four Evangelists in a form frequently portrayed in Romanesque sculptured doorways. There are also 5th-century mosaics on the nave walls and in the apse* of *S. Maria Maggiore*. The nave, which is flanked by antique columns, is original. In the Borghese Chapel is the *Black Virgin*, a work of great antiquity, traditionally attributed to the hand of St Luke.

In contrast with these two churches, the 5th-century basilica of *S. Sabina* is well-preserved and well-restored. It has classical columns and a timbered roof. The mosaic dates from the fifth century, as do the unique carved wooden doors depicting scenes from the Bible, the earliest Christian sculpture of this type. The juxtaposition of Old and New Testament scenes becomes quite common in church art of later centuries, e.g. the 11th-century doors at Hildesheim, the 12th-century doors of S. Zeno, Verona.

S. Maria Antiqua is another early Christian church. It is in the Forum, not far from the Temple of the Vestal Virgins, and was possibly originally a temple to their cult.† In it one finds remains of Roman painting from the late 6th to the 9th centuries. Some of the frescoes show Eastern influence, e.g. the *colobium* (long robe) worn by Christ in the Crucifixion is a Syrian iconographical feature. Others are more Byzantine in appearance. The narrative scenes are essentially Italianate.

The lower church of *S. Clemente* has important 9th-century (series of the life of Christ) and 11th-century frescoes. The latter, full of drama and movement, are masterpieces of Romanesque painting in Italy. Painters in many parts of Europe used Roman art of this period as a model. S. Clemente is one of the most fascinating churches in Rome. There are three building levels. At the lowest level are the remains of a 3rd-century *titulus*, or parish church. Above is an early Christian basilica partly enclosed within the walls and foundations of the present structure. This gives us a clear idea of the standard basilica of *c.* 380. The upper church was built after the destruction of its predecessor by the Normans in 1084.‡ The apsidal mosaics are of about the same date. There is also a chancel in traditional style, dating from 872, and a handsome Cosmatesque baldacchino.

Other churches with early mediaeval and Romanesque fresco remains are: *S. Maria Egiziaco* (late 9th century), *S. Bàstaniello* (9th–10th centuries), *Sant'Urbino* (11th century), and *S. Croce in Gerusalemme* (12th century). The 8th-century (?) frescoes of *S. Saba* have been entirely repainted. They show

* Until quite recently the apse mosaics were thought to belong to the 13th century.

† Its date of consecration is doubtful, but might be anterior even to S. Maria Maggiore, which would make it the first church dedicated to the Blessed Virgin.

‡ It is indicative of the conservatism of mediaeval Roman building that the present structure was mistaken for the 4th-century basilica, until the ruins of the latter were discovered and excavated in the mid-19th century.

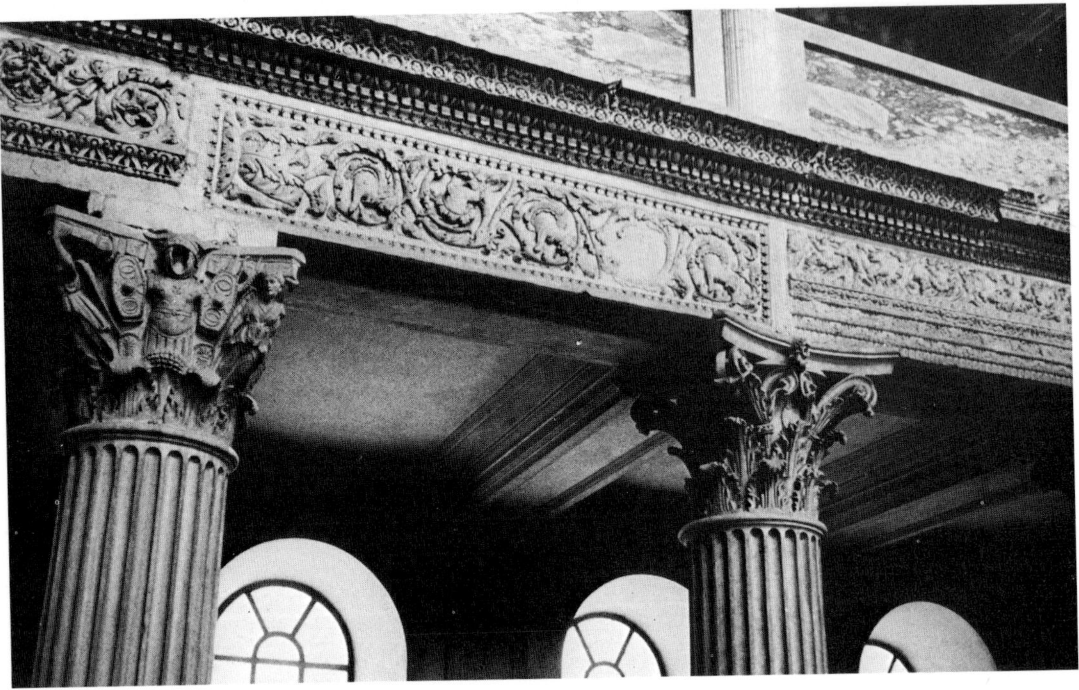

Detail of interior of S. Lorenzo fuori le mura, Rome.

strong Eastern influences. A panel of the Virgin was uncovered in *S. Maria Novella* some years ago.

Later mosaics can be seen at *Ss Cosmas e Damiano* (7th century), *S. Teodoro* (7th century), *S. Agnese* (7th century), *S. Pietro in Vincoli* (7th century), the *Vatican Crypt* (705–7), *S. Maria in Domnica* (9th century), and *S. Stefano Rotondo* (7th century). The last mentioned church is a much-debated structure showing both pagan and Christian origins. *S. Lorenzo fuori le mura*, which is a combination of two early churches, 432 and 578, with antique columns, has a 6th-century mosaic on the triumphal arch. The best preserved early mediaeval mosaics are in the chapel of S. Zeno in *S. Prassede* (rebuilt in 822). They are of exceptional quality. Mosaics and frescoes from the 6th century onwards were influenced by Byzantine art. But the Roman work is less refined and has a stronger feeling for drama and narration.

S. Maria in Cosmedin is an old basilica which has been well restored to its mediaeval condition of about 1120. It was used originally by Greeks living in Rome. Inside the church are antique fragments, and inscriptions built into the walls. There is also a museum of ancient fragments. The columns are antique. High up on the walls are 11th-century fresco fragments. There are also fragments of an 8th-century mosaic in the sacristy. The 12th-century Cosmatesque floor is of superb quality. The campanile, which is of the same

Capital from S. Lorenzo fuori le mura, Rome.

date, is very fine. Nearby is the so-called *House of Rienzi*, an extraordinary early 12th-century brick tower base.

In the rebuilt S. Maria in Cosmedin and S. Clemente we see the conservatism of mediaeval Roman architecture. This is also apparent in the church of the *Santi Quattro Incoronati* (reconstructed in the late 11th and early 12th century) and *S. Maria in Trastevere* (finished *c.* 1150). The tower of S. Maria in Trastevere is one of the best in Rome. Inside the church there is 13th-century mosaic work by Cavallini and a handsome Cosmatesque baldacchino. The only really Romanesque looking church is *Ss Giovanni e Paolo*. The original 5th-century building, which was in the form of a Greek cross, was one of the many churches which suffered destruction at the hands of the Normans in 1084. It was rebuilt in the 12th century in the Lombard style, but the 13th-century tower is Roman. Excavations under the church have uncovered pagan and Christian frescoes of the 2nd to the 6th centuries; also a chapel with frescoes of the 9th and 11th centuries.

There are interesting frescoes in churches a little way out of Rome, at **Tivoli** in *San Silvestro* and at the nearby **Marcellina**, in *Santa Maria in Monte Domenico*. A little further on, at **Palombara Sabina**, is the Benedictine abbey church of *S. Giovanni in Argentella* (12th century). The interior contains both 'barbaric' and Roman features.

Southern Italy

In southern Italy and Sicily we find some of the most interesting local variants of the Romanesque style. Here there is to be found an extraordinary multiplicity of cultural influences. Shortly before the conquest of England by the Normans in 1066, another Norman, Duke Robert Guiscard, invaded Sicily. Some years earlier the Normans had taken over Apulia and Calabria and after the conquest of Sicily they returned to the mainland and extended their southern Italian possessions. Byzantine and Arab influences are strong in this region. The Byzantines had been ousted from Sicily by the Arabs some centuries before the Norman occupation. They had maintained a tenuous control over Apulia, Basilicata and Calabria until the early 11th century. In the west the independent duchies of Naples, Sorrento, Amalfi and Benevento had close contacts through trade with Byzantium and Islam.

The argument that the Normans introduced Romanesque into southern Italy needs some modification. In the first place it must be remembered that they arrived before the maturing of the Romanesque style in Normandy. Secondly, one must not overlook the influences coming down from the North, from Tuscany, Lombardy and France. These contacts were established through pilgrimage centres like Monte S. Angelo (shrine of the Archangel Gabriel) and S. Nicola at Bari, which contained the remains of St Nicholas of Myra (Santa Claus). The Crusades were another means of contact, since southern Italy provided ports of embarkation for the Holy Land.

The artistic traces of the Norman period in these parts are numerous and of a particularly interesting character in the welding of so many different elements. The conception and pictorial subject matter of the great mosaic wall-decorations are Byzantine. However, the mosaic geometric decorations of columns and walls are clearly Arab. The buildings show the influence of Norman ideas. Cathedral doors of the finest Byzantine bronze decorate many of the church entrances, but sculptured figures are comparatively rare.

Fifty miles south of Rome is the town of **Anagni**. The late 11th-century *Cathedral* has an exterior in the Lombard style, but the Roman effect of the interior is heightened by the Cosmatesque work. In the crypt are very conservative mid-13th-century frescoes. They were probably influenced by the nearby Benedictine monastery of *Monte Cassino*, destroyed in the last war. Founded in 580 it was most powerful in the 11th century during the abbacy of the learned Desiderius. He imported Greek craftsmen to embellish his church, thus helping to spread the influence of Byzantine ideas and techniques not only in Italy but also over the rest of Europe.*

Inland from Monte Cassino at **S. Vicenzo** is a half-sunken cruciform chapel, all that remains of a large Benedictine abbey. It contains some very

* It has been argued that Monte Cassino had a role in the evolution of the Gothic style. Abbot Hugh of Cluny visited Monte Cassino in 1083, and adapted its architectural innovations, including the pointed arch, for Cluny. See, K. J. Conant, *Carolingian and Romanesque Architecture*, 800–1200 (Penguin Books, 1959), p. 223.

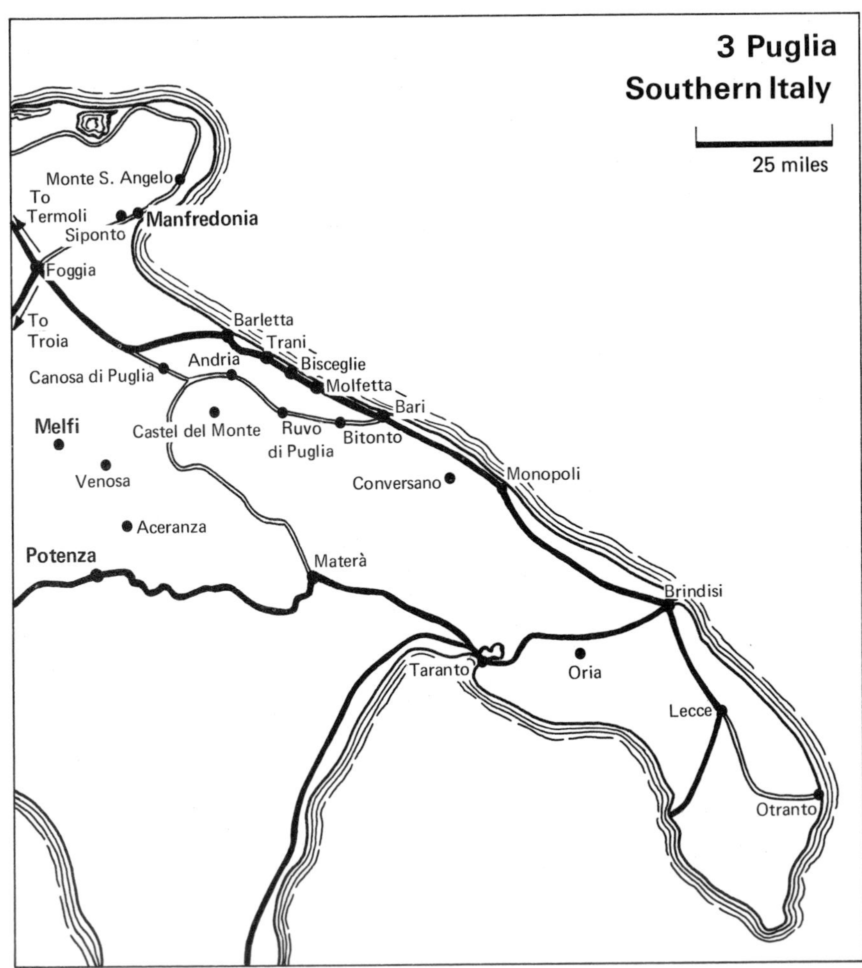

interesting 9th-century frescoes. There are also important frescoes (*c.* 1100) in *S. Angelo in Formis*, five miles north of Capua. Their Byzantine character probably reflects the influence of Monte Cassino.

The *Cathedral* of **Sessa Aurunca** has a rich façade which is antique in feeling. Inside there is an impressive 13th-century pulpit. The museum of the *Cathedral* of **Gaeta** contains a most unusual 13th-century Paschal candlestick. It consists of a marble column, covered with a series of reliefs, resting on a pedestal of four lions.

At **Caserta Vecchia** there is a beautiful *Cathedral* with a Moorish type cupola and Norman interlacing arcades. The church furnishings are of very high quality.

The *Cathedral* of **Benevento**, begun in the 11th century, was reduced to rubble in the last war. It has now been rebuilt. Fragments of the bronze door are preserved in the cathedral *Treasure*. The campanile dates from the 13th century. Next to the church are 11th-century cloisters with richly decorated capitals. The *Museum* is a 13th-century structure. The circular church of *S.Sofia* was founded in the 8th century during the period of Longobard domination. There are also remains of the Longobard town walls.

S. Felice, **Cimitile** near Nola, is an early foundation which has kept the remains of its 8th-century porch. The mediaeval pulpit apparently incorporated older panels with 'barbaric' style beasts against Byzantine-type foliage.

The entrance to the *Cathedral* of **Salerno** is through an atrium with pillars taken from ancient temples at Paestum. The campanile is like that of the cathedral of Amalfi. Inside there is a late 12th-century mosaic in the lunette above the entrance door and two splendid mosaic-worked pulpits (1173–81). Like other churches of this region, the plan of the cathedral is of a conservative, basilican type.

Amalfi is a mediaeval port with arched streets and climbing alley-ways. The *Cathedral*, though of mediaeval construction, has a Baroque interior. The façade has been (badly) restored in a 13th-century style. The campanile and small cloister show Arab-Norman features. There are fine Romanesque carvings in the cloister. The Byzantine bronze doors of *c.* 1066, now almost completely destroyed by fire, inspired similar doors in southern Italy. The *Cappuccini Hotel* and the *Hotel Luna*, formerly monasteries, have Arab-Norman cloisters.

Ravello is another mediaeval town high above the Mediterranean, six miles from Amalfi. *Castle Rufolo* is a partly 12th-century ruin consisting of a tower and open court in the Arab-Norman style.* The *Cathedral*, rebuilt in 1137, has bronze doors (1179) by Barisanus of Trani. His other doors are at Trani and Monreale. Inside there is a 12th-century pulpit, Roman in style rather than Campanian. Two other churches of the period are *S.Giovanni del Toro* and *S.Martino*. The garden of the *Belvedere Villa* is adorned with Romanesque sculpture.

At **Cava dei Tirreni** is the abbey of *Trinità della Cava*. It is from here that William II drew monks for his foundation at Monreale in Sicily.

Further south towards Sicily is *S. Michele*, **Potenza** (11th–12th centuries), and a Byzantine cross shrine and the remains of a Norman castle at **Cosenza**.

Sicily is justly famous for its exotic mediaeval buildings. The *Cathedral* of **Cefalù** (began in 1131) is the most western and least exotic looking, with its two massive towers flanking the 13th-century façade. The mosaic in the apse (1148) is the oldest in Sicily.

The *Cathedral* of **Monreale** is one of the marvels of mediaeval architecture and decorations, and certainly the most beautifully located building in Italy.

* Wagner wrote *Parsifal* here and Klingsor's Magic Castle (Act II of *Parsifal*) is based upon the mediaeval portions of this castle.

Animal carving from the pulpit of S. Felice, Cimitile.

It was begun in 1174. The interior reveals one of the largest displays of mosaics to be seen anywhere, covering an area of over 6000 square metres. They have suffered much at the hands of restorers. The bronze doors at the main entrance are by Bonnanus of Pisa (1186). They have very fine low-relief carvings of Old and New Testament scenes. The doors on the north aisle are by Barisanus of Trani (*c.* 1186). The beautiful cloisters (1174–89) belonged to the Benedictine monastery. The 216 columns are decorated with mosaics, and almost all the designs are used only once. The carvings of the capitals are most varied and interesting.

The *Cappella Palatina* in **Palermo** is another example of the way in which the Norman rulers adopted the arts of the civilizations they displaced: the Byzantine and Arab. This chapel (1132–43) is richly decorated with mosaics, its columns supporting tall, slightly pointed Arab arches, and it has an elaborately compassed marble floor. Other Arab features are the angle columns, the squinches with receding steps in the zone of the drum, and the magnificent stalactite ceiling over the nave. The lectern is one of the finest examples of the antique-influenced style in Italy.

S.Giovanni degli Eremiti (1132) is a small church with mosque-like pointed domes and Arab arched cloisters. It is an exotic creation of great style and atmosphere, one of the outstanding examples of the Sicilian-Byzantine style.

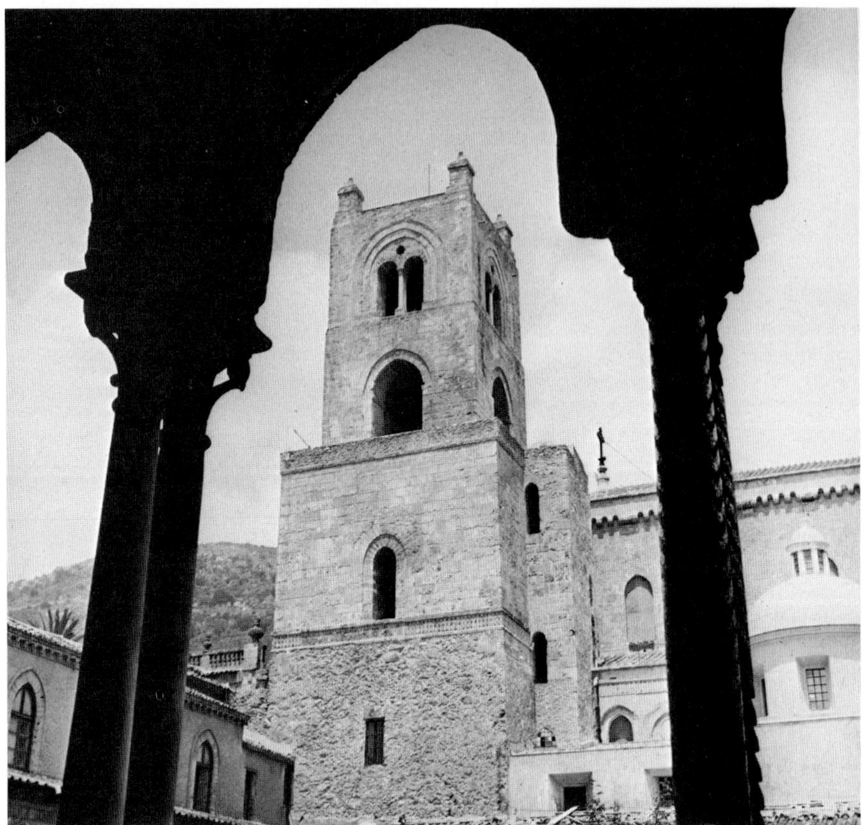

Exterior view of the Cathedral of Monreale.
Begun in 1174.

S.Cataldo, was restored in 1884. It is essentially similar to S.Giovanni. The much altered *Cathedral* of Palermo has retained its 12th-century southern façade. *S. Maria dell' Ammiraglio* (1143–51) was restored in 1869. The plan is purely Byzantine. The *Chiesa dei Vespri* dates from the second half of the 12th century.

In the *Royal Palace of Palermo* the *Stanza di Ruggiero*, or Norman stanza, is decorated with attractive mosaics. *La Ziza*, *La Cuba* and *La Piccola Cuba* are examples of Moslem-influenced Norman secular architecture.

Two other churches built during the Norman occupation are worthy of note. The first is the *Chiesa della Trinità di Delia* at **Castelvetrano** in the south-west corner of Sicily. It was discovered in 1880 and well-restored. A few miles from Caltanisetta is the *Badia di S.Spirito* (1153), which has changed little.

Opposite
The apse of the Cathedral of Monreale.

Paternò has a good example of a Norman castle. It is a small fort built by Roger I in 1073.

Earthquakes have destroyed most of the Romanesque cathedrals of Calabria.

There are, however, some interesting examples of small Byzantine churches which have been quite well preserved. *La Cattolica* (10th century) at **Stilo** belongs to this group. There are both Byzantine and Norman remains at **Gerace**. The 11th-century *Cathedral*, which shows Arab influences, has been restored. *S.Giovanello* is another church of the period. **S.Severina** includes the ruins of a Byzantine-Norman fortress and a Norman castle. There is a baptistery (6th–9th centuries). Armenian influences are discernible in the church of *S. Filomena*. The abbey of *S. Giovanni in Fiore* (1189) is a Byzantine basilican church 3,000 feet up in the mountains. It is from here that Joachim issued his prophecies towards the end of the 12th century. In the *Cathedral Library*, **Rossano**, is the important 6th-century *Codex Rossano*.

We now come into Apulia (today, Puglia). Here are the most important examples of Romanesque architecture on the southern Italian mainland. The 11th-century *Cathedral* of **Taranto** belongs to a group of Byzantine-inspired multi-domed churches. There is a late Romanesque *Cathedral* (1268–70) at **Materà**, and the perfectly preserved *S.Giovanni Battista* (completed in 1204). **Oria** has the Byzantine chapel of *Ss Cristante e Daria* and a castle built by Frederick II in 1233.

The interior of *Ss Nicola e Cataldo* at **Lecce** is Baroque, but the splendidly ornamented façade is late 12th century. In the early 11th-century *Cathedral* of **Otranto** is an attractive mosaic pavement of 1186.

The *Cathedral* of **Brindisi** begun in the 12th century has been much altered. *S.Lucia* has a Byzantine crypt. *S.Giovanni al Sepolcro* is a Templar church modelled on the Holy Sepulchre in Jerusalem. It contains Byzantine frescoes. *S.Benedetto* (1080) has an interesting portal and cloister. There is also a castle of Frederick II in **Brindisi**.

The *Cathedral* of **Monopoli** has one of the first portals with columns resting on animal bases. This became a typical feature of Apulian Romanesque art. **Conversano** is worth visiting for its Romanesque *Cathedral*, *Monastery* and *Castle*.

At **Bari** one finds yet another of Frederick II's castles (1233–40). The *Cathedral* is mid-12th century. Its model was *S.Nicola* (1087–1197), the most influential of the churches of Apulia, inspiring a whole series of similar structures. It was planned as a pilgrimage church. The eclectic design includes Lombard, Tuscan, Norman and local elements. Two towers flank the massive, cliff-like façade. The carvings on the portal reflect Lombard influence in style and subject matter. Inside there are low reinforcing diaphragm arches which somewhat spoil the effect of the interior. In the apse is a 12th-century tabernacle. The famous bishop's throne (*c.* 1098) shows strong Northern influences. There is also a very fine crypt.

The *Old Cathedral of S. Corrado* (1150–end of 13th century) at **Molfetta** is a notable example of an Apulian triple-domed church. **Bisceglie** has a 13th-century *Cathedral.* The handsome *Cathedral* of **Trani** (1094–1180) derives from S.Nicola at Bari. The bronze doors are by Barisanus of Trani.

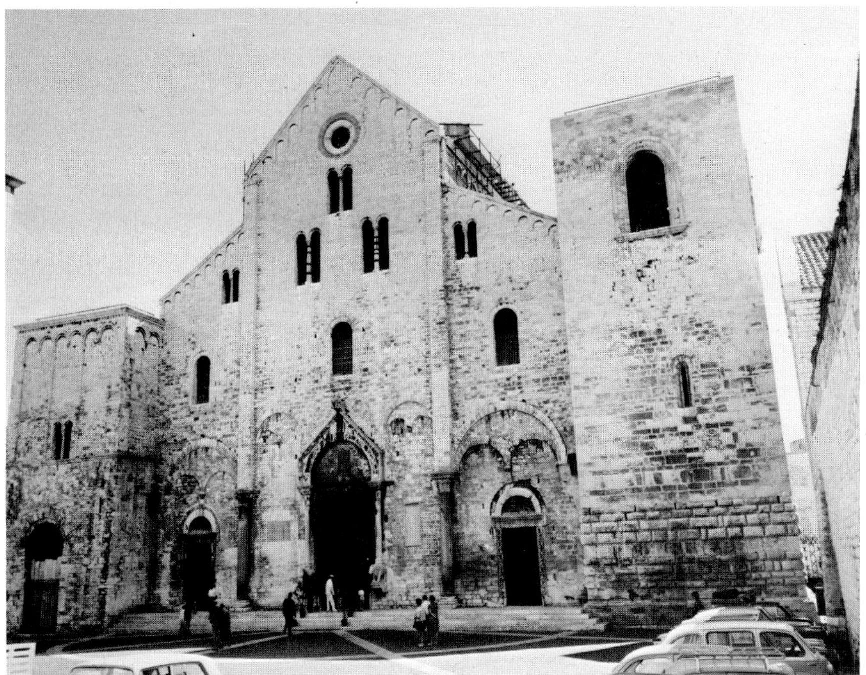

Façade of S. Nicola, Bari.
Begun in 1087.

In the portal there is a beautiful carved tympanum, a feature very unusual in Italy in comparison with France. It sometimes appears along the Apulian pilgrimage routes. Another example can be seen at the *Cathedral* of **Barletta** (12th century). Inside there is a fine baldacchino. The church of *S. Sepolcro* (13th century) has a colossal bronze statue.

The *Cathedrals* of **Bitonto** (1175–1200) and **Ruvo di Puglia** (13th century) are typically Apulian. The former has a magnificent rose window. Ruvo has a wonderful portal with two immense griffins projecting from the façade. **Andria** was a resort of Frederick II. There are Byzantine murals in *S. Croce*. *Castel del Monte* is the famous fortified hunting lodge of Frederick II. It is well-preserved.

At **Venosa** there are the imposing ruins of the *Abbazia della Trinità*, a 12th-century monastery markedly French in character. It has a Burgundian ambulatory with radiating apses. The neighbouring *Cathedral* of **Aceranza** is stylistically related to Venosa.

The *Cathedral* of **Canosa di Puglia**, dedicated in 1101, is the first and most important of the Apulian domed churches. The episcopal throne, resting on two elephants, is derived from an Eastern model. There is also a fine pulpit. On the south wall of the church is the tomb of Bohemond, hero of the First Crusade (after 1111). The *Cathedral* of **Foggia** shows French influence.

The *Cathedral* of **Troia** (*c.* 1093–1127) is a most unusual structure. It is virtually a replica of Pisa. The rose window is very beautiful. The interesting bronze doors on the façade (1119) and the south flank (1127) are by a certain Oderisius of Benevento. Inside there is a typical Apulian pulpit of 1169. Pisan influence spread from Troia to the abbey church of *S. Leonardo* at **Siponto**. It has Tuscan arcading on the exterior, but the portal is Lombard and inside, the nave is surmounted by two domes on squinches.

Monte S. Angelo, once the shrine of the Archangel Michael, has little of interest surviving, apart from a later campanile and a domed tomb or baptistery known as the *Tomba dei Rotari* (1180–1200). Next to this are the ruins of *S. Pietro* and the small Tuscan basilica of *S. Maria Maggiore*. At **Termoli** there is a 12th-century *Cathedral*.

The region known as the Abruzzi was always something of a backwater and local traditions remained strong even after the introduction of the Romanesque style towards the end of the 11th century. At **Fossacesia** there is the impressive Romanesque church of *S. Giovanni in Venere*. *S. Maria Maggiore* at **Pianella**, just north of Pescara, has a fresco in the apse and an interesting pulpit of *c.* 1160. There is another interesting pulpit in the church of *S. Angelo*. These are a special feature of Romanesque art in the Abruzzi. One of the best examples is in the abbey church of *San Clemente a Casauria* (mid-late 12th century) at **Torre dei Passeri**. The large carved rosettes are characteristic. One finds them again in the corners of the sculptured tympanum. The tympanum and portals bear an unmistakable resemblance to French cathedrals. On the bronze door (1191) of the portal is a pictorial catalogue of the former treasures of the monastery, which was founded in 871.

S. Pietro ad Oratorium, near **Capestrano**, is a beautifully situated church, now deserted. It was renovated in the Romanesque style in *c.* 1100. The baldacchino is a magnificent early 13th-century work. The wall and apse behind are covered with a 12th-century fresco.

At **Aquila**, a city founded by Frederick II, are a number of fine examples of late Romanesque architecture. At **Celano**, near Aquila, is another of his castles, accurately rebuilt in modern times.

Not far from Aquila is the town of **Bominaco** with several Romanesque structures: the monastic church of *S. Maria* (early 12th century); the *Chapel of Ease*, with late 13th-century frescoes and vigorous reliefs of animals in stucco on the choir screens; and the abbey church of *S. Pellegrino* (11th–12th centuries).

Central Italy

The glories of Romanesque in central Italy are concentrated in Pisa and Lucca. However, scattered all over this middle band of Italy are abbeys, churches and towers, the most interesting of which we shall discuss briefly.

About thirty miles north-east of Rome, near Nepi, is the abbey church of

Castel Sant'Elia. Its extensive 11th-century frescoes, the work of a Roman family, reveal remarkable imaginative powers and sensitivity of execution.

Further north at **Viterbo** are the churches of *Ss Giovanni in Zoccoli*, *S. Sisto* (restored), and *S. Maria Nuova.* In the latter there is a 13th-century painted tabernacle. Monumental crucifixes, altarpieces and tabernacles are common in central Italy and Spain. They were directly influenced by Byzantine icons, and were the precursors of the art of easel pictures. The *Piazza S. Pellegrino* is a perfectly preserved Romanesque square.

Parts of the *Cathedral* of **Tuscania** may date from the 8th century. The massive façade, with its carvings influenced from a variety of sources, is early 12th century. Inside there is an 11th-century fresco and an interesting crypt (end of the 11th century). *S. Maria Maggiore* (11th century–1206) has a similar façade. Next to the church is a free-standing square Lombard tower.

At **Montefiascone** is the double church of *S. Flaviano* (begun 1032). The elaborate capitals in the lower church (*c.* 1160) are most original in conception. The *Palazzo del Capitano del Popolo* (12th–13th centuries), **Orvieto**, is an excellent example of Romanesque secular architecture.

In the little town of **Ferentillo** is the church of *S. Pietro in Valle* (late 11th or 12th century). Its fresco fragments are rustic but vigorous. The frontal of the high altar is archaic looking, and may belong to the 8th century, when the church was founded. The campanile is in the Lombard style.

Spoleto is well-endowed with Romanesque monuments. The *Cathedral* was rebuilt in 1155 – from this period dates the ornamentation on the main entrance. The rose window (1207) is a Cosmatesque work. The early monumental crucifix in the sacristy is by Alberto di Sozio (1187). In contrast with later convention, Christ is shown as living. *Sant'Eufemia*, founded in the 10th century, has been well-restored. Among the 12th-century frescoes in the church and sacristy of *Ss Giovanni e Paolo* is a martyrdom of Thomas à Becket. The choir of the church of *S. Salvatore* dates from the period of its foundation in the 5th century. The building was restored in the 9th century and extended in the 12th century. It contains early Christian sculptures. *S. Pietro* has a 13th-century façade with splendid reliefs.

The *Palace of the Consuls* (*c.* 1270) **Bevagna**, is late Romanesque. The church of *S. Silvestro* (1195) has a simple, pleasing façade. The beautiful rose windows of the *Cathedral* of **Assisi** (11th–13th centuries) are 11th century. St Francis and the Emperor Frederick II were baptised in this church. The façade of the Benedictine church of *S. Pietro*, founded in the 12th century, is purely Romanesque. In the nearby town of **Gubbio** is the late Romanesque *Palazzo dei Consoli* (1300). At **Fabriano** is the 12th-century church of *S. Vittore delle Chiuse*, a centralized structure of Byzantine type.

On the east coast at **Ancona** is the 12th-century *Cathedral*, with zebra-work masonry, recalling Pisa. Near Ancona is the lofty church of *S. Maria di Porto Nuovo* (12th century), a very fine building indeed.

Inland once more we find at **Arezzo** the church of *S. Maria della Pieve.*

Façade of the Cathedral of Assisi. 11th–13th centuries.
Sketch by John Ruskin in the Ashmolean Museum, Oxford.

The façade (1210) is built in the Pisan style. Not far from Arezzo, in the little town of **Gropina**, is the parish church of *S. Pietro* (mid 12th century). It has an interesting archaic looking pulpit.

The abbey church of *Sant'Antimo* is situated near **Montalcino** in the Siena district. The abbey was founded in the 9th century, and the church was rebuilt from 1118 onwards. In plan and sculptural decoration it is very much indebted to France. The *Cathedral* of **Massa Maritimma** (1228–67) was built in the Pisan style.

The mediaeval town of **S. Gimignano**, like Avila in Spain and Carcassonne in France, is an example of a mediaeval community of the 12th and 13th centuries still virtually in its original state. It contains no less than thirteen towers which were used in the Middle Ages as dwellings and for protection. It is said that there were once seventy-six towers. The isolation of these dwellings exemplifies the individualism of the Tuscans.* The town contains numerous 13th-century houses. The *Cathedral* is of the 12th century. The façade and frescoes date from later periods. On the edge of the town is the church of *S. Pietro* (11th and 12th centuries), with fine 14th-century frescoes. Beneath the town walls are vaulted washing basins, probably of the 12th century. They are still in use.

Opposite
Façade of S. Maria della Pieve, Arezzo. 1210.
Overleaf
View of the towers of S. Gimignano.

* Florence had 150 such towers, Bologna, 180. Lucca 'rose like a forest'.

Above: Cathedral of Pisa from the north-west with the Leaning Tower in the background.
Below: Detail of the exterior of the Cathedral. Water-colour sketch by John Ruskin in the Ashmolean Museum, Oxford.
Opposite: Façade of the Cathedral of Pisa. 12th century.

The group of buildings at the Piazza del Duomo in **Pisa**, comprising the *Cathedral*, the *Baptistery* and the *Leaning Tower*, constitute the most finished and elegant group of Romanesque architecture that Europe possesses. The fine architecture of Pisa is the direct product of the nearby marble quarries and the great prosperity of the city when it reached great power as a maritime state.

The founding of the cathedral marked the victory over the Saracens by the Genoese navy at Palermo. It was begun in 1063 by Buschetto (who might have been a Greek) and altered in the 12th and 13th centuries. The distinctive features of the cathedral, progenitor of the Pisan Romanesque style, were the extensive use of marble panelling, the embellishment of the exterior with decorative arcading, and the façade with four storeys of small arcades. A variety of sources were drawn upon for the construction and embellishment of the cathedral, but they have been synthesized to form a highly original and surprisingly harmonious whole. The architectural design is basically Lombard, although there has been no attempt to use stone vaulting. The arcading on the façade recalls Lombard free-standing gallery work. The architects drew heavily not only on Roman buildings for material – the columns in the main aisle are antique – but upon Roman forms and architectural patterns, e.g., the decorative arcades on the exterior, the zebra work inside. There are also

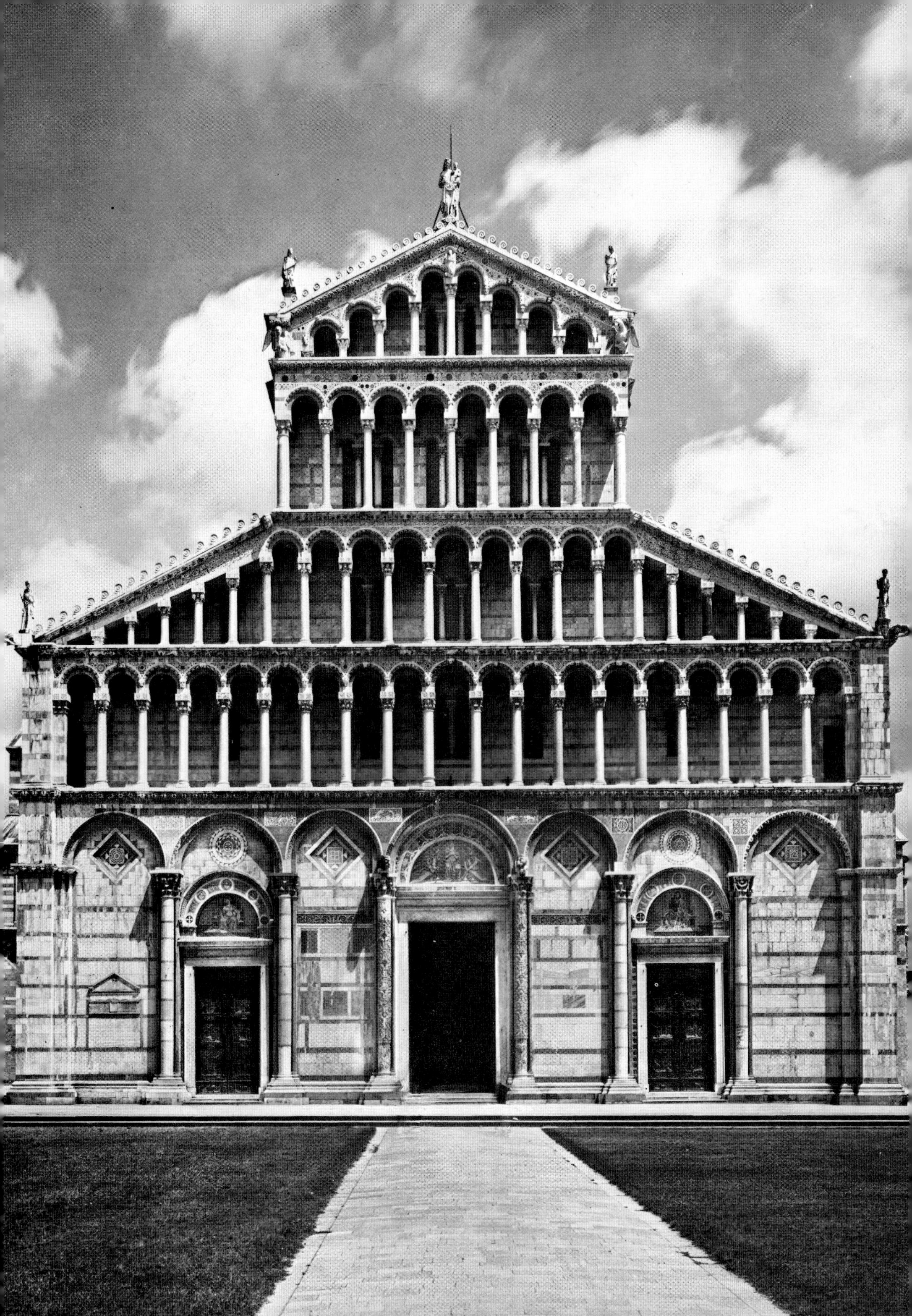

Façade of S. Michele, Lucca.
Completed 1143.

distinct Byzantine and Eastern overtones. The mosaic in the apse is in the Byzantine tradition. The iconography of the fine bronze doors by Bonnanus Pisanus (1180) is Byzantine, although the treatment is Romanesque. The dome shows Islamic influence.

The white marble baptistery was begun in 1152 and completed in the 14th century in the Gothic style. Inside there is a font by Guido da Como (1246) – a masterpiece. The campanile (Leaning Tower) was begun in 1173 and completed *c.* 1350. Its cylindrical form recalls the old belfries in Ravenna. *S. Paolo a Ripa d'Arno* (begun in 1210) is a simplified version of the cathedral.

Examples of the Pisan style may be seen in Apulia, Tuscany, and on the island of Sardinia, where many Pisan Romanesque basilicas were built from the 11th to the 14th centuries. Among these are *S. Gavino* at **Porto Torres**

Left : Detail of the façade of S. Michele, Lucca.
Right : Detail of the façade of the Cathedral.
Water-colour sketches by John Ruskin in the Ashmolean Museum, Oxford.

(late 11th century – *c.* 1111), *Trinità di Saccargia* at **Codrongianus** (1116–*c.* 1180–1200), and *S. Maria di Castello* at **Cagliari** (*c.* 1200–1300).

However, it is at **Lucca** that we find the best examples of the style outside Pisa. *S. Michele* (completed 1143) has a wonderful four storied façade with a statue of St Michael slaying a Dragon on the top. The façade of the *Cathedral* (begun 1160) is also very impressive. Inside is the famous equestrian statue of St Martin which used to be on the façade, and a splendid font by Guido da Como (*c.* 1246). Next to the cathedral, is an older campanile and a Romanesque *Episcopal Palace*. The church of *S. Frediano* (1112–47) is more obviously classical in spirit than the others. The mosaic on the façade (*c.* 1260) has been badly restored. The late 12th-century font inside has borrowed from Roman sarcophagus reliefs in an ambitious attempt to emulate the antique.

94 Façade of S. Frediano, Lucca. 1112–47.

Exterior of the baptistery of S. Giovanni, Florence. 11th–13th centuries.

The *Cathedral* of **Barga** (early 12th century) near Lucca, houses some very fine church furnishings. In *S. Bartolommeo in Pantano*, **Pistoia** there is a pulpit by Guido da Como.

While **Florence** saw its great artistic development a century after the high point of Romanesque art, it has certain examples of Romanesque art that are of great significance. Here the classicizing tendencies, which are never far below the surface of central Italian Romanesque, are most strongly expressed, in the basilica of *S. Miniato al Monte* (11th–12th centuries). The façade is sheathed in black and white marble. The colourful ornamentation inside reflects early Christian, Byzantine and Eastern influences. The crypt is very interesting.

The famous baptistery of *S. Giovanni* (11th–13th centuries), adjoining the cathedral, is a large octagonal structure, beautifully finished in marble. Its immense mosaic decorations (13th century) are the finest in central Italy. The extraordinary parti-coloured pavement is also 13th century.

The *Cathedral* of **Fiesole** (1028) is the oldest church in the environs of Florence. It is a fine solid structure. The antique columns in the nave are from nearby ruins. The late 12th-century façade of the *Badia* (begun *c.* 1090) has inlaid marble around the door, like S. Miniato.

Northern Italy

The north of Italy would be one of the most fascinating and complex areas for the study of Romanesque and its origins. There are well-preserved examples of early Christian, Byzantine, Longobard, and early and mature Lombard Romanesque art. The region was ideally situated to receive, absorb for itself and disseminate, influences coming up from Rome and the South, from the Byzantine and Islamic East, and from the North. For the first time we enter the mainstream of Romanesque art in Europe.

The vital core of northern Italy was the Milan-Como region, which managed to retain importance from Roman times, through the period of Longobard domination, into the Middle Ages. Here we find well-preserved examples of the so-called 'first Romanesque' style of *c.* 1000. These churches are small, substantially built, and partially or wholly vaulted. The exteriors are decorated with blank arcading and eaves niches.

Among the colourful theories concerning the origin of this architecture, is the theory of the Comacini master-builders. According to this theory a reference found in the laws of the Longobard kings to 'Magistri comacini', who are builders accorded certain privileges, justifies the inference that the stone masons from Lake Como constituted a guild of master-builders. This guild, it was argued, had preserved the secrets of the Romans in constructing vaults and dressing stone. However this romantic theory has not stood the test of critical evaluation and the word 'comacini' is now interpreted by scholars as meaning 'mason'.

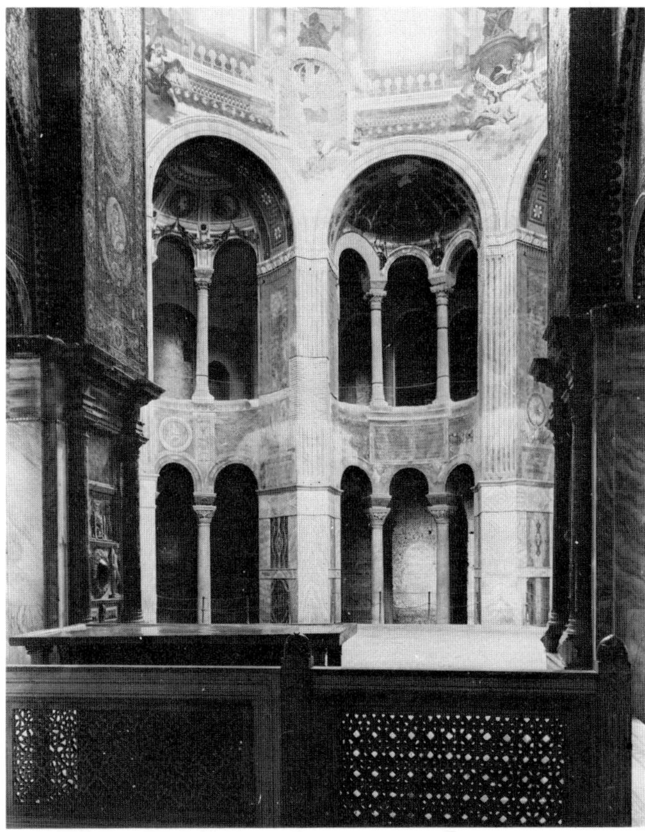

Interior of S. Vitale, Ravenna. 526–46.

The name of Lombard masons became in time synonymous with that of skilled builder-architects. In the later Middle Ages, Lombard masons travelled, building churches and castles in England, France, Germany and even in far off Russia. Parts of the Kremlin were built by them. They must have brought back ideas from their travels, for Lombard Romanesque building is not simply a development of the 'first Romanesque' but reflects also transalpine influences, particularly of the Empire. Romanesque architecture in what is now Piedmont, on the other hand, substantially derives from Burgundian and French models. These influences are apparent also in the sculpture of northern Italy.

The superb monuments of **Ravenna** illustrate the uninterrupted architectural history of this city from the 5th to the 8th centuries. There are three periods represented: Romano-Christian, Romano-Goth (476–538) and Byzantine (539–700). Ravenna was a bridge between the East and West and an important centre for the dissemination of early Byzantine influences in the north of Italy and from there throughout Europe.

The *Mausoleum of Galla Placidia* (*c.* 440) is a cruciform structure built of plain brick. Its interior is illuminated by transparent alabaster windows. The ceiling and walls are covered with mosaics of great delicacy. The *Baptistery of the Orthodox* or *Neon* (*c.* 425–58) is a domed octagonal building decorated with fine marble and a large mosaic ceiling of the 5th century. On the exterior we see an early example of pilaster strips flanking arched corbel tables. This was to become the hall-mark of the 'first Romanesque' style. *S. Giovanni Evangelista* is a basilica of the first half of the 5th century. It was rebuilt in the 7th and 12th centuries, and again after bombing in the last war. The *Baptistery of the Arians* is an octagonal building of the late 5th century.

Just outside Ravenna is the *Tomb of Theodoric* (*c.* 526) – a fine building, capped by a great monolithic dome. Theodoric was the most Romanized of the Gothic conquerors and made a notable effort to harmonize Roman and Gothic cultures. The basilica of *S. Apollinare Nuovo* (*c.* 490) was begun during the period of the Gothic occupation. It contains fine mosaics.

S. Vitale (526–46) is a domed cruciform building, Byzantine in design and showing Eastern elegance and sophistication. In its choir are two of the most famous mosaics extant, with the portraits of the Emperor Justinian and the Empress Theodora. The pilaster strips on the outside are bolder than those of the Baptistery of the Orthodox. S. Vitale exercized a powerful artistic influence in western Europe for hundreds of years. Its plan was copied in Charlemagne's chapel at Aachen.

The 6th-century *Palace of the Exarchs* is an excellent example of early secular architecture. Its use of arched windows and columns as decoration is suggestive of Romanesque architecture.

Near Ravenna is the basilica of *S. Apollinare in Classe* (*c.* 550), very well-preserved and with a lovely mosaic of the 7th century in its apse.

Some thirty miles to the north along the coast is the impressive basilican church of *S. Maria*, **Pomposa**. The nave is 8th century; the porch was consecrated in 1026. The beautiful campanile (1063) is a fine example of the mature Lombard tower. A little to the west is **Bagnacavallo** with *S. Pietro in Silvis*, a 6th-century building of the Ravenna type.

The *Cathedral* of **Ferrara** has a portal (*c.* 1135) by Niccolò, pupil of the famous Wiligelmo. The carvings resemble the work of southern France, especially Toulouse. In the *Diocesan Museum* is a series of the Labours of the Months, a popular theme in Romanesque sculpture.

At **Bologna** there is a centrally planned church of *S. Stefano* (*c.* 1150–60) with side court, and the church of *S. Pietro* adjoining.

Along and near the old pilgrimage route from France to Rome we find a series of splendid churches. The design of the *Cathedral* of **Modena** (1099–1106) shows Tuscan influence. The plan is simple, and the church was originally wooden-roofed – in contrast with the stone vaulting of Lombard churches. The sculpture on the façade is the work of Wiligelmo and his school, effectively marking the beginning of the resurrection of figure sculpture in

Opposite
Exterior view of S. Apollinare in Classe, *c.* 550.

Exterior of the baptistery of Parma. 1196–*c.* 1216.

Italy. The master's narrative gifts are clearly displayed in the vigorously portrayed scenes. On the archivolt of the *Porta della Peschiera* are figures from the Arthurian legend.

The *Cathedral* of **Parma** was rebuilt in the 12th century, after the earthquake of 1117, and completed in the 13th century. The façade is typically Lombard with its ascending and descending arcades and porch with columns resting on the backs of lions. Inside, the church has Lombard ribbed vaults. In plan it is more complex than Modena, and therefore more northern. The

Opposite
Detail of the patterned wall-work on the exterior of S. Stefano, Bologna. *c.* 1150–60.

Right : Relief figure of a Prophet, Cathedral of Modena. 1099–1106.

Below : Genesis relief, Cathedral of Modena, showing the creation of Adam and Eve. 1099–1106.

Opposite, above
Deposition panel by Benedetto Antelami, 1178. Cathedral of Parma.

Opposite, below
Genesis relief, Cathedral of Modena, showing the slaying of Cain. 1099–1106.

richly carved capitals are fine Romanesque specimens. The Deposition panel, now in the wall of the south transept, is by Benedetto Antelami. He was responsible for the fine sculpture, the font, and perhaps also the design of the octagonal baptistery (1196–*c.* 1216).

Near Piacenza is the collegiate church of *Castel'Arquato*, also rebuilt after the earthquake of 1117 and completed in 1122. On the façade of the *Cathedral* of **Borgo S. Donnino** is more sculpture by Antelami and his assistants. The niche statues of David and Ezekiel are particularly impressive.

Piacenza has two Romanesque monuments: *S. Savino* (dedicated 1107) and the *Cathedral* (1122–13th century). The cathedral has Gothic features but the overall feeling is Romanesque. The façade sculpture is by Niccolò and his assistants. Some of the capitals inside have lively scenes of guild life. The *Cathedral* of **Cremona** was begun in 1129–43, but there are extensive Gothic and Renaissance additions.

At **Bobbio** there was an important old abbey founded by the Irish monk, St Columban, in 612. In the crypt of the basilica of *S. Columbano* are relics of splendid early mediaeval church furnishings.

There are a few Romanesque monuments to be seen along the Ligurian coast. The *Cathedral* of **Genoa** was begun in 1199, but little of Romanesque has survived later alterations. The few surviving original features of the monastery of *S. Fruttuoso di Capo di Monte* show Byzantine influence, which is also strong in the well-preserved church of *S. Paragorio* (late 11th century) at **Noli**.

The 11th-century baptistery of *S. Pietro* at **Asti** is a circular building – a rare form in northern Italy. At **Vezzolano** in the Asti region is the abbey church of *S. Maria* belonging to a Benedictine monastery, supposed to have been founded by Charlemagne in *c.* 773. The present church was completed in *c.* 1189.

The *Cathedral of Sant'Evasio* at **Casale Monferrato** is very interesting. It was dedicated in 1107, and underwent alterations at the end of the century. Some scholars think that the compound vaulting of the narthex (part of the later alterations) reflects Armenian influence, via the Crusades. Others attribute it to Islam. Inside the church are splendid relics of floor mosaics. The *Cathedral of Sant'Eusebio* at **Vercelli** contains an Ottonian life-size gilt metal crucifix, and mosaic fragments.

The church of *S. Fede di Cavagnolo* at **Cavagnolo Po**, near Turin, belonged to an abbey founded by monks from Saint-Foy, Conques. Therefore the French character of this church with the three porches on the west front is not surprising. Overlooking the Val di Susa on the Mt Cenis road is the fortress-like *Sagra di S. Michele* (*c.* 1150). Its interior is essentially Gothic. The *Porta dello Zodiaco* is very interesting since the zodiacal symbols are probably the first representation of this subject matter in Italy.

In the Val d'Aosta are two early Romanesque foundations, the *Cathedral* of **Ivrea** and the *Cathedral* of **Aosta**, both dating from the beginning of the 11th

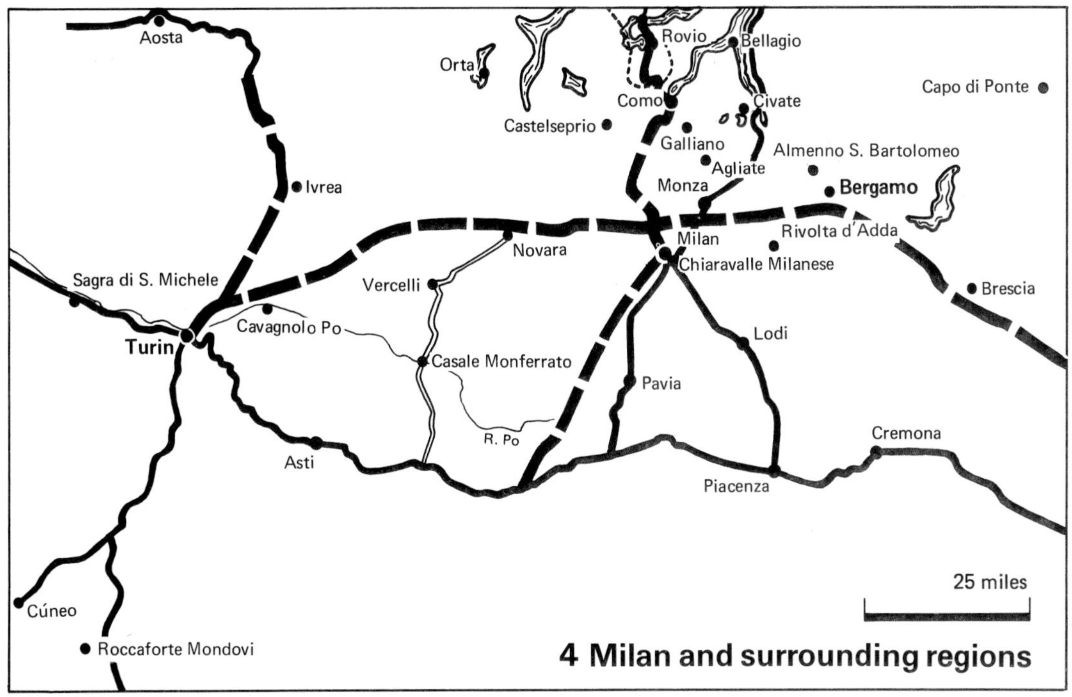

4 Milan and surrounding regions

century. Their towers are among the first built in Lombardy, probably derived from the belfries of the Exarchate at Ravenna. The cloister of the collegiate church of *Sant'Orso*, Aosta, has imaginatively worked figurative capitals (*c.* 1130).

South of Turin near Cúneo is the *Pieve di S. Maurizio*, **Roccaforte Mondovi**. The whole right side-aisle and the apse are decorated with 13th-century frescoes which show a mixture of Tuscan Romanesque and Byzantine influences.

The ancient basilica of *S. Giulio* at **Lake Orta**, near Novara, was rebuilt a little before 1000 by the priest architect, William of Volpiano. It has a fine early 11th-century black marble pulpit. In the former town hall of **Novara** (*c.* 1208) are frescoes depicting secular scenes in a very lively fashion. The paintings on the walls and vaults of the *Oratory of S. Siro* – all that remains of a Romanesque basilica destroyed in 1857 – are of exceptional quality. Those on the west wall were painted in the 13th century; the rest date from the second half of the 12th century.

At **Milan** we find a series of monuments from early Christian times to Romanesque. The most important of these is *S. Ambrogio*. This very remarkable agglomeration of styles is an almost inexhaustible storehouse of pre-Romanesque and Romanesque art. It was built on the foundations of a huge church laid out by St Ambrose in 385. Its remains can be seen below the present structure. The dating of the Romanesque church is fraught with controversy. The most general consensus of opinion would seem to be that the oldest portion is the apse, with its mosaic (9th century). The stumpy tower known as the *Campanile dei Monaci* belongs to the following century.

Somewhat later is the nave with its alternating piers and columns, a design of both strength and beauty. It was constructed early in the 12th century. The domed-up ribbed vaulting is probably of *c.* 1128. The 12th-century atrium may rest on the foundations of its 4th-century predecessor. However it uses the building conventions of its age.

The main portal has carved wooden doors of the 4th century. The animal carvings on the door jambs and atrium capitals are reminiscent of the 7th-and 8th-century work of Longobard sculptors. They are more likely to be 12th-century copies than originals.

The altar of Wolvinus is among the finest works surviving by early mediaeval goldsmiths. Its rarity is responsible for the controversy about its dating. To place it in the Carolingian period would seem to be reasonable. The sculptured pulpit has also created a good deal of controversy. Pieces of a very much earlier date were probably incorporated in a restoration of *c.* 1200, from which period the relief scenes would seem to date. Most baffling of all is the complex ciborium over the altar, which has been variously attributed to 9th, 10th, 11th and 12th centuries.

Three early basilicas much altered by later remodellings are *S. Lorenzo*, a vast cruciform domed structure of *c.* 370, *S. Simpliciano* and *S. Nazaro*, also of the 4th century. Inside S. Lorenzo are Romano-Christian and Byzantine mosaics, and early Christian carvings and sarcophagi. Adjoining the church is the chapel of *S. Aquilino* (4th century), a niched octagon originally used either as a baptistery or as an Imperial mausoleum. It contains the remains of a 4th-century mosaic.

The brick basilica of *S. Vincenzo in Prato* was rebuilt in such a conservative manner in the 11th century that it was for a long time accepted as the original church of *c.* 814–33. Here we see the characteristic features of the so-called 'first Romanesque' – the pilaster strips and the arched corbel tables, with arched recesses under the eaves of the main apse.

S. Satiro has a characteristic Lombard campanile of 1043 and a few 9th-century fresco fragments. Little of the original *S. Babila* (early 11th century) survives later rebuilding. *S. Celso* (10th–12th centuries) has a fresco fragment of the latter part of the 12th century. The apse of *S. Calimero* is 9th or 10th century. *S. Eustorgio* was rebuilt in 1178 with typical domed-up ribbed vaulting.

Secular Romanesque architecture in Milan is represented by the *Palazzo della Ragione* (1228) the *Loggia dei Mercanti* (1228–33), and the *Porta Nuova* (12th century).

Opposite: Detail of the pulpit, S. Ambrogio, Milan.

There are three museums with important mediaeval collections: the

Ambrosian Library, with its priceless illuminated manuscripts; the *Museo Archaeologico ed Artistico* which has a variety of stone carvings of the early mediaeval period; and the *Museum of Sant' Ambrogio*.

The most important Romanesque monument at **Como** is the beautiful Benedictine abbey church of *S. Abbondio* (1063–95), the cultural centre of late mediaeval Lombardy. It is a wooden-roofed basilica with a rib-vaulted sanctuary. The blind arcades and niches are a good example of what was to become the dominant decorative motif of Romanesque in the Rhineland and the Lombard influenced areas of Italy. The twin towers are Lombard in style, but their position – flanking the apse – follows the German pattern. The sturdy columns support cushion capitals. These were universally used in 11th- and 12th-century Rhineland architecture. It is not certain whether they first developed north of the Alps or in the Milan-Como region. In any case the capitals of S. Abbondio are among the first examples of this type.

Animal carving on the left side of the east portal of S. Fidele, Como. Early 12th century.

At *S. Fidele* (early 12th century) we have an early example of the developed Lombard eaves gallery. The trefoil plan of the church reflects transalpine influence. It has a sculptured doorway, and there are sculptured animals on the apse.

Other Romanesque examples in Como are the church of *S. Giacomo* (1095–1117), the *City Wall Tower* (1192), and the elegant *Palazzo del Broletto* (1215). In the *Museum* are works of Longobard and Romanesque art.

The Como region is dotted with early and mature Romanesque churches. The 13th-century chapel of *San Vigilio* at **Rovio**, in Italian Switzerland, has frescoes of the period in its apse. The campanile of *S. Maria di Loppia*, near Bellagio, is magnificent. The church is beautifully situated.

On a mountain-side near Lecco, about two hours walk from the village of **Civate**, is the church of *S. Pietro al Monte*. The original Longobard-Carolingian foundation was transformed *c.* 1040 by the addition of a west apse. It has a stone ciborium (*c.* 1093–7). The important stucco ornaments in the east apse and in the crypt show oriental influences. The frescoes (11th or 12th centuries) are archaistic, with Byzantine borrowings.

S. Vincenzo at **Galliano** is an early 11th-century reconstruction on the foundations of a 5th-century church. The frescoes are the oldest in Lombardy, and despite the vicissitudes they have suffered, are among the key works of Romanesque painting. They illustrate the transition from Carolingian to Romanesque painting.

Despite its humble appearance *S. Pietro* at **Agliate** (*c.* 875) is a church of some importance in the history of the evolution of the Romanesque style. It is a basilica, with two aisles carried on antique columns, quarter domes over the apses. The tunnel vaulting over the nave is an early attempt at stone vaulting. The baptistery is a near contemporary example of a building of the central type.

At **Monza** the Longobard Queen Theodolinda built a palace and a great church, which later gave way to a Gothic *Cathedral*. In its treasury are early

Opposite: East view of S. Abbondio, Como. 1063–95.

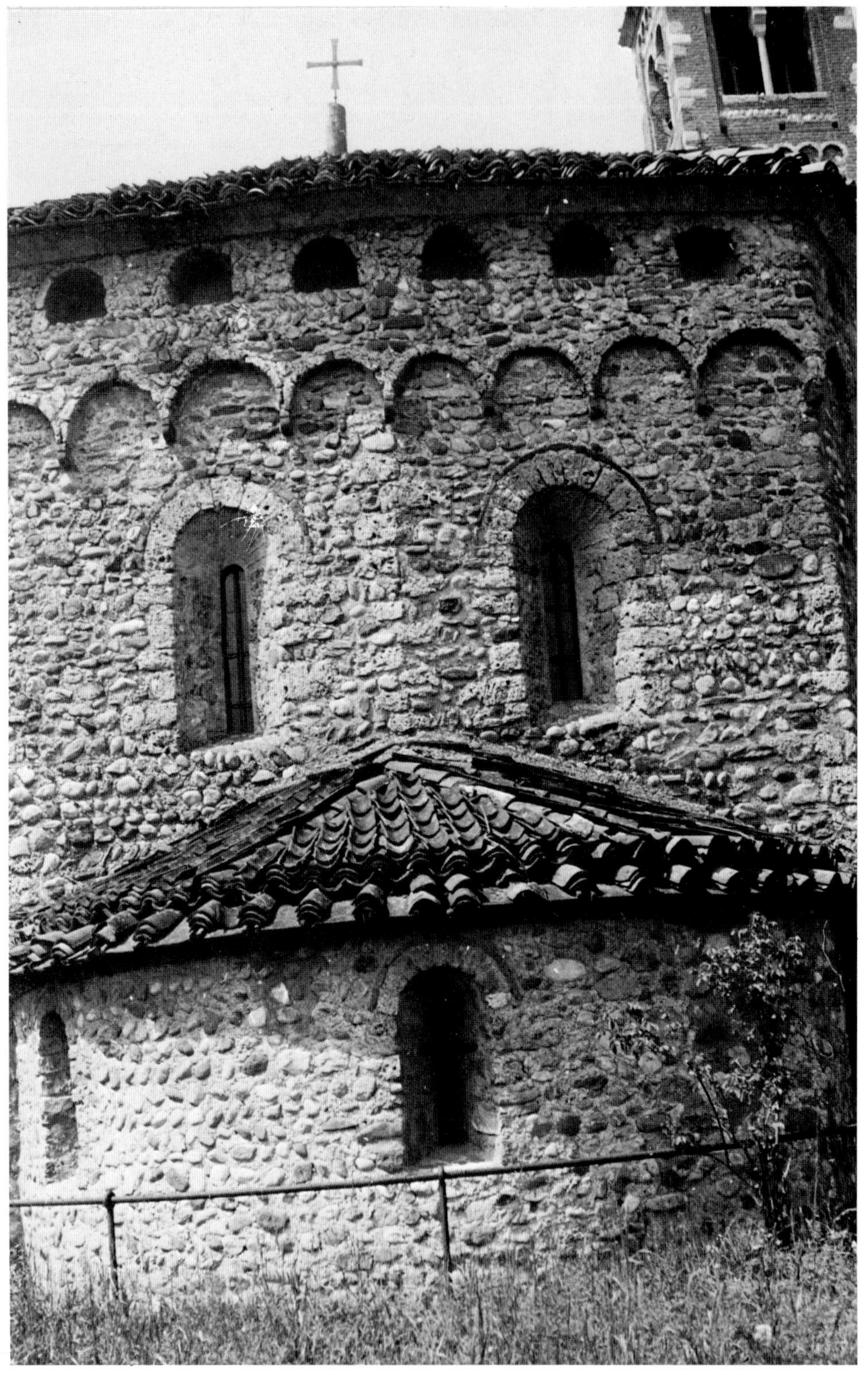

Exterior view of S. Pietro, Agliate, *c.* 875 (?).

Christian ivories, small decorated lead containers for oil or water brought from the Holy Land, and the Iron Crown used by Longobard kings and their successors, the mediaeval German Emperors. According to legend the crown was made from a nail used in the Crucifixion. *S. Sigismondo* (1099?) at **Rivolta d'Adda** is an early example of the Lombard domed-up ribbed vault.

The Cistercian abbey church of *Chiaravalle Milanese*, (begun in 1136) some miles south of Milan is another example of Lombard vaulting. It has a huge, exaggerated tower over its crossing. At **Castelseprio** is the church of *S. Maria* of uncertain date – anywhere between the 6th and 11th centuries, in fact. Its murals, discovered in 1944, are of a very high quality. They are probably Carolingian. Both church and frescoes show Byzantine influence. The inspiration of Burgundian models is apparent in the stone reliefs on the door jambs of the main entrance of the *Cathedral* of **Lodi** (1158–63).

At **Pavia** there are two interesting Romanesque churches. *S. Pietro in Ciel d'Oro* (dedicated in 1132, finished *c.* 1180) has a typical Lombard façade and an elaborately carved entrance. The simple interior has a raised apse, no transept and no gallery above the aisles. The cruciform *S. Michele* (1100–60) is more complex in design. The interior is dominated by two rows of massive pillars, each composed of an integration of individual vertical shafts, round and angular. The pillars are crowned with carved capitals representing figures and animals. As in S. Pietro, the apse is raised and decorated with mosaics (modern in both cases). The plain walls have small windows which was customary in 12th-century Italian architecture. The fame of S. Michele rests on its massive façade. This is divided by four pilasters, each of which is composed of a cluster of strikingly carved elements. The decorated pilasters carry the eye up to the rising arcade of arches which meets at the apex of the roof. The three entrances are magnificently decorated with sculpture. The façade is broken by horizontal friezes of wild animals, horses and human figures. Although badly weathered they have retained a certain primitive vigour, reminiscent of early Lombard sculpture, with its oriental influence.

Pavia was capital of the Longobard kingdom between 572 and 774 but the monuments of this period are hardly recognizable owing to later alterations. However the crypt of *S. Teodoro*, built in the Byzantine style, has been little changed and keeps its original capitals. In the *Museum* of Pavia is the sarcophagus of Theodota (*c.* 688–700).

Near Bergamo is the impressive 11th-century church of *S. Tomaso in Léminè*, at **Almenno S. Bartolomeo**. It is circular in design.

At **Brescia** we find the important *Civic Museum of the Christian Era* and two early Lombard monuments: the magnificent rotunda of *S. Maria*, built in the 11th century over earlier remains; and the church of *S. Salvatore*, founded in 753, with a splendid crypt, partially rebuilt early in the 12th century.

North of Brescia near **Capo di Ponte** is the Cluniac abbey church of

Griffin on the left side of the porch of S. Zeno, Verona. 12th century.

S. Salvatore built *c.* 1120 on a Burgundian model. It is the best preserved Romanesque building in the Brescia district.

Verona has the massive wooden-roofed basilica of *S. Zeno* (1125–78). The Lombard 'high choir', with the magnificent crypt beneath, represents the most monumental development of this system. The mid-12th-century statue of S. Zeno is one of the earliest sculptures in the round to survive in its original position. The bronze doors of the main entrance, with Old and New Testament scenes, resemble those of S. Ambrogio in Milan. The reliefs flanking the doors and in the tympanum are by Niccolò and his assistants. The campanile is one of the finest of the Lombard style. Sculpture by Niccolò can also be seen on the façade of the *Cathedral.* Inside the baptistery of *S. Giovanni in Fonte* is a remarkable font decorated with slabs of blood-red Veronese marble in high relief. The domed cruciform church of *Ss Apostoli* has an 8th-century crypt, dedicated to Ss Teuternia and Tosca, which resembles early Lombard and Visigothic buildings. *S. Stefano* was rebuilt in *c.* 990.

Recent excavations in the church of *S. Sofia* at **Padua** have uncovered a massive semicircular section of the choir which probably dates from the 8th century, i.e., from late Longobard civilization. The ground plan and capitals of the church are Byzantine. The nave is early 12th century, the vaulting late 13th century. The domed church of *S. Antonio* ('Il Santo'), begun in 1231, is somewhat similar to S. Marco at Venice.

S. Marco at **Venice** is not, properly speaking, a Romanesque building. Nor for that matter is it entirely Byzantine. It is a curious and original mixture of both styles. We need only describe the church briefly since it had little direct

Detail of the façade of S. Marco, Venice. Begun 1063 (?). Watercolour sketch by John Ruskin in the Ashmolean Museum, Oxford.

Choir screen panel, Cathedral of Torcello. 12th century.

Longobard carvings, Aquileia.

effect, with the exception of Padua's Il Santo, which we have just mentioned. The three-aisled basilica, with five domes and a Greek cross plan, was built on the site of a 9th-century church from the 11th to the 15th centuries. The four bronze horses before the west window were, like many of the other treasures of the cathedral, brought from Constantinople after the conquest of that city during the Fourth Crusade in 1204. The mosaics have been much restored. The method of construction and the carving of the capitals suggest workmanship from the West. The slight lengthening of the nave and the design of the chancel area show a certain Romanesque architectural influence.

Near Venice on the island of **Torcello** is the church of *S.Fosca*, a typical Greek cross octagon of the 11th century. The basilican *Cathedral* which took its present form in 1008 has beautiful 12th-century mosaics on the apse and west wall. The *Cathedral* (12th century) on the island of **Murano** is the finest surviving example of Veneto-Byzantine architecture. It has a beautiful Lombard arcaded gallery around the east end.

Aquileia is a small village on the site of a Roman frontier fortress village. Only the foundations have survived of the original cathedral, which consisted of two large rectangular halls, side by side, with connecting smaller rooms, founded in 314. This plan is interesting, since it reminds us that the basilica evolved from a diversity of architectural experiments. Excavations in 1909, and during the First World War, uncovered the floors of the cathedral which contained fascinating mosaics. These and the carvings in the museum garden are among the most important monuments of 4th-century art. Only the intersection of the nave with the choir and the transept remain of the Romanesque *Cathedral*, dedicated in 1031. Here we find important frescoes. Those in the apse, which belong to the first half of the 11th century, are a typical example of the art of painters trained in the mosaicists' school. They are also excellent examples of the Italian prototypes adopted in apsidal pictures north of the Alps, particularly in Germany and south-east France. The frescoes on the walls and vaults of the crypts are nearly two centuries later. They too are largely Byzantine in conception.

Nearby at **Grado** are other important early Christian remains. The *Cathedral* was built between 571 and 579, replacing a 5th-century structure. It has a complete choir screen with Longobard panels and an early mosaic floor. The *Museum* of the cathedral contains many Longobard stone sculptures. Three distinct periods of this art can be distinguished: flat bas-reliefs (as at Cimitile), crude faces and designs (as on the altar at Cividale), and perfected rope designs. There is also a frieze with figures under arches. The baptistery is 5th century.

At *S.Maria delle Grazie* (6th century) there has been preserved the original choir and the apse, consisting of a round bench, a high seat, and – most interesting of all – a double arched window with a 'romanico' column in between. Moreover, the interest of this church has been heightened by the barrel-vaulted ambulatory around the apse, said to be of Syrian origin.

Opposite, above Longobard carvings in the museum at Grado.
Opposite, below Interior of the 'Tempietto', Cividale, showing stucco reliefs. 726–76.

The power and originality of Longobard art is fully represented in **Cividale**. This beautiful spot, where the green Natissina River emerges from the Alps into the Lombard valley, was chosen by successive peoples from the Stone Age to the Longobard as their habitat. Numerous stone carvings attributed to the period 720–40 are preserved in the *Museo Archaeologico Nazionale*. In addition, there is the famous 'Ratchis' or 'Pemmo' altar from the church of *S. Martino* and the ciborium from the *Cathedral*. The first, which dates from *c.* 734–7, is an unselfconscious representation of pagan and Christian symbols, figures, angels and the Holy Virgin. The second is decorated with carvings of lively wild animals of great strength and beauty.

The 'Tempietto' at the end of the choir of the chapel of *S. Maria in Valle* is a remarkable little Longobard building, erected on the site of an ancient temple. According to tradition, it was founded by the Duchess Peltruda (*c.* 762–76). The nave is groin vaulted. The stucco mouldings and reliefs have been perfectly preserved. It bears some resemblance to Asturian and Mozarabic churches of Spain, and may have been subjected to Moslem influences coming up north from southern Italy.

Yugoslavia

We now travel along the Dalmatian coast of Yugoslavia where we find some interesting Italian-influenced Romanesque churches as well as remains of earlier periods. **Poreč** (Parenzo) is the principal archaeological city of this coast. Its earliest Christian feature extant is the mosaic floor of a private chapel of *c.* 305, with a symbolic fish set in the pagan pavement. There are also remains of a 5th-century basilica. It had three naves and instead of an apse there was a semi-circular bench for the clergy. The *Cathedral* has not only preserved the complete layout of a 6th-century basilica, including the atrium, but there is also a baptistery, bell-tower, martyr's chapel, and episcopal audience hall. The capitals of the church are Byzantine and were probably imported from Constantinople. There are also mosaics, both inside the church and on the gable of the façade. Much of this work is early, though those of the ciborium are 13th century and others in the side aisle are 15th century. Fragments of the original stucco decoration have also survived.

The ruined church of *S. Giovanni Battista*, **Arbe**, has an unusual ambulatory of the 11th century, perhaps inspired by S. Stefano, Bologna. Both Lombard and Pisan influences can be seen in the *Cathedral of S. Crisogono*, **Zadar** rebuilt in *c.* 1175. The former appears in the east end, the latter in the west end. Beside the cathedral is a Ravennate style tower of 1105. The early 9th-century church of *S. Donat* is circular in plan with a two-storied elevation. The apse of the massive exterior is decorated with blind arcading.

The *Cathedral* of **Trogir** (Traù) has a richly decorated west door by the Slav, Radovan. Despite its late date (1240) it is essentially Romanesque.

At **Split** (Spalato) is the *Palace of Diocletian* (300) which shows the Roman

Opposite above: Carved altar screen from the Palace of Diocletian. 9th century (?). *Opposite below:* Relief of a Croatian ruler in the baptistery at Split. 11th century.

Opposite: Fresco in S. Procolo, Naturno, showing St Paul's escape from Damascus. 9th century.

Left: Fresco in S. Procolo, Naturno. 9th century.

use of blind decorative arcading, a characteristic feature of the 'first Romanesque' and Ottonian styles, and later of Romanesque. Beside the cathedral, originally the mausoleum of Diocletian, is a tower in the Lombard style which has been almost completely restored. The church of *St Luke*, **Kotor** (Cattaro) is a good example of the aisleless barrel-vaulted churches common in this region. The baptistery was once the Temple of Jupiter.

Italian Tyrol

In the Italian Tyrol are a number of little churches with interesting fresco remains. The *chapel* of **Castel Appiano**, near Trento, has the most complete and least restored frescoes of this region, dating from *c.* 1131–80. They are very Byzantine-looking. In *S. Jacopo* at **Termeno** there are mid-13th-century frescoes. Some of them depict sea-monsters, grotesques, etc., illustrating that aspect of the mediaeval mind which delighted in the Bestiaries. At **Naturno**, in the church of *S. Procolo*, one finds one of the few extant examples of early Carolingian mural painting. They are most original works, owing nothing to either the antique, or to the stylization of the Christian East. If anything, they resemble the Anglo-Irish influenced manuscripts, executed at the abbey of St Gall towards the end of the 8th century. In *S. Benedetto*, **Malles**, there are 9th-century mural paintings, in *S. Jacopo*, **Grissiano**, late 12th-early 13th-century apsidal frescoes.

10 Germany, Switzerland, Austria, Holland and Belgium

The Alps rising to their majestic height are regarded as a barrier between central Europe and the Mediterranean. Yet ever since Hannibal's elephants crossed them, the passes through these mountains have served as a high road for invaders, pilgrims and merchants. A lively traffic persisted throughout the Middle Ages, joining Christendom's remotest outposts to Rome and the sea-ports of Italy. Many northern pilgrims to Rome, prior to the Arab conquests of the Near East, continued their voyage to Byzantium, the Holy Land, Alexandria and Asia Minor.

In ancient times the principal passes through the Alps were the Julia and the Brenner, passing through Chur and Innsbruck respectively. The St Gothard could not be opened for a long time because of the necessity of crossing a raging torrent by a suspended bridge. This was achieved in the early Middle Ages with the construction of the 'Devil's Bridge'. Near this crossing there stood the monastery of **Disentis** founded by Sigisbert, a follower of St Columban. Under the Ottonian Emperors this strategically situated monastery received important gifts. The monks were instrumental in opening the new route and offering shelter to travellers at Lucmanier after the bridge had been built.

These routes linked Italy and the Holy Roman Empire. Building masters and craftsmen moved freely between the two areas, which, in the 12th century, achieved a remarkable harmony of style. In the cultural interchange of the Romanesque period Germany gave much more than she took.

Romanesque building in the Teutonic lands is in direct line of descent from its Carolingian and Ottonian predecessors. Enough survives to enable this connection to be established, but the remains are scanty. However, the dearth of buildings is somewhat compensated by the wonderful manuscripts, ivories and goldsmiths' work to be seen in museums and libraries.

Romanesque churches are based on the basilica with important modifica-

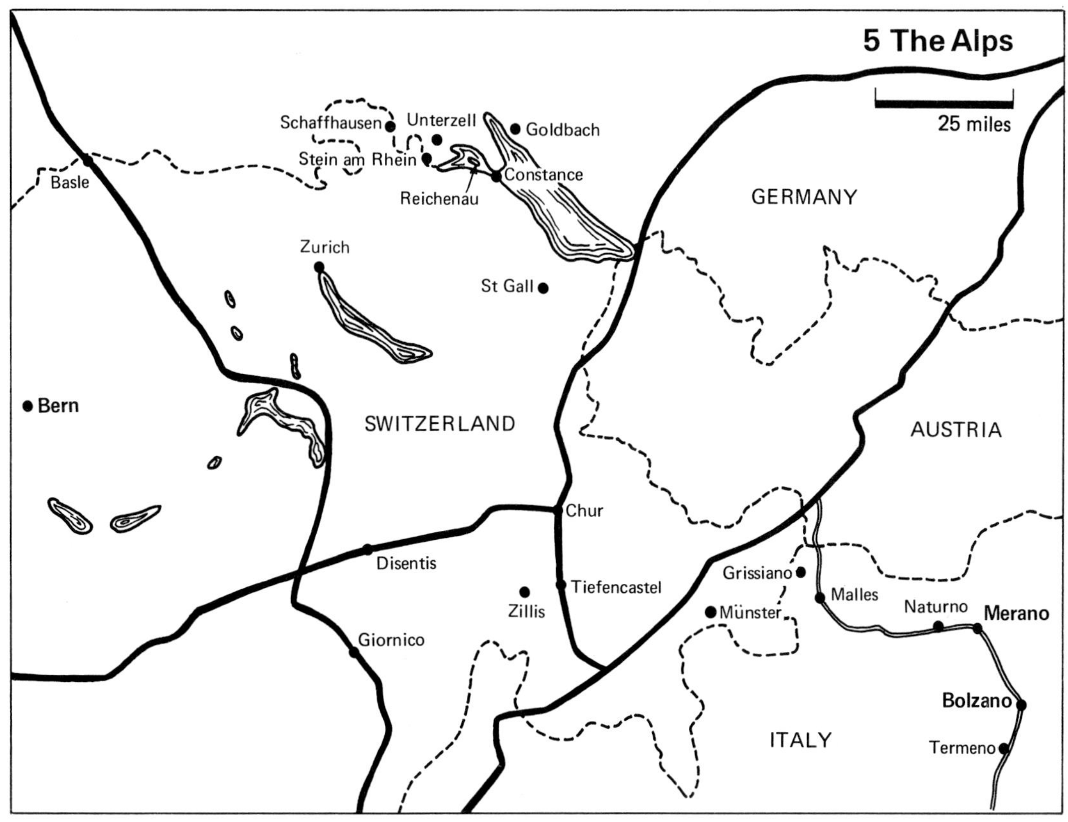

tions. The distinctive features are: massive west-work and a complex tower system; a double apse and double transept plan; a hall-crypt; a simple interior, generally double-storied, though there are notable three- and four-storied exceptions in the greater churches. Naves are usually wooden-roofed, but the cathedral of Speyer acquired great domical groined vaults, something like those of S. Ambrogio in Milan, when it was rebuilt towards the end of the 11th century. The exteriors relied on mass rather than detail for effect. Blank arcades and dwarf galleries around the apse are extensively used, the latter probably a development of the eaves niches common to both Ottonian architecture and the 'first Romanesque'.

Little has survived of Romanesque sculpture, much of which was apparently in stucco that has subsequently perished. In any case, until the end of the 12th century, there does not seem to have been that taste for architectural sculpture which we find in Italy and France. The simple cushion capital was preferred, while the double-apsed system eliminated that focal point for architectural decoration, the west door. Occasional animals, heads and figures appear on the exterior. On the other hand, there are a number of realistically sculptured crucifixes in wood and metal of great emotional depth.

It was in the art of metalwork that Imperial craftsmen excelled: cast bronze doors, candlesticks, fonts, statues and crucifixes, enamelled altar frontals and portable altars. The art reached a high level at Hildesheim in the early 11th century and continued throughout the 12th century with the remarkable works of the Mosan style, centred in Liège.

In wall painting a few Carolingian and Ottonian examples have survived. However, those of the Romanesque period have either entirely disappeared or have been disastrously restored.

Within the German land, three stylistic regions for Romanesque can be discerned. The first includes Switzerland (except for the western part which then belonged to the kingdom of Burgundy), the upper Rhine, southern Germany, Alsace and Austria. It is characterized by a simple basilican plan with square pier or column supports. The distinguishing feature of the second region, which comprises Saxony and Westphalia (most of which now lies in East Germany), is the 'Saxon' façade, i.e. two towers flanking an intermediate structure, sometimes higher than the towers.

The third and most important area is the lower Rhine, where we find the magnificent Imperial cathedrals, the envy not only of lesser rulers in France, Spain and Italy, but also of the enormously wealthy Order of Cluny. Within the Empire, their influence extended into the Low Countries. The exact nature of this original cathedral style is not easy to trace since all these structures suffered devastating fires and were rebuilt with embellishments in the following centuries. It is thought, however, that the essential spirit of the structures changed little and it may be fairly assumed that Worms, Speyer and Mainz afford us an insight into the enormous contribution of the Rhineland to cathedral building.

The German abbeys did not establish a style as did the Rhineland cathedrals. The monastic movement in Germany felt its upsurge in two waves: the first wave inspired by the Cluny reforms and a later wave inspired by the Cistercian reforms. The first never took deep hold, nor did it leave much in the way of Cluniac art, particularly sculpture. On the other hand, the Cistercian movement found deep roots in Germany and the severe style of the abbeys of this Order greatly influenced ecclesiastical architecture, not only throughout Germany, but in the whole of northern Europe as well.

The 12th-century castles of Germany stand in ruins, but in the remains of these great structures there can be found the decorative elements characteristic of Romanesque art in central Europe and made familiar to other generations through the scenery of Wagner operas and the 19th-century Romanesque revival in Germany, England and the United States. The castles are associated in large part with the personality of Frederick Barbarossa, who perished after a colourful life in the Third Crusade (1190).

Switzerland

St Peter, at **Tiefencastel** is a 9th-century triple-apsed church. The church at nearby **Müstail**, also dedicated to *St Peter*, has been attributed to the 8th century. If this dating is correct it is virtually an unique example of this style (triapsidal) and period. The *Cathedral* of **Chur** was built between 1178 and 1278 on the foundations of an earlier building. It has Lombard type ribbed vaulting. The choir screen is a work of the 9th century. Also worth noting are the interesting carvings on the Romanesque capitals.

At the church of *St Martin*, **Zillis**, on the old main road connecting Italy with Lake Constance, is the only Romanesque ceiling painting preserved almost in entirety. It dates from the mid-12th century and is one of the treasures of mediaeval art. The Lombard style church of *S. Nicolao*, **Giornico**, has an unusual open crypt. The completely plain entrance is also unusual in view of its late 12th-century date. There are some Romanesque fresco fragments.

The church of *St Johann* at **Münster** (Müstair) was founded by Charlemagne and parts of the original structure, which was triple-apsed, still remain. The apsidal frescoes repainted in the 12th century, are definitely Romanesque in character. The other frescoes date from *c.* 800. The general Western style and iconography is modified by the introduction of Eastern, particularly Syrian, elements.* The church contains a life-size statue, probably of Charlemagne, of *c.* 800. This is a rare example of Carolingian sculpture in the round.

The abbey church of **St Maurice** was founded in 515 on the site of an early Christian basilica and was subsequently rebuilt many times. Excavations have uncovered Roman, Merovingian and Carolingian substructures, and relics of these periods can be seen in the *Treasure* of the church. The altar is 8th century and the frescoes in the church are Carolingian. The tower dates from the 11th century.

On the shores of Lake Geneva is the famous Romanesque castle of **Chillon**, built in the 12th century and enlarged in the following century.

The abbey church of **Romainmôtier** was founded in the 5th century and rebuilt in the late 10th and early 11th centuries on a Cluniac pattern. The heavy circular piers and tunnel vaulting over the nave date from this period. The church has a rare 8th-century pulpit. The east choir, apse and porch are Gothic.

The design of the abbey church of **Payerne**, begun in the 9th century, was also influenced by Cluny when the monastery joined the Reform. The church was completed towards the end of the 12th century. The transept, crossing and choir are Romanesque. There are interesting capitals archaic in character. The simple exterior of the church has great dignity.

Of the 11th-century *Minster* at **Basle**, only the north wall of the nave and

* Many of these frescoes are now in the *Zurich Museum*.

Capital, church of Payerne.

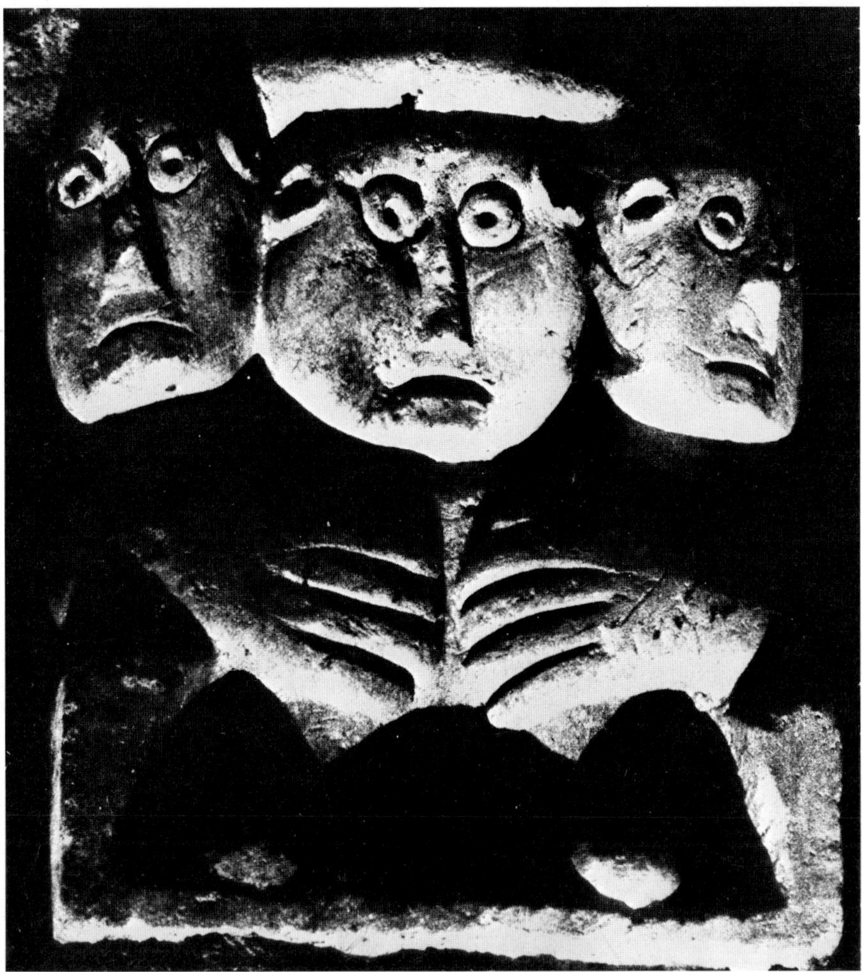

Plinth, church of Payerne.

the lower two storeys of the north tower still stand. The church was destroyed by fire in 1185 and rebuilt in the early 13th century. It was the first church in the Rhineland area to have an ambulatory around the sanctuary and to be entirely roofed with a ribbed cross vault. In fact, it stands midway between the Romanesque and Gothic styles. The late 12th-century sculpture shows French influence.

At **Schaffhausen** is the abbey church of *Allerheiligen*, a Romanesque basilica founded in 1103. The flat ceiling, transepts, and choir with a rectangular apse reflect the influence of the abbey of Hirsau, the Cluniac centre for Germany. On the other hand, the simple two-towered façade resembles Strasbourg.

Nothing remains of the ancient monastery of **St Gall**, founded in 614 by the Irish monk, St Columban. It was one of the monasteries on the routes linking Italy with the North which served the pilgrims and radiated the faith among the peoples of the mountain regions. St Gall's period of greatest eminence was in the 9th and early 10th centuries, when it enjoyed Imperial favour. Thereafter its influence declined. In the library of St Gall are a number of important and beautiful manuscripts, produced by the monastery's scriptorium, the most famous of which is the *Golden Psalter* (890–920). The library also contains a manuscript plan for a monastery, of *c.* 820. It is a source for our understanding of the complex structure of the Carolingian monastery, and of the design of the church. Like the Bayeux Tapestry, the plan at St Gall is an unique document, providing us with a key to the mediaeval mode of life.

Very little remains of the 11th-century building of the *Cathedral* of **Constance**. Traces can be discovered in the hall crypt, with its heavy cushion capitals decorated with lightly carved acanthus leaves.

Southern Germany

Just across the border, on the German side of Lake Constance, is the simple monastery church of **Stein am Rhein** (*c.* 1100).

The island of **Reichenau** was the home of an ancient and venerable monastery, a leading school of illumination in the 10th century. Of the original abbey, founded in 724 by an Anglo-Saxon missionary, not a vestige remains. Three early churches are, however, intact: the abbey church at **Mittelzell**, *St Peter* at **Niederzell**, and *St Georg* at **Oberzell**.

The 8th-century foundation at Mittelzell was replaced by a larger church, consecrated in 816. Part of the chancel of the first church still survives. It was further enlarged in the 10th century, and acquired a western apse and tower, decorated with Lombardic arcading, in 1048.

St Peter at Niederzell was founded in 799 and enlarged in the 11th and 12th centuries, the original building becoming the choir of the new church. In the east apse there are 12th-century murals. The interior of the church was altered in the 18th century.

The abbey church of St Georg was built *c.* 890 and altered at the end of the 11th century. It is a triple-aisled basilica with a tower over the crossing. The crypt, which retains its original columns, is one of the earliest examples of the typically German 'hall' crypt. The frescoes in the church are incomplete and, unfortunately, have suffered 19th-century restoration. They are usually attributed to the second half of the 10th century. Their monumental dignity and refinement look forward to mature Romanesque painting. The *Last Judgement* on the outer wall of the western apse is early 11th century.

The church of *Ss Peter and Paul* at **Unterzell**, near Reichenau, has 10th to 11th-century frescoes, but they are in very poor condition. Better preserved are the frescoes in the little church of *St Sylvester* at **Goldbach**, one mile west of Überlingen. They are in the apse and on the walls of the nave.

Exterior view of St Georg, Oberzell.
c. 890 and later.

Stylistically they resemble the frescoes at Reichenau, and date from the 10th century.

Near Balingen is the church of **Burgfelden** with an unrestored fresco fragment of the *Last Judgement* on the east wall. Christ is depicted as beardless, which is unusual. The style of the mural, e.g., the elongation of the figures, is not unlike that of Reichenau manuscripts and wall paintings.

The abbey church of **Alpirsbach** was built between 1095 and 1127. There are also Gothic additions, and later reconstructions. The abbey was associated with Hirsau, geographically, ecclesiastically and stylistically. The church has a flat roof and no crypt. There is also an interesting carved wooden bench attributed to *c.* 1000. It has carvings of oriental inspiration. A few sculptures are scattered around inside the church, and there are interesting metal reliefs on the great doors.

At **Hirsau** are the imposing ruins of the abbey church of *Ss Peter and Paul.* This was the mother chapter of Cluny west of the Rhine. The church completed in 1091 became a model for Cluniac building in Germany. Its

Fresco of bust of St Florian from the convent of Nonnberg, Salzburg, *c.* 1154.

influence can be seen at Schaffhausen, Alpirsbach, Paulinzella and Prüfening. The church had a clearly defined cruciform plan with a deep atrium. All that remains is one tower which has some interesting animal sculpture. In the same village are the ruins of *St Aurelius* (1038–71) with heavy cushion capitals on round columns.

The abbey of **Maulbronn**, mostly Gothic, is in a very good state of preservation. The Cistercian movement was brought east of the Rhine early in the 12th century by Count Walter von Lomersheim, who wanted to build a monastery for the Order on his property at Eckenweiler. Twelve monks and an abbot came from Alsace to found this abbey, but the selected spot did not suit them and through Bernard of Clairvaux they prevailed upon the bishop of Speyer to grant them a new site for their monastery. This was Maulbronn, far from human habitation in a deep forest. Maulbronn became the centre of the Cistercian movement in Germany and many abbeys were founded under its supervision. The elaborate buildings surrounded by a wall give a very complete impression of what a mediaeval monastery was like. There are a few vestiges of Romanesque architecture (1146–78), but the main interest lies in the totality of the preservation.

Wimpfen was originally a Roman fort guarding the Neckar Valley. It became a city of the Franks and a Christian centre. The church of *St Peter*, destroyed by the Hungarians in the early 10th century, was rebuilt under Emperor Otto the Great in 965 in the style of the Palace Chapel at Aachen. Two towers, with Lombardic detail, remain of the early structure. The church was rebuilt in the Gothic style.

The city also has some fine Romanesque structures: a 12th-century dwelling known as the *Steinhaus*; the *City Gate* and the *Blue Tower*, 12th–13th centuries; and the 13th-century *Emperor's Chapel*, of which only the walls remain. On the edge of this walled city, overlooking the Neckar, is the *Palace of Barbarossa* (late 12th century). Part of the outside wall, with a fine arcade of columns, still stands. The entrance is through the Youth Hostel. The entrance to the *Red Tower* (1180–90) is some twenty-four feet above the ground, reached by a retractable ladder. It contained the apartment used by the Emperor and a secret passage leading outside the walls.

The Romanesque *Cathedral* of **Augsburg** was transformed in the Gothic period. The bronze doors, however, are mid-11th century. **Munich** has no Romanesque monuments, but in the *Staatsbibliothek* there are early manuscripts, notably the *Codex Aureus of St Emmeran* (from Reims or St-Denis), *Henry II's Pericope* (early 11th century) and the *Gospel Book of Otto III* (late 10th century), both the work of the Reichenau school. Not far from Munich, at **Moosburg** is the 12th-century *Cathedral*, with a beautiful Romanesque portal.

Austria

Just across the border at **Reichenhall** there is a church with interesting Romanesque sculpture. Nearby **Salzburg** was a leading centre for south German manuscript illumination in the 12th century. The convent of *Nonnberg* has important mid-12th-century frescoes. They show a close acquaintance with Greek or Byzantine models – this influence probably coming north from Aquileia or Venice. But, far from being slavish imitations, they reveal a considerable degree of individual interpretation.

To the south, at **Teurnia**, we find a rare example of antiquity in central Europe. All that remains of the 5th–6th-century basilica of *St Peter am Holz* are the foundations, with a mosaic floor. The basilica had a short central apse and two side apses, one of which contains a fine mosaic. In the *Museum* there are many Roman fragments and remains of the basilica, said to have been destroyed around 600.

The vast and remote monastery of **Gurk** (1160–1200) seems artificially planted by some great exterior power to impress the natives, rather than an expression of the locality and its population. A number of different and unhomogeneous styles can be discerned. The exterior and the main nave (architecturally) are strongly 'classical Romanesque'; that is to say, the masons* either knew, or were guided along, classical lines. Lombard arcading can be seen on the outside of the church. The base of the walls, the columns and the arches of the entrance are copied from some Roman structure. Only the frieze of the external wall, with its involuted and complicated design of endless pattern, has a suggestion of barbaric antecedents.

* Forty-eight masters left markings on the stones.

The spacious hall crypt has a hundred thin columns supporting its vaults, raised as in the manner of the Sicilian Romanesque structures built by Arab craftsmen and reflecting, it would seem, the Mozarabic formulae. In this elaborate forest of columns is to be found a tomb resting on three heads. To inspect these one must perform something like an Arab genuflection, richly rewarded by an unusual side view of a lifesize woman's head, in the Byzantine tradition, and the head of a bearded man, Etruscan in style.

The murals of the *Bishop's Chapel* (*c.* 1167), situated over the 'Paradise' entrance, present a striking contrast to the church's interior. The rooms are covered, from the tips of their vaulted ceilings to the floor, with frescoes of high artistic quality. The ceiling of the inner room has four Garden of Eden frescoes. The general theme of the paintings is taken from Augustine's 'City of God'.* Their green and brown tones have survived. It is said that the frescoes have not been retouched and show what is left of the work of approximately 800 years ago. This in itself is something quite remarkable.

Modling, outside Vienna, has an example of the round chapels which were numerous in Austria and southern Germany in the 12th and 13th centuries. They served as charnel houses or cemetery chapels, and were often richly decorated.

In the *Secular Treasury* at **Vienna** there is the gold German Imperial crown and the famous *Vienna Evangeliary*, on which the German kings swore their coronation oath. It is a late 8th or early 9th-century work, probably from Aachen, and one of the most classically influenced of the Carolingian manuscripts. At the *National Library* is the outstanding *Gedhardt Bible* (first half of 12th century), an example of the work of the Salzburg school of illumination, and the 6th-century *Codex of Genesis*.

North of Vienna is the convent church of **Klosterneuburg**. The magnificent enamelled altar in the chapel of *St Leopold*, by Nicholas of Verdun, dates from 1181. He was an outstanding master of the Mosan style, which was influenced by the antique.

The abbey church of **Lambach** has late 11th-century frescoes. The iconography is derived from Byzantine sources. The technique is archaic, but there is an impressive boldness in the handling of details.

We now come back into Germany to **Regensburg**, in ancient times the terminus of the transalpine road. It has a 'Roman tower' of very fine stonework. In the Middle Ages the town was an important centre of manuscript illumination. There were two Benedictine establishments; the *Niedermünster*, which has a fine Romanesque tower, and *St Emmeran.* St Emmeran was founded in the 8th century, but was rebuilt after a fire in 1020. It has now lost much of its Romanesque character through further rebuilding. The plan follows the simple basilican type common to early Romanesque churches in southern Germany, although it has a western transept and chancel. In the big rectangular western apse are fresco scenes (*c.* 1052) markedly Byzantine in

* Other 'City of God' frescoes can be seen at Regensburg Cathedral and Prüfening.

Opposite
Detail of the exterior of the abbey church of Gurk (1160–1200), showing apse with decorative arcading.

character. The atrium is composed of fine columns, built into a wall. The capitals have varied geometric designs. There is interesting sculpture in the lateral porch. The crypt lies entirely outside the church to the east of the main building. This scheme was extensively used in late German Romanesque, particularly in the south.

The 'Schotten' portal of *St Jakob* is decorated with some of the finest and most elaborate sculpture in Germany. It bears some resemblance to the carvings at S. Michele, Pavia. The most varied figures of beasts and men seem to be of eastern Mediterranean inspiration. There are also echoes of Chinese (i.e. Buddhist) work in the human figures.

The chapel of *Allerheiligen* (12th century) in the cloister of the *Cathedral* of Regensburg is covered with frescoes, on the 'City of God' theme. In spite of 19th-century alterations one can still see the Byzantine influences, especially in the paintings on the cupola. The chapel is lavishly decorated with Lombard arcading.

The abbey church of **Prüfening**, near Regensburg, is a Cluniac foundation, and its plan follows that of Hirsau. Here, too, the frescoes on the walls and vault of the choir (*c.* 1150) have suffered at the hands of 19th-century restorers, but the Byzantine influences are still discernible.

The Romanesque castle at **Nuremberg** has been reconstructed. In the *Germanisches Museum* is the handsome manuscript known as the *Codex Aureus Epternacensis* (*c.* 1035–40). The cover, consisting of an ivory panel set with enamels, pearls and precious stones, is of exceptional quality. The manuscript was executed at the former abbey of Echternach, the cover comes from Trier.

The stone church of *St Maria*, **Würzburg**, was built in imitation of an Italian or Dalmatian circular building with niches. The early dating formerly given to it, *c.* 706, is now doubted since it was not until the Carolingian age that stone came to be used widely as a building material.

East Germany

The territory which is now included in the East German state has some monuments of great significance for the study of Romanesque. For it was in Saxony that the Ottonian Emperors established their dynasty and attempted to revive the dignity and tradition of the Carolingian Empire.

The most distinctive feature of the Romanesque style in Saxony and associated regions is the arrangement of the west-work – two towers flanking a central structure which often rises above them. The effect is massive, even fortress-like. A simple basilican plan is preferred, as in southern Germany, with alternating column and pier supports.

Just inside the border, and now almost inaccessible, is the Hohenstaufen castle of **Eger** (1180–90). It is in a very good state of preservation. There is a fine two-storied chapel – a descendant of the Palace Chapel at Aachen.

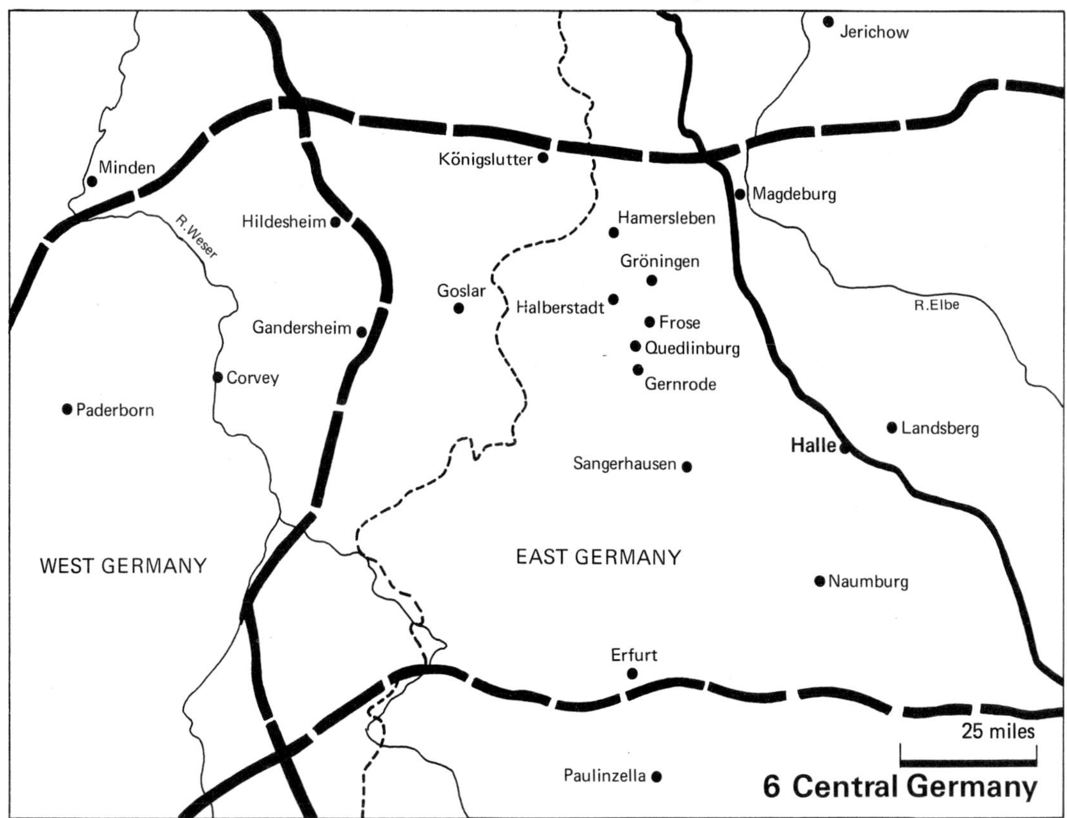

6 Central Germany

At **Paulinzella** was the finest example of a church, built under the influence of Hirsau, now a beautiful ruin. The abbey church of *St Peter*, **Erfurt** (1103–47) was one of the first churches in Germany to have cross-ribbed vaulting.

The remarkable sculpture of the Golden Portal at the *Cathedral* of **Freiburg** (Silesia) dates from the early 13th century; yet it is Romanesque rather than Gothic. The Germans were almost as conservative as the Italians in their adherence to the Romanesque style. Nearby, the church of **Krosingen** has frescoes of the life of St John which, though fragmentary, are valuable as a rare example of unrestored painting in Germany. At **Naumburg** is the half-Gothic four-towered *Cathedral*.

In the castle of **Landsberg** there is an Aachen-inspired double chapel. The first two storeys are late Romanesque (*c.* 1174–86), the third, Gothic. In the main portal on the north side there is a tympanum relief, derived from a Rhineland prototype. *St Ulrich* at **Sangerhausen** was founded *c.* 1083. The cross groined vaults over the side aisles are 12th century, the vault over the main aisle is Gothic.

St Cyriakus, Gernrode, from the south-west.
961 and later.

Quedlinburg was an important Ottonian city. The abbey church was founded in the 9th century, rebuilt in the 10th–11th centuries, and rebuilt again after a fire in 1070. It was consecrated in 1129. There are a few Gothic additions. The present church retains in its essentials the Ottonian plan of its predecessor. In the crypt are much restored frescoes of the late 11th century. The small church of *St Wipert*, converted into a barn in 1806, was recently restored. This simple pillared basilica was built in *c.* 1146. Excavations have uncovered remains of the hall church of *c.* 936. The early 11th-century ambulatory crypt, included in the chancel of the present church, is very unusual and must have derived, ultimately, from France.

The abbey church of *St Cyriakus* at **Gernrode**, founded in 961, has retained its austere Ottonian character, although the western apse, transeptal galleries, and exterior arcading are Romanesque. It is the earliest example of a three-storied building in this area. It is also the earliest existing example of alternating piers and columns in the nave. The badly restored frescoes date from *c.* 1118. The stucco reliefs of the Holy Sepulchre appear to be large-scale reproductions of ivory work. They probably belong to the early 11th century, although they are sometimes attributed to the mid-12th century. Underneath the choir is a vast crypt.

The monastery at **Frose** was founded some time before 959. In 1170 a new building replaced the Ottonian abbey church. It is a cruciform basilica with alternating supports and the characteristic Saxon west-work. The church of the *Holy Virgin*, **Halberstadt**, founded in the mid-12th century, has now been restored after bomb damage. The stucco screen, also restored, is a very fine late 12th-century work and reflects the influence of Byzantine miniatures.

The foundations of the original abbey church of **Gröningen** (936) were discovered in 1934. The present church dates from *c.* 1100. Worth noting are the Italianate architectural decorations. Instead of the usual alternating supports, the abbey church at **Hamersleben** (*c.* 1112–mid-12th century) has columns with magnificent foliage capitals.

Magdeburg was another important Ottonian city. The *Church of our Lady* was founded by Archbishop Gero of Cologne early in the 11th century. The nucleus of the present building dates from the late 11th – early 12th centuries. It was rebuilt again in the early 13th century, when it acquired the Gothic vaulting which dominates the interior. The church was badly damaged in the last war, but has now been restored.

Not far from Magdeburg is the abbey church of **Jerichow** (*c.* 1150–1200), the most important of the earlier brick buildings in north Germany. It is basilican in plan, wooden-roofed, and round-arched. The crypt is open, after the Italian system.

We now return to Western Germany, though still within the Saxon stylistic area of influence. The abbey church of **Königslutter** (1135) was the first church in Saxony to follow the Speyer example of cross-vaulting. The exterior eastern apse is richly carved. Next to the church is a double-aisled cloister, with lavishly decorated columns.

Northern Germany

At **Goslar** is the old *Pfalz*, built *c.* 1050 by the Ottonian Emperor Henry III, whose favourite residence it was. It acquired its Romanesque character after 1132, and in the 19th century was inaccurately restored. The large two-naved wooden-roofed main hall is on the upper level. The throne-room and side parts open onto an outdoor assembly place through arches. At the south end of the building are the Imperial apartments which contain the two-storey chapel of *St Ulrich*. Near the palace is the *Lady Chapel*, also two-storied, which was built after 1035.

The church at **Gandersheim** has a handsome façade, with twin octagonal towers (late 11th century), reflecting the influence of the Strasbourg façade scheme.

Hildesheim was one of the most important centres for Ottonian art. Here remarkable bronze works were cast, under the patronage of Bishop Bernward, who founded an atelier on his return from Rome early in the 11th century. Its most famous product are the bronze doors, made for the church of St Michael but now preserved in the *Cathedral Museum*. Here also is the Easter

Detail of the bronze doors at Hildesheim, showing the meeting of Adam and Eve. 1015.

column, made before 1022, and other minor works of the atelier. They are so far ahead of any other works of art of this period that the attribution to Bernward's workshop was long a matter of doubt. Today there no longer is any question that they are truly the product of the early 11th century, surpassing the finest contemporary work from Byzantium, preceding the fine work of the Meuse school, unparalleled and unrivalled for at least a century. Doors from this atelier reached Novgorod in Russia and Gnesen (Gniezno) in Poland.

The Hildesheim doors have sixteen panels cast partly in high relief, a technique thought to be wholly unknown to the period. The figures are full of movement and expression and are grouped in dramatic scenes. Equally extraordinary is the fact that the doors were cast, not in small sections, but in two wings.

The doors resemble S. Sabina in Rome, and the column, Trajan's column. Bernward would have known these from his Roman visit. Yet this connection scarcely explains the phenomenon of the atelier at Hildesheim mastering the highly intricate art of bronze casting on a large scale, when no such work was being done in Rome itself, or in Milan where Wolvinus was creating his great altar in low relief. For this innovation credit must go to Bernward, ranking him as one of the greatest patrons of art in the Middle Ages.

Detail of the Easter column at Hildesheim, showing Christ healing the sick. Before 1022.

The church of *St Michael* (1001–33) was severely damaged in the last war. However, one compensation was that during restoration the accretions of centuries were removed to give us back the church as it was in the early Middle Ages. We see most of the characteristic features of the early Romanesque in Germany: the simple basilican plan, the double transept and double chancel, the multiple towers. Beneath the choir, raised as in Lombardy, is the crypt with the tomb of St Bernward. The cushion capitals of the church are richly decorated. The stucco choir-screen reliefs (*c.* 1186) are the work of the school of Cologne. They show both classical and Byzantine influences.*

St Godehard (1133–72) is somewhat similar to St Michael, although it has a masonry apse vault, and a Burgundian-type ambulatory with radiating chapels. The tower complex is also different. The stucco tympanum has been preserved. It is worth remembering that stucco was a very popular form of decoration in Germany, though few examples of work in this most perishable material have survived.

The *Cathedral* at **Minden** has a handsome 'Saxon' façade. Inside there is a solemn half life-size crucifix in copper gilt, *c.* 1070. The abbey church of **Corvey** was rebuilt in the Baroque period. However the west end, built

* The interior was almost completely covered by murals, a few vestiges of which remain; great bronze circular chandeliers were suspended over the aisle, adding a Byzantine note to the interior.

129
182

between 873 and 875, which still forms the entrance to the church, has been restored to its original condition.

At **Paderborn** there are three interesting Romanesque churches – all the work of Bishop Meinwerk. The *Cathedral* was begun in 1009. Fortunately it is still intact, in spite of the heavy bombing which the city suffered during the war. The church has a western transept and a characteristic western choir in the massive square tower. The tall steepled spire is of later date. Near the cathedral is the unusual chapel of *St Bartholomäus* (1017), constructed by 'Greek' workmen. It is a triple-aisled church, with pendentive dome vaulting, for which there is no known prototype, although it is clear that contacts with Byzantium influenced the design. The carved capitals of the columns are of exceptional quality.

Minden Crucifix. Copper gilt. *c.* 1070.

Bishop Meinwerk went to Rome with Emperor Henry II. There, in 1014, he met Abbot Odilo of Cluny. As a result of this meeting the **Abdinghof** *Monastery* was refounded as a Cluniac priory in 1016. It was dedicated in 1036, and partly rebuilt in 1058–68 after a fire. The church is interesting as a Cluniac-style building in north Germany. Recent excavations have uncovered pre-Ottonian foundations dating from *c.* 777–99. The *Franciscan Church* has a small, exquisitely worked portable altar of *c.* 1100, originally in the monastery. In the *Diocesan Museum* there is a small wooden statue of the Virgin – one of the earliest free-standing representations – known as *Bishop Imad's Madonna* (*c.* 1060). It was originally sheathed in precious metals.

In the choir of the *Cathedral* of **Soest** are retouched frescoes of *c.* 1160. The Christ in Majesty in the apse of *St Petroklus* has been completely repainted. The original dates to *c.* 1166. The church was built in the second half of the 12th century, from which period dates the Lombard style rib vaulting. The extraordinary looking west tower is *c.* 1200. The façade of the abbey church of **Freckenhorst** is even more astonishing. It was built *c.* 1116–29. The central mass rises, like a great protective wall, to a tall hip roof.

The half-Gothic *Cathedral* of **Münster** which was vaulted in the rebuilding of 1225–65, demonstrates the conservatism of German mediaeval architects. In the *Landesmuseum* there is early Romanesque sculpture (*c.* 1070) and an altar front from St Patroklus, Soest, dedicated to St Walpurga in *c.* 1180.

In the late 12th-century church of *St Norbert*, **Xanten** there is interesting sculpture of St Victor and St Gereon. The crypt of *St Martin*, **Emmerich**, near the Dutch border, has mid-12th-century frescoes (retouched) of the life of Christ.

The Low Countries

Just inside Holland at **Nijmegen** is a 12th-century church, built on the lines of the Palace Chapel at Aachen. *St Peter's*, **Utrecht** (*c.* 1030), has been well preserved. It has a long sanctuary and a vast crypt almost on a level with the floor of the church. In the university library is the famous *Utrecht*

Opposite
Nave of St Michael, Hildesheim. 1001–33, 1162. After reconstruction.

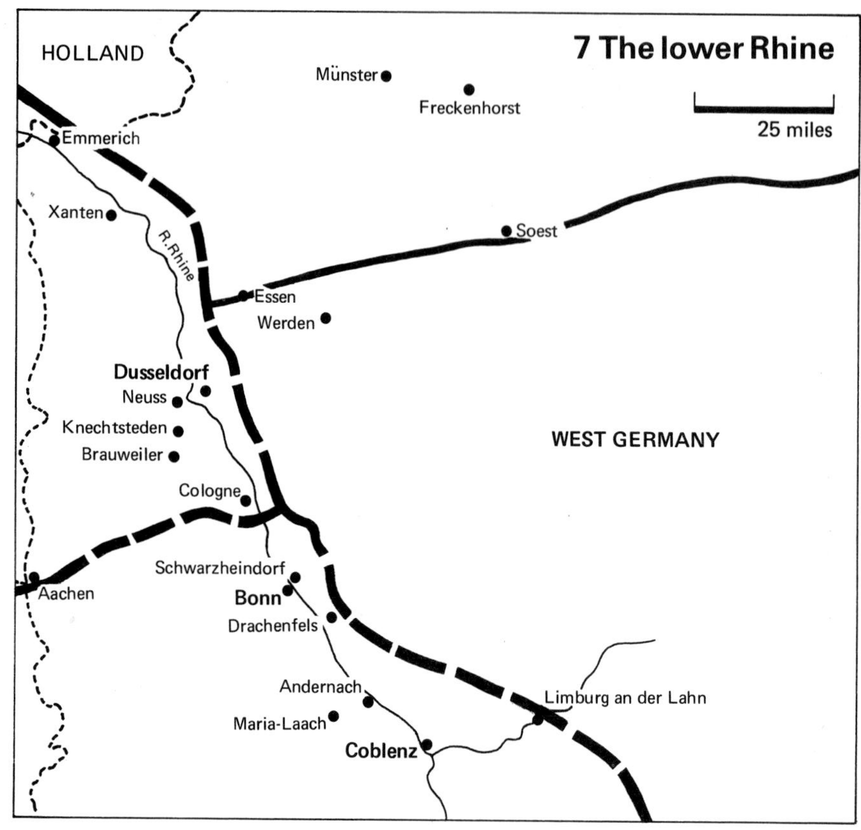

Psalter, a Carolingian work of the school of Reims. It shows how indebted were the Carolingian illuminators to late antique art. The *Minster* at **Roermond** was built in the 12th century. Its vaulting is Gothic. At **Susteren** is the well-preserved church of *St Sauveur*. It was built in the 11th century on the foundations of an 8th-century structure.

The *Cathedral* of **Maastricht** (12th century) has an apse with two towers – we shall meet this form again in the Rhineland. At the west end is a spacious narthex with an elaborate chapel above it. The *Church of Our Lady* (mostly *c.* 1150) also has an apse with two towers. The most striking feature of this building is the massive, fortress-like west front. In the choir are carved capitals. Both these churches have Rhenish style interiors and Gothic vaulting.

The church of *St Denis*, **Liège**, (972–1008) has been rebuilt several times. Portions of the original walls of the transept and nave remain. The façade dates from the 12th century. *St Barthélemy* was founded in 1010. Although the present basilica is later, its interior has preserved the original layout. The bronze font by Rainier of Huy (*c.* 1114) is one of the most remarkable works of the Romanesque period. The font is an example of the Mosan style. It lost its cover during the Napoleonic wars. The rotunda of *St John the Evangelist*, inspired by Aachen, has been altered beyond recognition. The city *Museum* has some interesting mediaeval remains, such as the so-called *Dom Rupert's Madonna* (*c.* 1180).

St Ursmer at **Lobbes** was the cemetery church of the abbey, founded in Carolingian times. The church was enlarged at the end of the 11th century, when it acquired a western tower, crypt and a new choir decorated with Lombard bands.

Tournai was once the Merovingian capital city. The present *Cathedral* was built in 1110, from which period dates the round-arched wooden-roofed nave. It is unusual in having four storeys. The trefoil apse is part of the extension work begun in 1165 and is derived from St Maria in Capitol at Cologne. In the north transept is an 11th-century fresco cycle (much repainted). The *Shrine of Our Lady* (1205) is probably the work of Nicholas of Verdun.

The solemn dignity of Ottonian architecture is beautifully represented at *St Gertrude*, **Nivelles** (Nyfels). This church was damaged during the war. Restorers have removed Gothic and Baroque additions so that now we see the church as it was built in the 11th century with its 12th-century façade. The plan is typically Ottonian, with two transepts and the west-work.

West Germany

In West Germany once more, we travel down through the Rhineland coming first to **Aachen** with its important *Palace Chapel* of Charlemagne (796–804), now incorporated into the Gothic *Cathedral.* It is a two-storied polygon, 105 feet in diameter, covered by a dome. The outer polygon has sixteen sides, the inner one eight. The treatment of the interior and floor plan follows that of S. Vitale in Ravenna. However Aachen is not an exact copy, and the final effect lacks the elegance and subtle feeling for space of the Byzantine church. The bronze railings of the gallery are the only original fittings to survive. In the vaults of the lower ambulatory aisle are animal and human figure sketches which are also Carolingian. The *Treasure* of the cathedral contains wonderful examples of mediaeval craftsmanship: Carolingian and Ottonian manuscripts, ivory work, the golden antependium from the principal altar of the cathedral (*c.* 1020), and the pulpit of Henry II (before 1014). This pulpit is elaborately decorated with classical, oriental and Islamic 'spoils'. Most curious of all is the Lothar Cross (*c.* 1000) which incorporates an antique cameo of the Emperor Augustus.

The ancient city of **Cologne**, founded by the Romans, was the capital of Romanesque art in Germany. It has twelve Romanesque churches, all badly damaged in the war and now more or less restored. The city walls of the 12th century, and earlier, still stand in part. This was the largest fortification of the Middle Ages, rivalling Justinian's great wall at Constantinople.

The foundation of *St Gereon* is attributed to St Helena, mother of

Left: Interior of the Palace Chapel, Aachen. Late 8th century.
Right: Detail of the Shrine of the Three Kings, Cologne. Late 12th or early 13th century.

Constantine, in commemoration of the martyred Roman legionary Gereon. The original structure is included in the decagonal main room of the Romanesque church of the 12th century, when the building was enlarged. The apse and two great towers were also constructed at this time. There was further extensive rebuilding in the 13th century. The Gothic ribs were added in the 14th century. The frescoes in the apse (late 12th century) have been retouched. The church also contains two fine sculptured heads of 1025.

St Maria in Capitol was founded in the 7th century on the site of a late Roman secular building. It was rebuilt in the 11th century, though part of the west end is of earlier date. The sanctuary is 13th century, and the plan is trefoil. This unusual type had no immediate influence, but we find it again in the 12th century in the churches of St Aposteln and Great St Martin in Cologne, and in the cathedral of Tournai. The church has an early example of a hall crypt, with interesting late 12th-century frescoes. The 11th-century carved wooden doors were inspired by S. Sabina in Rome.

The *St Aposteln*, founded in the 11th century and rebuilt towards the end of the 12th century, has been completely reconstructed. There is blind arcading on the interior and exterior of the east end, and eaves galleries. The *Great St Martin* has now also been rebuilt. It was founded in the 10th century, and altered in the 12th and early 13th centuries.

St Cäcilia has very fine 11th-century carved wooden doors. The carving on the tympanum was executed *c.*1150. *St Ursula* has a flat-roofed nave with galleries and vaulted aisles. The Romanesque tower is very impressive. *St Pantaleon* (*c.*970) was one of the first Rhineland buildings to show the German version of Lombardic pilaster strips and arcading. Only the westwork with its three towers has retained its original character. A famous atelier of enamellers was associated with this church.

In the *Treasure* of Cologne Cathedral are the *Gero Cross* (973), the *Shrine of the Three Kings* (1180–1226) – probably by Nicholas of Verdun, and some fine manuscripts. The *Schnütgen-Museum* contains many examples of German Romanesque sculpture.

The Benedictine abbey church at **Brauweiler** is magnificently situated, high above the surrounding countryside. It was founded in 1024, but except for the crypt and parts of the transept, nothing remains of the 11th-century structure. Of the 12th-century abbey buildings there remains the cloister court, the Medardus chapel, and the interior of the chapter-house covered in wall paintings of *c.*1175, unfortunately repainted in the 19th century.

In the monastery church of **Knechtsteden** there are retouched 12th-century frescoes – Byzantine influenced, with German modifications. The west apse has some good sculpture. The magnificent south porch was added towards the end of the 12th century. *St Quirinus*, **Neuss** (1200–42) shows the affection the Germans had for the Romanesque style. Note, for example, the arcaded galleries and blind arcading on the outside. *St Peter* at **Werden**, founded in the mid-10th century and subsequently enlarged and modified, has some interesting early frescoes. The Carolingian crypt of *St Lucius* has been preserved. In the 11th-century choir is an early example of the alternating pier and column system. There are also remains of an extensive fresco cycle (11th century). The church has a bronze crucifix (*c.*1070) from Helmstedt monastery.

Detail of the wooden doors of St Maria in Capitol, Cologne.

The western part of the *Minster* at **Essen** dates from the 11th century. The double-storied apse is reminiscent of Aachen. The octagonal crossing over the tower is roughly contemporary. In the hall crypt are niches and elaborately moulded piers. The *Golden Madonna* (*c.*1000) is the earliest statue of the Virgin Mary preserved in Germany. The seven-branched bronze candlestick, of about the same date, is a very fine piece of work indeed. The 12th-century frescoes, like so many others in Germany, have been spoiled by 19th-century restoration.

The abbey of **Schwarzheindorf** was begun by the chancellor of Emperor Barbarossa, Arnold von Wied, around 1140–50, and is of distinct interest in having the rare upper and lower church. The dominant features are the large

Abbey church of Maria-Laach from the north-west.
1093–1156.

tower over the centre of the building and the Lombardic arcade with sculptured capitals which girdles the entire structure. The interior, lit by small windows, contains some valuable 12th-century frescoes – valuable from an iconographical, not aesthetic point of view. 19th-century restoration has destroyed their original character. Worth noting is a portrait of Emperor Conrad III, uncovered in the last century.

About six miles south of Bonn is the ruined castle of **Drachenfels**, situated on one of the peaks of the 'Siebengebirgen', which was the fabled scene of the battle of Siegfried and the dragon, as well as the home of Snow White and the Seven Dwarfs of the fairy tale. The four-towered abbey church of **Andernach** has some interesting late Romanesque frescoes.

The Benedictine abbey church of **Maria-Laach** was founded in 1093 and completed in 1156, except for the sanctuary (1177). It was renovated in the 19th century. The church is a rare example of homogeneous Rhineland Romanesque, with six towers. It has an elaborate east end, a western choir, and two transepts. The western apse, which was used as a mausoleum, has two storeys. The stone vaulting dates from the mid-12th century. There are lively capital carvings in the narthex.

The abbey church of *St George*, **Limburg an der Lahn**, was founded early in the 10th century, but rebuilt in a transitional style, 1220–35. The exterior, with its seven towers and magnificent west façade, is purely Romanesque. *St Severus* at **Boppard** contains an extensive fresco cycle on the walls of the nave depicting the legend of the Saint. This must have been an outstanding work before it too fell into the hands of 19th-century restorers.

The ancient city of **Trier** was founded by the Emperor Augustus. It was the capital of the Western Empire under Diocletian and the home of the father of Constantine. In 324–48 Constantine built a large three-aisled basilica. A second basilica was later built beside the first, connected to it by annexes. Sandstone arches and brickwork from the sanctuary of the second structure survive in the fabric of the present church, a great agglomerative mass with Romanesque, Gothic, Baroque and 19th-century elements. The 11th-century Romanesque west front displays one of the first developed uses of blind arcading in the Rhineland. In the *Landesmuseum* are late 9th-century paintings from the crypt of the sanctuary of *St Maximin*. They come close to contemporary miniatures in subject matter, arrangement, and linear treatment. There is also a late 9th-century crucifix from the same crypt. The *Frankenturm* (*c*. 1050) is an example of a Romanesque tower house, with single superimposed rooms.

The vast *Cathedral* of **Mainz** was begun in 978, and rebuilt after a fire of 1081. Rebuilding continued into the 12th and 13th centuries. The cathedral has two apses, two transepts and six towers. As in many other Rhineland churches, the square piers are without capitals.

The earliest use of the connected tower, rather than the separate campanile, occurred at about the same time in the Rhineland cathedrals and Lombard churches. Italian craftsmen almost certainly helped to build the churches of the Rhineland. They worked at Speyer, at Worms and many other places. On the other hand German craftsmen worked in Italy and their names are associated with metalwork and sculpture there.

The lower part of the Carolingian nave of the abbey church of **Höchst** has been preserved. The capitals are simplified versions of the classic 'Composite', and are very beautiful in shape.

The small village of **Münzenberg** (north of Frankfurt) is dominated by the ruins of a huge castle. Two great towers of the 12th and 13th centuries stand intact. These are the remains of a fortress built for the Emperor Barbarossa, one of a chain of castles built against the Hungarians. The great outside walls are built of huge stones fashioned in the Italian style – huge blocks of stone with rough, pointed, unfinished sides, apart from the joints. The 12th-century *Palace* has a wall containing arched openings with sculptured columns. It shows concern for the ornamental and beautiful. It speaks not of

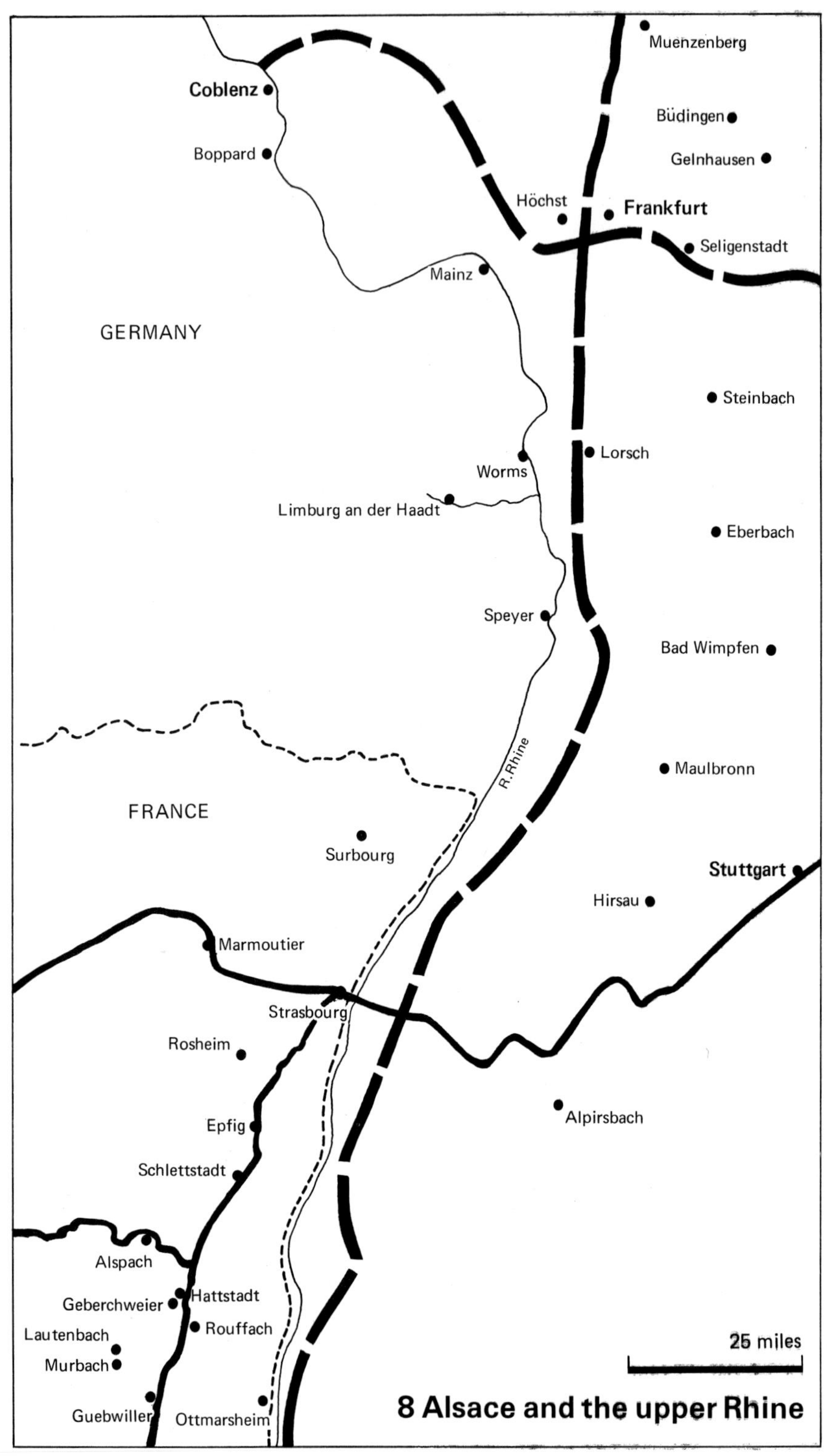

8 Alsace and the upper Rhine

war, but of peace. It is in such Hohenstaufen castles that the awakening of German Romanesque art, influenced by Italian monuments, can be seen. It is here that the Age of Chivalry, of the Crusades, of the dawn of refinement, of the first Minnesingers, of the earliest evidences of lay architecture, can be studied.

At **Hersfeld** are the impressive ruins of an abbey, destroyed in the 18th century. The outer walls of the nave and transept of the church still stand, and the Ottonian choir. The abbey church of **Fulda** was replaced in the Baroque period, but the church of *St Michael*, in the monastery grounds, has been preserved. It was built in 820–2 as a sepulchral chapel on the pattern of the Holy Sepulchre in Jerusalem. The gallery storey, built in the Ottonian era, adopted the Aachen prototype. The nave was added later, in the 11th century. The church of *St Andreas* in the suburb of **Neuenberg** was consecrated in 1023. The Byzantine-influenced frescoes in the crypt are comparatively well-preserved, and show a fine feeling for colour and design.

The castle of **Büdingen** is an inhabited building containing significant portions dating from the 11th and early 12th centuries. The oldest parts of the castle are the tower and adjacent wing, the abandoned chapel with a small sculptured tympanum, and the walled-in columns in the 'Byzantine Room' and in the library (11th and 12th centuries). The outer walls reveal stonework similar to that of Barbarossa's famous castle at Gelnhausen.

Büdingen was one of a series of castles built as a defence against the Frankish tribes who settled in these parts in the 5th century. The existence of an early Frankish settlement in this location is revealed by the fact that the stone church (of uncertain date), not far from the castle, is dedicated to St Remigius, who in 496 converted and baptized the Merovingian King Clovis.

The castle was started by the knights of Büdingen in 934. Its enlargement and embellishment were effected by a knight in the service of Emperor Barbarossa, Hartmann von Büdingen. The Hohenstaufen style here exemplified was influenced by Italian architecture. It was a revolutionary change from the previous dungeon-like construction of fortified dwellings. Note the open arcades on the outer wall of the castle.

At **Gelnhausen** are the ruins of the 12th-century *Palace*. The legend tells of how Barbarossa came to build a palace in this wild place. While hunting for boar, he came upon a beautiful girl called Gela. He fell deeply in love with her and married her. The castle was built near the spot in the forest where they met. To please her he called the castle 'Geln-hausen' – Gela's House. So that she should not feel too lonely when he went away, he formed a community there. The place was named after the castle. The town seal shows the Emperor and his wife under an arch, an incident described in another legend. The Emperor and Gela were in the palace one day, when they were surprised by the town council which had come to ask his advice on the design of the town seal. The council found the pair standing at one of the beautiful windows that survive in the ruins, gazing at a circling eagle. Barbarossa was

Gatehouse of Lorsch, *c.* 800.

annoyed at being disturbed. When told of the business he said simply, 'Take what you see'. In their confusion, the council saw only the Emperor and his wife standing against an arched window, looking sternly at them. They took the words literally: the seal shows the Imperial couple in this position. In the town of Gelnhausen is the Romanesque church of *St Maria*.

The 9th-century abbey church of **Seligenstadt** has recently been restored as far as possible to its original condition. The basilica has a broad-aisled nave with pier supports, an apse with an ambulatory, and a vaulted passage leading down to the tomb of the martyrs Marcellinus and Peter. At **Steinbach** there is another Carolingian church, completed in 827. The main aisle, apsidal chancel, the chapel on the north side, and the remarkable cruciform crypt all survive. As at Seligenstadt, piers were used owing to the shortage of stone suitable for columns in the Rhineland.

The *Gatehouse* of **Lorsch** is attributed by various scholars to a range of centuries, from the 8th to the 11th. The pilastered columns and finely cut capitals have a great sophistication. The refined style and excellent masonry work of this small building make it a unique monument, if it is given the earlier date. The stone work is hard to match up with other Carolingian structures. Analogous treatment of the straight-sided arch and capitals in manuscript painting and sculptural details, here illustrated would, however, served to confirm its earlier origin.

The design and decoration of the gatehouse show obvious eastern and classical influences. The triangular gables are reminiscent of the timbering on early northern wooden churches. In the upper room, late 9th-century mural paintings have survived. They are derived from the antique tradition of architectural decoration, and are strongly classical in spirit.

The *Cathedral* of **Worms** (1016–1181) has the characteristic double apse. This made the principal entrance appear at the side, and not, as in other European cathedrals, at the west end opposite the apse and altar. The effect of this architectural plan was to emphasize a symmetry between the two ends of the long nave. The construction of pairs of towers at each end of the structure, in addition to a larger tower over the crossing of the transept, gave the silhouette of the vast structure a massive symmetry of somewhat heavy appearance – as we see at Worms.

The magnificently severe eastern apse has three enormous round-arched windows decorated with a profusion of animals. Its simplicity is in striking contrast to the exuberance of late Romanesque architecture in Germany, e.g., at Mainz or Speyer. There is very little Romanesque sculpture in the interior of the cathedral. Worth noting, however, is the mid-12th-century 'Flight into Egypt' relief.

It has been argued that the Benedictine monastery of **Limburg an der Haadt** (1025–48) was the first truly Romanesque church in Germany because it reveals a new concept of architectural design. The walls, instead of merely confining space, are broken up into structural groups by piers, half-columns and pilaster strips. It is now in ruins. All that remains are parts of the crypt, chancel, transept, walls of the nave and the west end.

At **Eberbach** is the very large 12th-century Cistercian monastery, containing an entire monastic community within a fortified wall. Founded by Cistercian monks in 1147 and subsequently enlarged and rebuilt, it illustrates the economy of the 12th-century monastery with its cloister, refectory, barns, workshops and adjacent cultivated walled vineyards and gardens. The abbey church (1186) is built in the severe Cistercian style. It is almost entirely

Above: Lion decorating the exterior of Worms.

devoid of sculpture and ornamentation. The Cistercians did not favour the double-apsed system and the church has a square west end. There have been a few later alterations, e.g., the chapels flanking the nave date from the 14th century, but the Romanesque character of the building is well-preserved.

The abbey is situated in a small valley overlooking the Rhine on the site of the famous Steinberg vineyard. The Cistercians are credited with having regenerated the skilled cultivation of the vine in the Rheingau. The vineyards are now state property and are among the finest of the region.

The *Cathedral* of **Speyer** was the burial place of early German Emperors. Like St-Denis in France and Westminster Abbey in England, it is a national shrine. At the time of its construction it was the largest building in Europe. It is the leading example of Romanesque in Germany.

Work on the present cathedral started *c.* 1039, and building continued into the early 12th century when the nave was vaulted. Most of the eastern portion of the church and the remarkable hall crypt date from the initial period of construction. The cushion capitals are typical of German Romanesque. Speyer is famous for its six towers, its great massive bulk, and beautiful stone colours ranging from pink to deep red. The Lombard arcading which encircles the apse and whole body of the church is possibly the work of Donatus, an Italian architect, and Lombard stonemasons who worked on the reconstruction of Speyer late in the 11th century. The church is unusual in having no western apse.

Opposite: Cathedral of Worms, from the west, 1016–1181.

Two finely decorated windows in the south transept remain from *c.* 1100. A very curious and primitive-looking sculpture of about the same date is located in a pilaster on the exterior of the apse.

11 France

It is a tragedy that much of the greatest architecture, sculpture and painting of the Romanesque period in France has been destroyed and forever lost. Of the hundred odd churches that have been cathedrals, less than seven are entirely Romanesque in style. Romanesque architecture in France is pre-eminent in the abbeys. These superb creations, stripped of all portable art treasures since the Revolution, still reveal the fullness of the French artistic genius of the 11th and 12th centuries. Their harmonious composition and decoration, their arcades and quadrangles inspired and challenged to emulation the builders of hundreds of monasteries and secular buildings throughout Europe. Situated outside cities, along pilgrimage routes, in remote areas of the mountains and by the sea, these outposts of mediaeval civilization have a unique beauty and atmosphere. At the other end of the building scale are the many little village churches which have survived and which, in their humble way, are as much a testimony to the vitality of French Romanesque art as the great abbeys.

Nowhere was Romanesque more varied than in France. In the past scholars described regional groups as 'schools', but today such a classification is considered far too rigid. However a number of regional styles did emerge, formed by such factors as inherited traditions and prevailing local influences, as well as geography, geology and climate. Cutting across local boundaries was the art and architecture of the two Burgundian monastic orders, Cluny and Cîteaux, and of the great churches along the pilgrimage routes to the shrine of St James at Compostela.

The development and expansion of French architecture and decoration was truly prodigious. In a period of less than a hundred years these arts rose from obscurity to achieve a series of unrivalled masterpieces. Reverberations of this artistic resurgence were felt throughout Europe. In England the Normans replaced Saxon art with their own monumental churches. Burgundian art was emulated in Spain and in far-off Sicily, Norman conquerors, after absorbing the wonderful abstract art of the Arabs and the splendour of Byzantine mosaics, built great structures in a mixed Norman and Eastern style. Then at the end of the 11th century the Crusaders, who conquered Palestine, were followed by French masons into the Near East and there they constructed castles and churches and decorated them with the sculptures of Burgundy.

Alsace and Northern France

Romanesque building in the north of France was influenced by Rhineland and Carolingian architecture. German influence is dominant in Alsace where we find the German tower arrangement, alternating pier and column nave supports, and occasionally the 'double-ender' plan. Further to the west, German elements mingle with more typically French characteristics. However Champagne and the Ile-de-France are very poor in Romanesque, since the early development of Gothic here led to the destruction of many churches and their reconstruction in the new style. Barbarian and Celtic motifs predominate in sculptural decoration, although towards the middle of the 12th century we can see echoes of the revival of figure sculpture.

The *Cathedral* of **Strasbourg** was the most important Romanesque building in Alsace until its reconstruction in the Gothic style. Its original façade scheme was adopted in a number of churches in nearby areas – at Basle, Constance, Schaffhausen, Hirsau and Marmoutier. The hall crypt of the 11th-century minster is essentially the same today as when built. It contains some very fine capitals. The present church was begun in 1176 and the late Romanesque choir dates from this period.

The countryside of Alsace is dotted with country churches which retain Romanesque columns and capitals, and in some cases are completely intact. The choir, transept and east bay of the nave of the church of *Sts Peter and Paul*, **Neuweiler** are Romanesque (second half of 12th century). At **Marmoutier** is an abbey church, with a west front and towers belonging to the 11th and 12th centuries. The decoration is Lombardic, but the general plan is reminiscent of Carolingian and Ottonian façades.

The *Heldenhaus* at **Rosheim** was built in the 12th century, which makes it the oldest surviving house in Alsace. The church of *Sts Peter and Paul* is of the same period, except for the top of the tower (rebuilt in the 14th century) and the two-storied chapel flanking the choir (a survival from an earlier church). The church has Lombard bands and arcadings. The carvings in the round – for example, the symbols of the Evangelists over the east window – are the first in Alsace. They have been much restored.

The abbey of **Andlau** was founded by Richarda, the wife of Charles the Fat, in the 9th century. The legendary story tells of her accusation of infidelity, her demonstration of innocence by the trial by fire, and her subsequent flight to the forest, where in a vision she is told to found an abbey at a spot that will be shown her by a bear. The abbey long kept bears in a pit in her honour. After Richarda's canonization in the 11th century the abbey became a pilgrimage centre. The 12th-century abbey church has fine, archaistic portal sculpture. It is the most complete collection of Romanesque sculpture in Alsace.

The chapel of *Ste-Marguerite* (11th–12th century) at **Epfig** is cruciform, with barrel-vaulted arms and a dome over the crossing. The long porch extending around the west and south sides was added in the 12th century. The decorative details of *Ste-Foy*, (second half of 12th century) **Sélestat** (or Schlettstadt) are very sculptural in feeling. Much of the ornament seems to have been inspired by Italian examples.

Carolingian influence is obvious in the 11th-century convent church of **Ottmarsheim**. It is eight-sided with galleries over the aisles, and derives from Aachen. The late Romanesque church of **Guebwiller** was faithfully restored in the 19th century. Its gable is decorated with a criss-cross pattern.

Set in a narrow valley is the partly destroyed Cluniac monastery church of **Murbach**. The abbey was founded in the 8th century. All that remains of the 12th-century church is the square chancel, flanked by two high square towers and the transepts. The exterior is richly decorated with arcading and pilaster strips. There are also carved reliefs.

St-Abrogast (12th–13th centuries) at **Rouffach** contains some fine capitals. The upper parts of the west-work of the Romanesque church at **Lautenbach** were considerably restored in the 19th century. The lower stages of the towers flank a well-preserved, handsome porch.

These are the most important of the Romanesque buildings in Alsace. Of lesser interest are the churches at **Geberchweier**, **St Jochann**, **Surbourg**, **Feldbach**, **Dorlisheim**, **Arolsheim**, **Alspach** and **Hattstadt**.

To the north-west of Alsace, at **St-Dié**, is the mid-12th-century church of *Notre-Dame*, separated from the cathedral only by a cloister. The *Cathedral* of **Verdun** is a 'double-ender'. As the result of damage during the First World War the Romanesque church was discovered beneath its 18th-century casing and restored. It dates from the 11th and 12th centuries. The large choir reflects the influence of the Burgundian style. Beneath it is a fine crypt. The almost perfectly preserved church of *Notre-Dame*, **Mont-devant-Sassey** is a small scale version of the cathedral of Verdun.

St-Remi, **Reims**, is named after the early saint who founded a monastery in Reims. It was St Remigius, who in the fifth century baptized Clovis, king of the Franks, thus introducing Christianity into the Frankish lands. The present church, built over the foundations of a number of earlier churches covering the saint's tomb, was begun in 1005. Thus it considerably pre-dates the famous cathedral. It was vaulted in 1180 and has been reconstructed in part since – including an elaborate Gothic choir. In the Baroque façade, antique columns may be distinguished. The pair of façade turrets are of

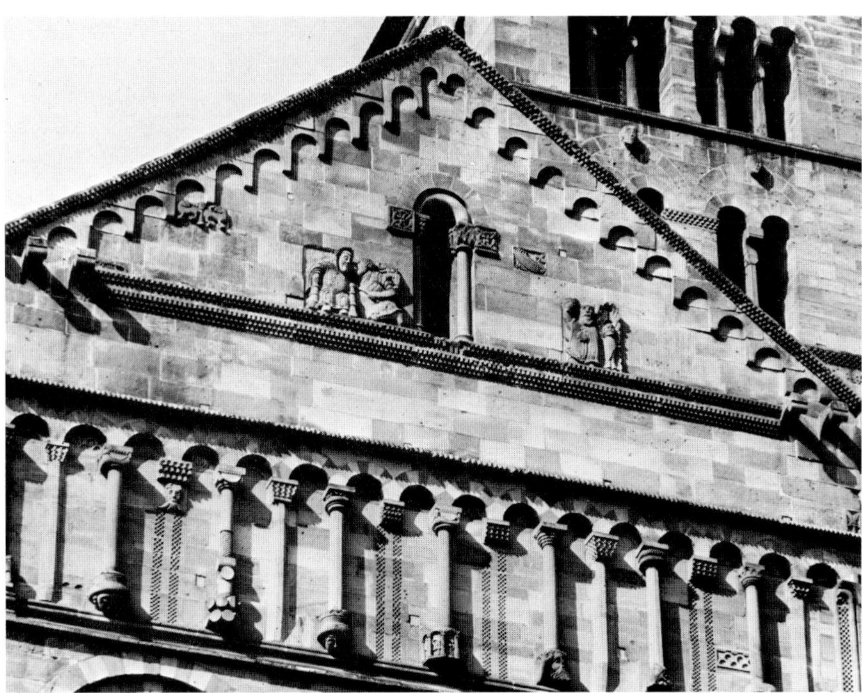

East gable of the choir of the abbey church of Murbach. 12th century.

Romanesque origin. In the course of alteration St-Remi acquired some of the earliest flying buttresses in France.

At **Cerny-en-Laonnais** near Laon is a Romanesque church of *c.* 1100. The nave is spanned by attractive-looking diaphragm arches. The church of **Nouvion-le-Vineux** has a beautiful 12th-century tower. The spire is modern. At **Laon**, the *Manecanterie* dates from the 12th century. About seven miles south of Laon, at **Urcel**, is a church which is Romanesque. It has a fine porch extending across the west front. Above the porch is a three-storied tower.

The abbey church of **Morienval** is beautifully situated. The present structure appears to have been begun in the late 11th century. The east end was rebuilt in the 12th century in the early Gothic style. The pair of towers flanking the apse reflect German influence.

St-Étienne, **Beauvais** belongs to the early 12th century, except for the sanctuary, which is later. Above the rich lateral portal of the north transept is a famous representation of the Wheel of Fortune.

At **Pontpoint**, which is near Point-Sainte-Maxence, there is a late 11th-century church. The church of **St-Vaast-de-Longmont** has a good Romanesque tower. The great *Cathedral* of **St-Denis** just outside Paris, in which the kings of France were buried, is notable as the first definitely Gothic construction in France.

France

Like all modern capitals save Rome, **Paris** has long since destroyed its early Christian and Romanesque architecture. The only Romanesque building in Paris is a part of the abbey of *St-Germain-des-Prés* dating from the 12th century. The foundation of the monastery dates from Merovingian times. During the 6th and 7th centuries, before the formation of the French kingdom, it served as the burial place for the kings and queens of Neustria. The Merovingian structure, now completely vanished, was described by contemporaries as shining with gold, covered with fine murals and gorgeously decorated with marbles.

The handsome entrance tower of the present building dates from about 1000, the nave and aisles from *c.* 1050. This makes the church (except for its Gothic choir) one of the oldest in France. The capitals of the columns in the nave are some of the earliest capitals, depicting stories, to be found anywhere. They are moreover sculptured in a vigorous and skilful manner. The originals of the capitals that have survived are kept in the *Cluny Museum*, the ones in the church being copies.

The Cluny Museum is devoted specially to mediaeval arts in France. The chief treasures of this museum are Visigothic crowns, Byzantine ivories and ancient oriental textiles which were used as models for early Romanesque art, and the Altar of Basle – a gorgeous gold altar frontal presented by the Ottonian Emperor Henry II to the cathedral of Basle in *c.* 1020.

In the *Louvre* there is a gallery of Romanesque sculpture. It contains some important pieces of work, including fine sculptured heads from the pre-Gothic St-Denis. In the gallery devoted to goldsmiths' work is a bronze statue of Charlemagne.

The *Bibliothèque Nationale* has a very rich and comprehensive collection of illuminated manuscripts – early Christian, Merovingian, Carolingian, Ottonian, and Romanesque. The *Musée des Monuments* (Trocadero) is a Romanesque museum second in importance only to Barcelona – in Europe – and The Cloisters in the United States. Here may be found full-size casts of individual capitals and complete portals. The second floor of the museum contains reproductions in colour, also full-size, of some of the finest Romanesque wall-paintings of France.

Some miles east of Paris at **Jouarre** is an important 7th-century Merovingian crypt. This small burial chamber shows sculptured capitals of considerable refinement and mid-7th-century tombs. The tomb of the Abbess Theodechilde, who died in 655, is the finest surviving French sculpture dating from a period stretching over several centuries. A small portion of the original wall reveals great skill in stone cutting and setting, an art sometimes held to have been lost in most of Europe during the 'Dark Ages'.

Longpoint, to the south, was an ancient pilgrimage centre. A Cluniac priory was founded there in the 11th century. The present church of *Notre-Dame* was begun in the 12th and finished in the 13th century.

The 11th-century *Cathedral* at **Chartres** was replaced by an early Gothic

Central portion of the altar retable from Carrières St-Denis.
c. 1170. Paris, the Louvre.

structure (1135–80). All that remains of the Romanesque building is the huge crypt completed in *c.* 1024. The elongated figures of the *Portail Royal* must be considered proto-Gothic rather than Romanesque, if only because they are not contained within the columns to which they are attached.

The glass of the three lancets of the west façade of the cathedral dates back to about 1130–40. It is almost contemporary with the Suger glass (now destroyed) in St-Denis. Of all the stained glass at Chartres, these early 12th-century windows are the best, and the north lancet the finest of all. The glass is designed without perspective. The treatment of colours is very sophisticated. Blue is the basic colour; this was the colour of the fine 'Tree of Jesse' window. All tones in the windows are repeated in the borders.

The south lancet window represents the Passion. Henry Adams in his book, *Mont-St-Michel and Chartres*, argues that it was made either by a Greek or by somebody who had before him a Byzantine missal, enamel or ivory. To him, the figure of Christ, the treatment of the fish, the figure pulling out the nails fastening Christ's feet, are all Greek.

Normandy

We shall now look at some of the churches and castles of Romanesque Normandy, leaving Norman building in England until a later section. Norman Romanesque is one of the most distinctive of the Romanesque styles. Its development was influenced chiefly by Ottonian architecture, but there were also elements characteristic of the nearby Loire region, and of Burgundy via the Cluniac monks. Norman building spread, with the Norman conquests, to Sicily and England. It is indeed a fitting expression of the energy and intelligence of these people. The western façade scheme differed from its Ottonian precedent in the emphasis given to the two massive square towers flanking the central portion. There is a strong feeling for vigorous simplicity and a grand scale, for the clear articulation of parts, vertically by the use of column shafts rising from the ground to the roof, horizontally by the use of a triforium gallery, often 'blind', above the nave arcade. Cushion capitals are preferred. The predilection of the 'Norsemen' for geometrical and abstract forms is reflected in decoration. Until the turn of the 11th century the naves of the churches were wooden roofed. However Norman architects at Durham had an important role in the development of ribbed vaulting.

The Normans were great warriors and much of their early architecture was military. *La Roche Guyon* (11th century) in the valley of the Seine is an example of their 'impregnable' castles. The great Romanesque builder, Abbot Suger, described it as the 'odious castle'. It was carved out of a high rock. The halls, storage and water reserves and the stairway giving access to the formidable tower above were contained within the living rock itself. In the 12th century this little Gibraltar was expanded to include outside structures. The great French archaeologist and restorer of mediaeval structures, Viollet-le-Duc, regarded this fortress as one of the most powerful of the early Middle Ages.

The ruin of the famous fortress, *Château Gaillard* (1196), illustrates the methods of construction used in the early Middle Ages. Three main lines of fortification can be traced: first, a huge enclosure protected by a thick wall and moat, then a second enclosure shielded by a scallop-shaped wall of great strength and beauty, and finally the interior keep with enormously thick walls, battlements, and void of windows except on the side of the sheer cliff overhanging the Seine. These windows are reminiscent of the contemporary Hohenstaufen fortresses in Germany, which likewise permitted this luxury.

The castle was built by Richard the Lionheart to control Normandy. Despite its strength it was captured eight years later by King Philip Augustus. It was the scene of many battles in the years following and of at least one savage mediaeval punishment: the strangulation for adultery of the wife of King Louis X.

The Norse invaders of the 9th century destroyed most of the existing abbeys and churches. Once converted to Christianity and settled (when they

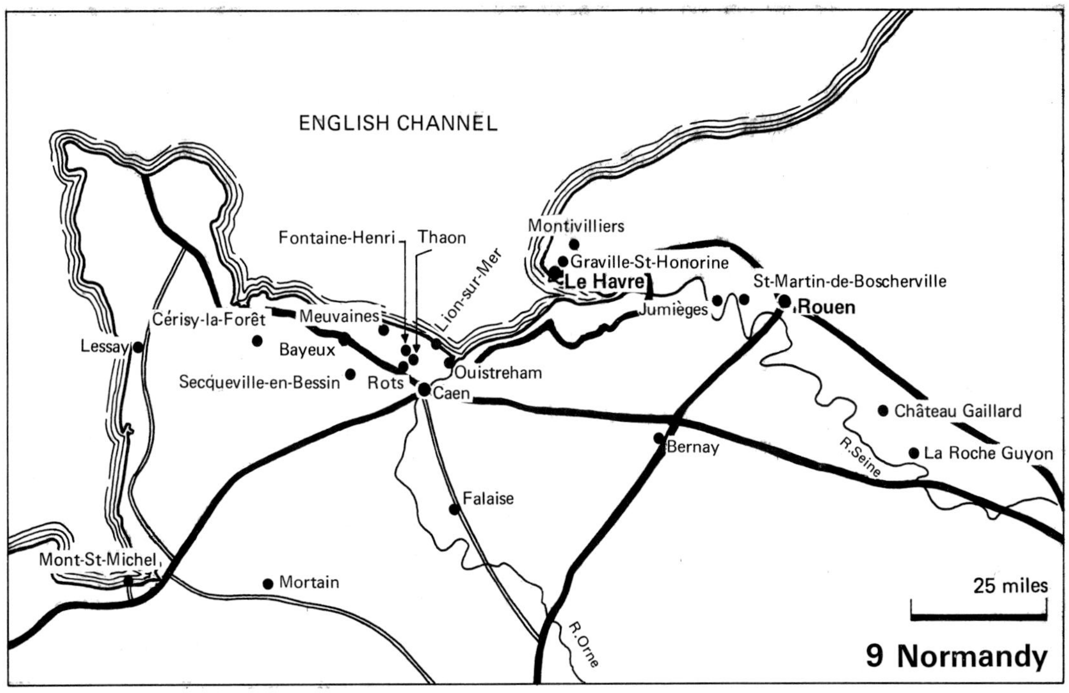

became 'Normans'), they set about rebuilding and establishing new foundations. At **Jumièges** are the ruins of two early abbey churches they rebuilt: *St-Pierre* (10th century) and *Notre-Dame* (1037–66). Although only two bays and the west end survive of the first, the vigour of the Norman builders is apparent. The western portion of Notre-Dame illustrates a stage in the evolution of this section. The porch tower, a feature of Carolingian building, has almost merged with the nave, and it is framed by two sturdy octagonal towers. Worth noting in the nave are the articulating column buttresses.

The former abbey church of *St-Georges*, **St-Martin-de-Boscherville** is a well-preserved and majestic building of the first half of the 12th century. The chapter-house which dates from 1170 has survived.

The abbey church at **Graville-St-Honorine** (now part of Le Havre) is 12th century, except for the north transept and tower over the crossing which are 11th century. The exterior is decorated with typically Norman intersecting arches. The conventual buildings now house a museum of archaeology and sculpture.

The abbey church of *Notre-Dame* at **Montivilliers**, although it has been altered, damaged and restored several times, has managed to preserve its Norman character.

In expiation of their uncanonical marriage, William the Conqueror and

Matilda founded two great abbeys at **Caen**: the *Abbaye-aux-Hommes* and the *Abbaye-aux-Dames*. The church of the latter, *Ste-Trinité* was begun in 1062 and completed early in the 12th century, when the nave was vaulted. The arches of the three-storied nave are decorated with a Greek key pattern.

The abbey-church of *St-Étienne*, just out of Caen, is the most impressive example of mature Norman architecture on the Continent. It was begun in *c.* 1067 and vaulted early in the 12th century. The church exhibits almost all the typical features of Norman building. The austere and majestic west front is the fulfilment of earlier developments. William the Conqueror was buried here in 1087.

To the east of Caen are the ruins of the 11th-century abbey of **Bernay**. To the south is the massive 12th-century castle of **Falaise** with its enormous central keep. Small rooms are constructed in the thickness of its walls. Falaise was the birthplace of William the Conqueror.

In a number of towns near Caen there are interesting Norman examples. The church of **Ouistreham** (11th–12th centuries and later) has a finely proportioned three-storied façade with thick walls, small windows, and a deeply recessed doorway reminiscent of the churches of central and southern France. It carries geometric ornament. The interior is similar to that of the Norman churches of Caen. The cylinder columns of the nave, which alternate with compound piers, are particularly massive.

The church of **Lion-sur-Mer** has some very curious old capitals in its garden, depicting beasts, snake-like vegetation, and crude figures in weird postures – all suggestive of pagan influences. At **Rots** there is a 11th to 12th-century church with very interesting arcading on both inside and outside walls. There are also many small pieces of sculpture.

Contemporary with Rots is **Fontaine-Henri**. The use of carving is subdued, and the proportions of the two-storied arcading most beautiful. The church of **Secqueville-en-Bessin** is mostly 11th century, except for the choir and its aisles, which were recast in the 17th century. The spire is Gothic. Its tower served as a fortress in 1105.

The abandoned church of **Thaon**, picturesquely situated in a little valley, is a 12th-century masterpiece. It is beautifully designed and highly decorated – in general more so than the great churches of Caen. Under the eaves there is a carved corbel-table. The blank arcade is decorated with numerous carvings of high quality. Inside, the nave clerestory has an ornamental arcade. The capitals are of most primitive design – perhaps anterior to the 12th century. According to Viollet-le-Duc the belfry was used for military purposes.

The west front of the church of **Meuvaines** has two little figures in the arcade below the west gable, and a much decayed Last Supper on the lintel of the north door of the west front. This is most unusual since Norman architecture in general had little use for figurative sculpture.

Bayeux *Cathedral* was built in the 11th century, but the original structure

Opposite
Façade of St-Étienne, Caen. Begun *c.* 1067.

Detail of the Bayeux Tapestry.
11th century.

has been greatly modified by Gothic additions. Its nave and fine towers, however, are early Norman. The nave walls are decorated with basket-work motifs or little discs, and in the spandrels are reliefs of Scandinavian inspiration.

The *Bayeux Tapestry* is one of the leading pictorial works of art of the 11th century and certainly the most famous. Wrongly attributed by some to Queen Matilda, wife of the Conqueror, it was more likely executed under the direction of William's brother, Bishop Odo, shortly after the Conquest, by Saxon needle-workers. It consists of a strip of canvas sixty yards long depicting in variety and detail the events leading up to the Battle of Hastings and the Battle itself. It is essentially a 'propaganda film' justifying the Conqueror's acts. It shows elaborate scenes of contemporary life in some fifty episodes, utilizing 626 human figures and hundreds of animals.

The tapestry is notable not only as a work of art, but also for archaeological reasons. It shows the design of the ships as pagan Nordic; the trees seem to derive from Irish manuscripts; the architecture has Byzantine elements. The more abstract designs reflect patterns of Near Eastern textiles and illuminations.

As an archaeological document the tapestry is priceless. It describes contemporary life in the manner of a contemporary historian. Such details as ships, houses, and costumes are illustrated – as is the manner of cooking, of harnessing horses, of the use of wine, of constructing ships and their navigation. We also see the different forms of dress, armour, arms and the various types of warfare.

Near Bayeux, at **Cérisy-la-Forêt** is a fine abbey church begun in the mid-11th century. At **Lessay** there is another fine building, founded about the same time. This abbey church of *La Trinité* suffered serious damage during the Battle of Normandy in the last war, but has now been excellently restored.

The island abbey of **Mont-St-Michel** on the boundary between Normandy and Brittany is one of the greatest of all mediaeval monuments. While the greater part of the structure is Gothic, there is an appreciable amount of Romanesque in the older portions of the church (the south side of the nave is 11th century, the north side, 12th century) and in the lower halls.

The Cistercian foundation at **Mortain** has kept its church, chapter-house, and two cloister walks.

There are few Romanesque survivals in Brittany. In the north at **Dinan** the church of *St-Sauveur* is partly 12th century – the lower stage of the west front, the south side of the nave, and some of the transept. The most important Breton Romanesque building is in the south. This is the abbey church of *Ste-Croix* at **Quimperlé**, a rotunda ultimately derived from the Holy Sepulchre in Jerusalem, although the more immediate inspiration was probably Neuvy-St-Sépulcre. At **Redon** is the 11th–12th-century church of *St-Sauveur*, with a crossing tower resembling those of the south-west of France. The church of *St-Tudy* at **Loctudy** is contemporary with Redon.

The Loire and South-western France

The Loire region and the south-west covers a vast area of France. Scholars have attempted to break it up into different 'schools', but because of the interpenetration of influences, there appears to be little consensus of opinion. For our purposes it is simpler to treat this part of France as a unit, though a far from homogeneous one, and describe regional peculiarities as we come to them. One common factor is the predominance of unaisled over aisled churches. Another type of church, centred in Poitiers, has aisles almost as high as the nave. One important difference is that in the north, churches are generally wooden-roofed, in the south (where timber was more rare), barrel-vaulted or domed. In the south-west sculptural decoration is particularly lavishly applied, though the churches here have no tympana. There are also a number of churches which have preserved their frescoes – more than anywhere else in France. In general they are of subdued colour against a light background. Finally we should mention the pre-Romanesque architectural remains which, though few, are significant.

The west front, and west bays of the abbey church of *Notre-Dame d'Avénières*, **Laval** were rebuilt in the 19th century in the neo-Romanesque

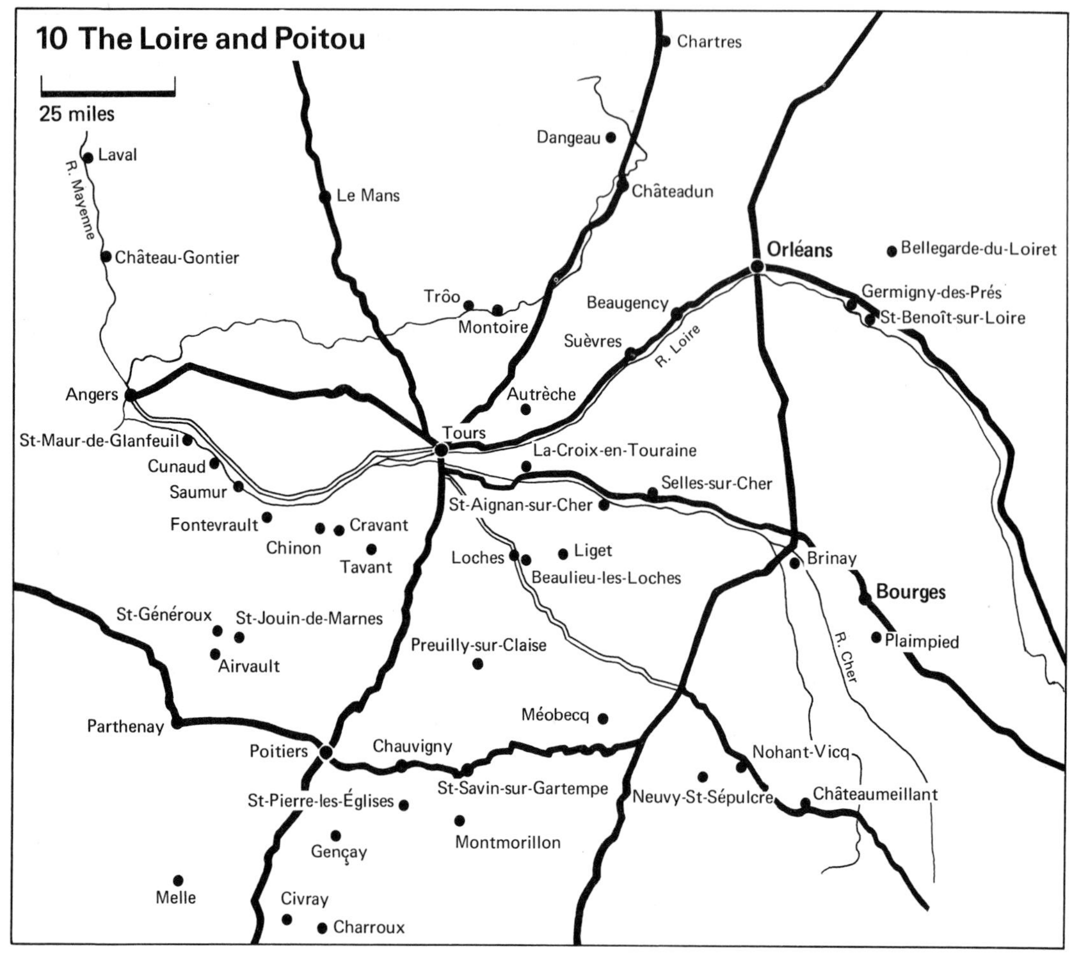

style. The rest of the church, however, is late 11th–12th centuries. Of about the same date are the abbey churches of *La Couture* and *Notre-Dame-du-Pré* at **Le Mans**. But they have been much altered. The Romanesque *Cathedral* is better preserved. Worth noting is the patterned wall-work on the exterior, ultimately inherited from antique constructions, like the baptistery at Poitiers.

The church of *St-Jean-Baptiste* at **Château-Gontier** was bombed during the last war, but has now been restored. Between the clerestory windows there are fresco remains, and in the transepts there is a Genesis Cycle, recently uncovered. These date from the late 11th or early 12th centuries. They resemble the great frescoes of St-Savin-sur-Gartempe. The pendentive dome over the crossing is like that of St-Martin at Angers.

Fresco of Saul (?) in the crypt of St-Nicolas, Tavant. 12th century.

St-Martin, **Angers** was built in 1012 on an aisleless cross plan. However, the only surviving parts are the nave and the pendentive dome, (*c.* 1075) reputedly the oldest surviving French Romanesque dome in existence. From this the great domed-up early Gothic ribbed vaults of the *Cathedral* probably derived. It was founded early in the 11th century and rebuilt between 1150 and 1240, from which period the vaulting dates. Like St-Martin it has a simple aisleless cross plan. All that remains of the 12th-century abbey church of *St-Aubin*, destroyed during the Revolution, is the massive, austere tower. The large and well-preserved *Town Hall* of Angers dates from 1175.

South-west of Angers near Nantes was the important pre-Romanesque abbey of **St-Philibert-de-Grandlieu**, named after the founder of Jumièges and Noirmoutier and during the 9th century, the repository of his earthly remains (which ended their wanderings at Tournus in 876). All that survives of the 9th-century church, important as an early mediaeval solution of the problem of providing additional altars and an easier approach to the relics, is the nave with its horseshoe arches. And some scholars would attribute even this to the 10th century.

The gable of the abbey church of **St-Maur de Glanfeuil**, near Angers, dates from the 9th century. It is decorated with a large cross composed of interlacing. At **Cunaud** there is a 12th-century abbey church, comparatively well restored in the 19th century. The relics of St-Philibert rested here for a while.

Notre-Dame de Nantilly, **Saumur** is a good, typical example of the churches of the south-west of France. It was built in the first half of the 12th century. The very wide aisleless nave is barrel vaulted. The capitals, some historiated, some animal and floral, are of very fine quality.

The abbey of **Fontevrault** was founded in about 1100. The only important part of the conventual building to survive is the kitchen – an octagonal tower with a hollow spire as a roof and a pinnacle at the top. There are pinnacles also clustered around the lower stage. They closely resemble the corner turrets of Notre-Dame at Poitiers. The abbey church is a curious amalgam of a choir with radiating chapels, derived from the system of the pilgrimage churches, and an aisleless nave roofed by four domes.

At **Chinon**, on the Vienne, there is a Romanesque castle. The church of *St-Mexme* has a 10th-century relief on its façade. The early 10th-century church at **Cravant** is decorated with unusually well patterned wall-work. In the choir and crypt of *St-Nicolas*, **Tavant** are 12th-century frescoes. Those in the crypt are of especially exceptional quality, in fact, the work of a man of genius. They reflect the influence of contemporary English art.

The great pilgrimage church of *St-Martin*, **Tours** was destroyed in the Revolution. The porch tower of *St-Julien* dates from the 11th–12th centuries. In the environs of Tours there are a number of interesting Romanesque survivals. **La-Croix-en-Touraine** has a typical 12th-century village church. The church of **St-Aignan-sur-Cher** (early 12th century) has some fine carved capitals on the ambulatory columns. In the large crypt there are early and late 12th-century frescoes.

The apse arrangement of the abbey church of **Selles-sur-Cher**, like that of St-Aignan, derives from St-Benoît-sur-Loire, the most influential church of the Loire district. On the exterior of the apsidal chapel is a double frieze of sculpture, rather naïve, but full of life. It dates from the early 12th century. Of the same date are the fine frescoes in the choir of *St-Aignan*, **Brinay**. The figures recall those of St-Savin and Tavant, which share their Carolingian characteristics. There is also a certain Ottonian influence.

Within the great keep of **Loches** is the church of *St-Ours* (11th–12th centuries). In about the middle of the 12th century its timber roof was replaced by two hollow eight-sided pyramids, which give the church an unusual appearance, both inside and out. They are obviously connected with the domed churches further to the south. The magnificent porch is decorated with polychrome sculpture. The chapel of *St-Jean* near **Liget** is a circular domed building, to which a nave, now in ruins, was added in the 12th century. The frescoes in the chapel are in very poor condition. At **Beaulieu-les-Loches** is a partly ruined 11th to 12th-century abbey church, with a remarkably sculptured north transept gable.

North of Tours there are also some interesting churches. The parish church of **Autrèche** is a good example of the wooden-roofed nave and chancel type structure widely built in the 10th century. The priory church of *St-Gilles*, **Montoire** (11th century) is trefoil in plan – most unusual for France. The 11th- or 12th-century frescoes in the apse show Carolingian influence. The nave is half-ruined. At *St-Jacques-des-Guérêts*, **Trôo**, there are frescoes of the second half of the 12th century. Their expressionistic quality is enhanced by the unusual colours.

Châteaudun has two Romanesque churches: *St-Jean*, which is mostly 11th and 12th centuries, and *La Madeleine*, which is 12th century except for the 16th-century choir. *St-Georges* (*c.* 1100) at **Dangeau** is a homogeneous structure, ably restored a few years ago.

We now return to the Loire. The church of *St-Lubin*, **Suèvres**, has an early 11th-century tower. Within the precincts of the castle of **Beaugency**, with its splendid 12th-century tower, is the abbey church of *Notre-Dame*, rebuilt in the first half of the 12th century. The choir is a miniature version of St-Benoît. The church of **Bellegarde-du-Loiret** has a richly worked Romanesque west front with a deeply recessed doorway.

Three miles from St-Benoît at **Germigny-des-Prés** the Abbot Theodulf built a villa in 806. This is now destroyed, but the oratory remains. It is a vaulted, centralized little structure with a tower and triple apses. A Byzantine prototype is sometimes sought, but since Theodulf was a Visigoth, Arab influence is more likely. The stucco and mosaic decoration in the east apse, on the other hand, do reflect a strong Byzantine influence. The oratory was cruelly restored in the 19th century.

Porch capital, St-Benoît-sur-Loire. Second half of 11th century.

The abbey of **St-Benoît-sur-Loire** was founded in the 7th century when relics, believed to be of St Benedict, were brought there from Monte Cassino, desolated by the Lombards. The abbey became a pilgrimage centre. It also became a great educational centre under the abbacy of Theodulf in Charlemagne's time. After the ravages of the Normans, St-Benoît went into a decline, from which it was rescued by Abbot Odo of Cluny.

The present church, replacing one burnt down in 1026, was begun in 1067 and finally completed in 1217. It is in an almost perfect state. The porch beneath the west tower is open and carried on sturdy columns with Corinthian capitals inhabited by little men. The spacious rib-vaulted nave (probably wooden-roofed originally), with groin-vaulted aisles, leads to the crossing which is surmounted by a handsome tower. Apsidioles are attached to the transepts. The apse has an ambulatory with four radiating chapels. Particular note should be made of the lively historiated capitals in the blind arcade below the clerestory in the choir. The well-preserved tympanum is now shown in the south transept.

We now leave the Loire, since the churches and abbeys on its lower reaches are within the Burgundian area of stylistic influence, and turn south. Not far from Bourges at **Plaimpied** is the abbey church of *St-Martin*. It is much altered, but there is excellent 12th-century decoration on the wall arcades in the apsidioles, on the capitals of the choir, and on the exterior of east end. At **Châteaumeillant** is the dignified and elegant abbey church of *St-Genès*. It has a spacious sanctuary of the 'Benedictine plan', i.e. with apsidioles laid out in steps.

The rotunda of **Neuvy-St-Sépulcre** was modelled on the Holy Sepulchre in Jerusalem. It was built in *c.* 1045. In the church of *St-Martin* at **Nohant-Vicq**, a little further up the Indre from Neuvy-St-Sépulcre, there are frescoes of the second half of the 12th century. They are in the choir and on the wall dividing the choir from the nave. They are quite rustic, but the figures have a dynamic exuberance. The choir of the abbey church of **St-Genou** resembles St-Benoît. On the columns of the north and south walls there are lively historiated capitals. At **Preuilly-sur-Claise** is a much restored late 11th to 12th-century church. It is tunnel vaulted, with diaphragm arches. There is no direct lighting, a common feature in the churches around Poitiers. The church of **Méobecq** has late 12th-century frescoes in the choir which are very well preserved.

The province of Poitou is exceptionally rich in Romanesque art. The centre is **Poitiers**. It was an important city under the Romans and in early Christian times. In the Middle Ages it was on one of the main pilgrimage routes to Compostela – the Paris-Orléans-Bordeaux route – and this contributed to the spread of Poitevin influence elsewhere.

The baptistery of *St John* was founded in the 4th century, and later altered. It reveals a Roman core with three Merovingian appendages and a later polygonal apse (11th century). The outside walls show most interesting Roman and mediaeval stonework. There are also fragments from Roman buildings. The *Hypogeum of les Dunes* is a 7th-century structure.

The church of *Notre-Dame-la-Grande* (*c.* 1130–45) is famous for its rich sculptured façade with a deeply recessed doorway and arcades enclosing figures. It is flanked by two low towers, each consisting of a bundle of shafts with pinnacles. The nave is barrel vaulted and the aisles, which rise almost to the same height, have groin vaults. The apse has an ambulatory with three radiating chapels. There is no direct lighting.

St-Hilaire was begun in *c.* 1025–30 and was transformed into a fire-proof building in the 12th century when it acquired a series of octagonal vaults over the central part of the nave. These have definite Eastern undertones, perhaps Moslem. There are some striking remnants of late 11th- or early 12th-century frescoes. *Ste-Radegonde*, a pilgrimage church like St-Hilaire with ambulatory and radiating chapels, has a spacious nave with Gothic domed-up ribbed vaults. Its tower-porch is characteristic to this region. *St-Porchaire* has a particularly fine example of the 11th or 12th century.

Around Poitiers there are many fine monuments. **St-Pierre-les-Églises** has some Romanesque fresco fragments. The church of *St-Pierre*, **Chauvigny**, is between two ruined mediaeval keeps. It dates from the 12th century, except for the 13th-century tower over the crossing. The church is famous for its rich interior and exterior decorations.

Opposite
Façade of Notre-Dame-la-Grande, Poitiers, *c.* 1130–45.

In the church of **St-Savin-sur-Gartempe** is the most important and magnificent ensemble of Romanesque paintings in France. They date from the 11th and 12th centuries, and managed to escape restoration in the 19th century. The best-preserved are those covering the barrel vault of the nave. They depict in thirty-six scenes the Creation, the Fall, Cain and Abel, and the stories of Noah, Joseph and Moses. The paintings in the crypt are of inferior quality. Stylistically the St-Savin frescoes resemble the mural and miniature paintings of Ottonian Germany and Anglo-Saxon England. The church itself is a very elegant piece of work, tall and narrow proportioned with a continuous barrel-vaulted roof resting on aisles almost as high as the nave. The capitals in the nave are finely and vigorously worked.

In the crypt of the church of *Notre-Dame*, **Montmorillon**, there are also some well-preserved frescoes. The graceful figures look forward to Gothic painting. Also worth noting at Montmorillon is the 12th-century octagonal funerary chapel of the hospital, *Maison Dieu*.

The 11th-century church of the abbey of **Charroux** is now in ruins. It was an interesting attempt to integrate a Latin cross plan with that of the Holy Sepulchre. All that survives is the handsome tower which stood at the intersection of the transept and nave, over the crypt. Among the sculptures in the imposing façade of *St-Jean*, **Civray**, are the remains of a statue of a horseman, resembling that of Marcus Aurelius in Rome, but most likely representing Constantine trampling down paganism. There are a number of churches in the area with this feature. **Gençay** boasts an interesting Romanesque church.

Parthenay, to the east of Poitiers has three 12th-century churches. The abbey church of *St-Pierre* (*c.* 1100) **Airvault**, is basilican in plan with ambulatory and three radiating chapels. The domical vaults replaced the Romanesque vaults in the 13th century. Note should be taken of the statues on brackets immediately below the upper row of columns in the nave. **St-Jouin-de-Marnes** is similar in plan to Airvault. At **St-Généroux** is an important little church with excellent (though restored) examples of plain and patterned wall-work.

South-west of Poitiers at **Melle** there are two fine examples of Poitevin Romanesque, *St-Pierre* and *St-Hilaire*. The church of **Aulnay-de-Saintonge** (*c.* 1130–60) is one of the masterpieces of Romanesque. The sculpture around the deeply recessed doorway is brilliantly integrated with its architectural setting. There is a handsome tower over the crossing. Inside, the nave is covered with a pointed tunnel vault. It leads to a dignified apse. The capitals are decorated with heavy foliage, heads, animals and monsters.

Saintes, like Poitiers, was one of the important halts for pilgrims travelling down to Compostela. The *Abbaye-aux-Dames* was consecrated in 1047 and enlarged and altered in the 12th century, when the nave was vaulted with domes. The main door (pre-1150) is richly arcaded, like Notre-Dame-la-Grande at Poitiers. The capitals are marvellously carved. The crossing tower

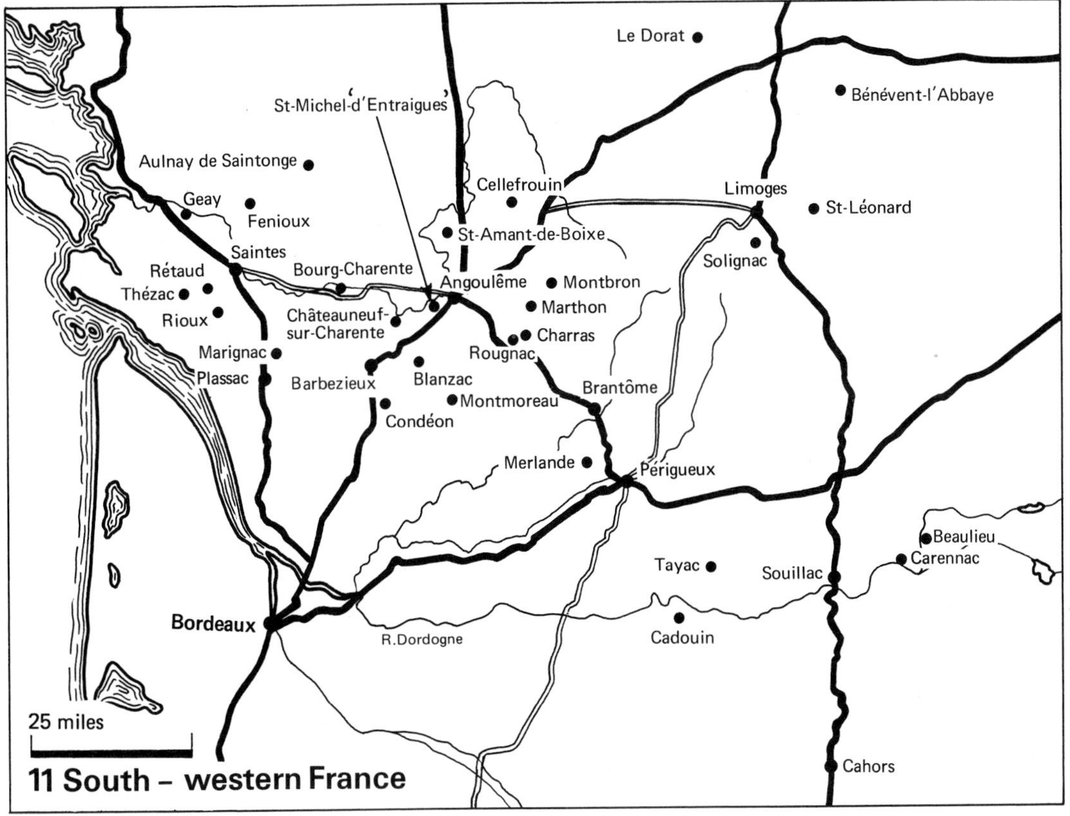

11 South – western France

also resembles that of Notre-Dame. The Clunaic priory church of *St-Eutrope* (11th–12th centuries) has a remarkable, elaborately planned, early vaulted crypt, with columns carrying Byzantine-type capitals. The hall-church above has been much altered. The elaborate carving on the exterior of the eastern apse inspired similar work in a number of churches near Saintes.

One finds it, for example, in the late 12th-century church of **Rétaud**, to the south-west. Near Geay is the remotely situated church of *Notre-Dame*, **Fenioux**. The west front, which dates from the third quarter of the 12th century, has a very deeply recessed doorway which fills the whole of the ground stage.

To the south of Saintes at **Marignac**, is the church of *St-Sulpice* (late 12th century). It has a trefoil plan east end, which is unusual. The decorations on the outside use classical motifs. *Notre-Dame*, **Rioux**, has a lavishly ornamented east end after Saint-Eutrope. So does the church of **Geay**. The most interesting part of *Notre-Dame*, **Thézac**, is the attractive 12th-century tower.

Angoulême *Cathedral* is one of the most famous of the domed buildings of the south-west of France. The nave is partly covered by a file of four domes, reminiscent of the old oriental system of reduplicated domes, although we cannot say if the influence was direct or not. It was an alternative solution to the problem solved by ribbed vaulting, namely the safe roofing of a large area of space. The apse of the cathedral has four radiating chapels. The tunnel vaulted transepts have eastern apsidioles and cruciform domed chapels at the end. The façade is another rich Poitevin example.

Angoulême is circled to its south by a series of village Romanesque churches. These are: **Montbron, Charras, Marthon, Feuillade, Grassac, Rougnac, Montmoreau, Condéon, Blanzac, Barbezieux,** and **Plassac.**

There are other interesting churches in the area. The façade of the church of **Châteauneuf-sur-Charente** (mid-12th century) has an equestrian Constantine, like Civray. The church is aisled, which is unusual in this region. *St-Jean*, **Bourg-Charente** is perfectly preserved. The aisleless nave carries two pendentive domes. Over the crossing is an ovoidal dome, capped by a tower. Nearby is **St-Michel-'d'Entraigues'**, an octofoil chapel of 1137 with a relief of an archangel conquering his enemy.

North of Angoulême is the late Romanesque abbey church of **St Amant de Boixe**. Its admirably articulated front bears purely geometrical decoration. At **Cellefrouin** is the church of *St-Pierre*, founded in 1025.

Limoges has lost its great pilgrimage church of *St-Martial* which was yet another victim of the French Revolution. However there are a few churches worth seeing in the Limousin region. The church of **St-Junien**, some miles to the west, has a sturdy looking west front with a diminishing staged tower flanked by two turrets. The door is deeply recessed but does not carry any sculptured decoration.

North of Limoges at **Le Dorat** is the impressive and robust-looking church of *St-Pierre* (12th century). It has two axial towers – as did St-Martial – a staged lantern tower over the crossing, and a sturdy porch tower with a dome underneath. The handsome portal is carved with four orders of cusped arches, which reflect Moslem influence. Inside the nave is barrel vaulted. The choir follows the pilgrimage church system. The church of **Bénévent-l'Abbaye** resembles Le Dorat in many respects.

The finest feature of the church of **St-Léonard** is the tower of *c.* 1150 adjoining the wall of the north nave. It is a type quite common in the Limousin region. The transition from the square lower stages to the octagonal spire is beautifully achieved. The abbey church of *St-Pierre*, **Solignac** (11th–12th century) is domed. It resembles Angoulême and Souillac to the south.

The domed churches of the south-west of France form a distinctive sub-group within the Romanesque style. Seventy-seven churches are known to have been built, and over sixty of these have survived. The church of *St-Étienne* at **Périgueux** was probably the oldest to be vaulted with a file of domes (*c.* 1100–30). The finest and most distinctive example is *St-Front*. The present Cathedral, built after 1120, was an enlargement of an earlier structure.

Left : Interior of St-Front, Périgueux. 12th century, rebuilt in 19th century.
Right : Detail of the trumeau of the church at Souillac. 12th century.

Unlike the other churches, it is built on a Greek cross plan, and was probably inspired by S. Marco at Venice. The entrance to the cathedral is through an imposing tower porch, the passage to the nave being roofed by two elaborate domical vaults, like those over the nave of Le Puy Cathedral.

The abbey church of **Brantôme** has a tower like that of St-Léonard. The priory church of **Merlande** (*c.* 1150) is fortified. It has recently been restored. Another example of a fortified church is at **Tayac** to the south of Périgueux. Below Tayac is the powerful, massive and austere Cistercian abbey church of **Cadouin** (12th century).

At **Souillac** we have another example of a domed church (*c.* 1130). The tall shafts of the arcade around the apse have historiated capitals. The fragmentary remains of the great portal are to be seen inside the church on the west wall. The prophet Isaiah resembles the famous portal figures of Moissac. The column supporting the lintel depicts beast devouring each other and the sacrifice of Abraham. It has a somewhat nightmarish quality.

The *Cathedral* of **Cahors** (1100–35 and later) is also domed. The lateral portal is in the Burgundian style. It was the model for Souillac. Cahors is our southernmost limit for the present, and we turn north again to travel through Auvergne and Burgundy. En route we visit **Carennac**, along the river from Souillac, with its 12th-century portal and 11th-century nave capitals. The cloister on the south side of the church is partly Romanesque. A little further along is the 12th-century abbey church of **Beaulieu** with a famous tympanum representing the vision of the Apocalypse.

Auvergne

The Auvergne region, in the centre of the Massif Central, created its own well-defined style. In plan the large churches followed the pilgrimage type with an apse with ambulatory and radiating chapels. They are aisled, and the nave is barrel vaulted. There is no clerestory and lighting is therefore indirect. The most distinctive feature of church building here is the crossing lantern tower set on a central mass which is raised above the transepts and nave. The west front is usually simple, but transept ends and the apse exterior are adorned with patterned wall-work. Many of the designs betray Moorish influences and we shall find other instances of this in Auvergne. There is little in the way of monumental sculpture, and stone carving is usually restricted to capitals and lintels.

Le Puy was an important pilgrimage centre in the Middle Ages. The present *Cathedral* dates from the 11th and 12th centuries, the earlier portions being the choir, transept and dome over the crossing, and the two eastern bays of the nave with octagonal squinch domes. The tower resembles those of the Limousin, such as St-Léonard. The west front, approached by a huge stairway, is richly adorned with patterned multi-coloured masonry work and decorative arcading. Moorish influence is particularly in evidence at Le Puy, in the cusping on arches and doorways, the zebra stripings, Cufic inscriptions and capital carvings. The file of domes rest on squinches (in contrast with the pendentives of the south-west), of a type very common in the south of Spain.

Remains of a large and elaborate fresco sequence have recently been discovered in the north transept. The south-east porch, known as the *Porche du For*, contains an unique feature of separate arches sprung from separate columns. No close parallel is known. The south part of the cloister is 10th century, the rest 12th century. Byzantine (or Islamic) influence is noticeable in the polychrome and in the capitals similar to those in Ravenna and Salonica. It was heavily restored in 1850.

St-Michel de l'Aiguille (11th century), on top of a pinnacle of basalt rock, was one of the places of assembly for Crusades and pilgrimages to Compostela. The entrance doorway is decorated with a mosaic of coloured stones and carved with grotesque beasts. In the vault there are mediocre Byzantine influenced 11th-century frescoes.

To the north of Le Puy there are a few Romanesque monuments of interest. At **Chamalières** is the rather sombre 12th-century church of *St-Gilles*. The tower is modern, but the weathercock is as old as the church. The end wall of the church of **Lavadieu** is covered with a huge fresco of the

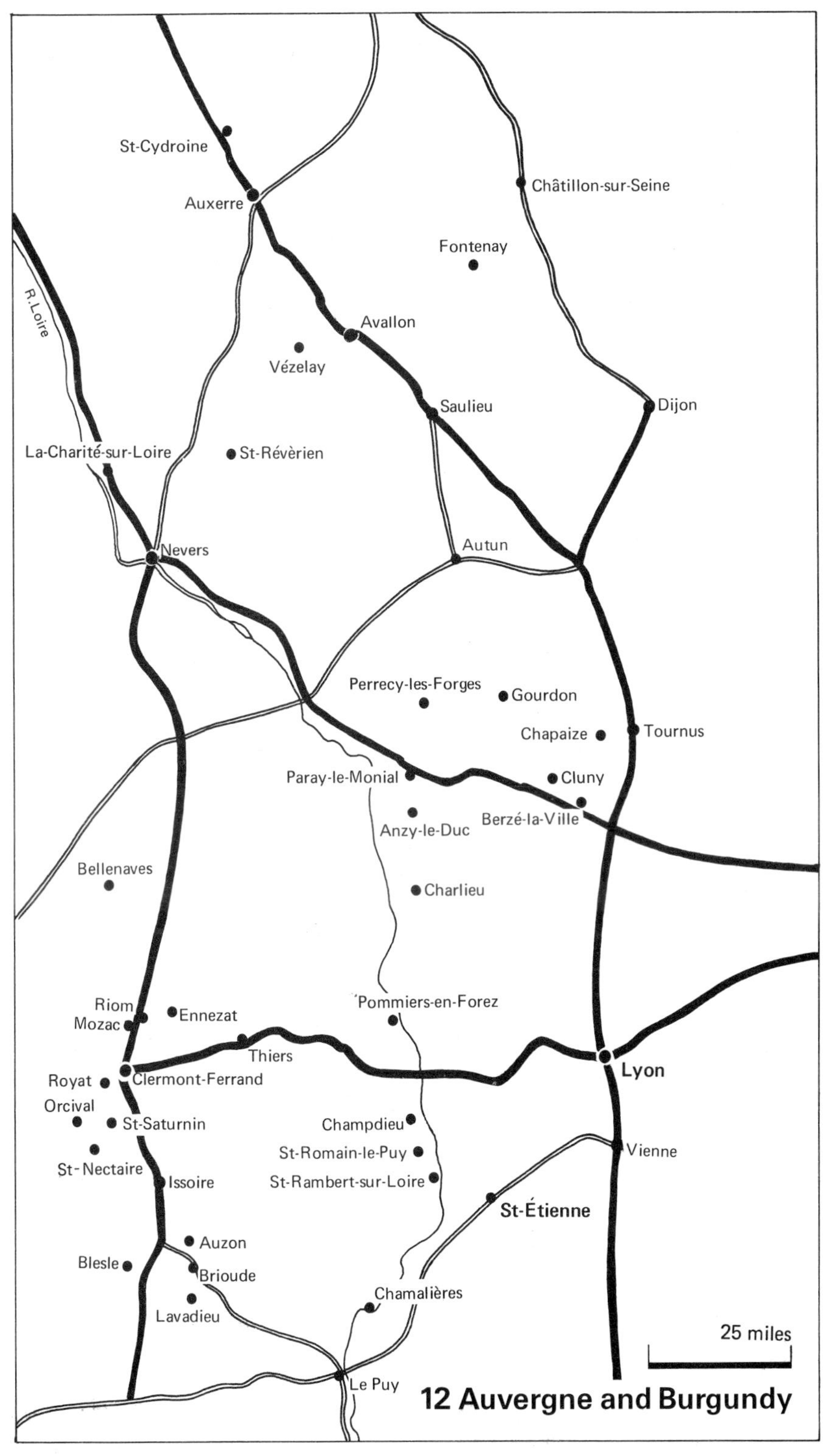
St-Cydroine
Auxerre
Châtillon-sur-Seine
Fontenay
R.Loire
Avallon
Vézelay
Saulieu
Dijon
La-Charité-sur-Loire
St-Révèrien
Nevers
Autun
Perrecy-les-Forges
Gourdon
Chapaize
Tournus
Paray-le-Monial
Cluny
Anzy-le-Duc
Berzé-la-Ville
Bellenaves
Charlieu
Riom
Mozac
Ennezat
Pommiers-en-Forez
Thiers
Royat
Clermont-Ferrand
Lyon
Orcival
St-Saturnin
Champdieu
St-Romain-le-Puy
Vienne
St-Nectaire
Issoire
St-Rambert-sur-Loire
St-Étienne
Auzon
Blesle
Brioude
Chamalières
Lavadieu
25 miles
Le Puy
12 Auvergne and Burgundy

France

Church of St-Paul, Issoire, from the south-east. 12th century.

Tympanum of Notre-Dame-du-Port, Clermont-Ferrand. 12th century.

12th century. Byzantine influence is very strong. The cloister next to the church has been well-restored. **Blesle** has some 12th-century houses. The large church of *St-Julien* (12th–13th centuries) **Brioude**, though more or less rebuilt, is well-preserved. There is particularly fine polychrome masonry work on the exterior apse. The warm golden pink stone of the interior is very pleasing. Important frescoes have recently been discovered on the nave piers. *St-Laurent* (second half of 12th century) at **Auzon** is a simply planned structure. On the south wall is a monumental porch with fine carved capitals. Inside the church is a Romanesque crucifix.

To the north-east of Le Puy, following the Loire, we find **St-Rambert-sur-Loire** (11th–12th century), the early Romanesque **St-Romain-le-Puy** with archaic looking carvings in the choir, **Champdieu** (first half of 12th century), and **Pommiers-en-Forez** (12th century).

West of the Loire on the road to Clermont-Ferrand is **Thiers** and the early 12th-century church of *St-Geniès* – typically Auvergnat in style. In the side chapel, off the south side, fragments of a 6th-century mosaic floor from an earlier church have been discovered. They are Roman both in style and subject matter.

Notre-Dame-du-Port at **Clermont-Ferrand** may be considered as the 'typical church' of Auvergne. The present church was begun in the first half of the 12th century and finished towards the end of the 13th century. The lantern tower with its associated work is a particularly good example. There is elaborate patterned wall-work on the exterior. Inside it is much simpler. The arches of the gallery arcades are cusped. In the choir there are fine historiated capitals. Beneath the choir is a much restored crypt. It was from Notre-Dame-du-Port that the French Pope Urban II preached the First Crusade in 1095.

Within a twenty mile radius of Clermont-Ferrand are a number of churches closely resembling Notre-Dame-du-Port. South of the town there are: *Notre-Dame*, **Orcival** (mid-12th century), centre of a famous pilgrimage to the Virgin; **St-Saturnin** (12th century), though without radiating chapels; **St-Nectaire** (*c.* 1080) whose historiated capitals in the choir are among the most famous in Auvergne; and **Issoire** (*c.* 1130–50), with remarkable carvings of the signs of the Zodiac above the windows of the east end.

In the opposite direction we find: **Royat**, a handsome fortified church of the 12th century; **Mozac**, a Cluniac priory; **Ennezat**, begun *c.* 1061–78, which makes it the oldest of the group; and **Riom** (begun in 1160), beautifully situated.

Burgundy

The French Romanesque architecture, which had the widest influence – apart from Norman – was that of Burgundy. This fertile country with its superb vineyards and its robust people produced a magnificent style of architecture and sculpture. Its important place in the history of European art was, however, assured by two additional circumstances. In the first place, Burgundy was admirably situated to receive influences from the various architectural trends, current in the 10th and 11th centuries. In the second place it was the home of the two greatest mediaeval monastic Orders, Cluny and Cîteaux, with their hundreds of chapters. The two Orders were headed by men of genius in the 11th and 12th centuries, who were endowed, moreover, with exceptional taste. Cistercian architecture and, to a lesser extent, that of Cluny, spread all over Europe.

Within Burgundy itself we do not find the same homogeneity in Romanesque building as we have seen in Auvergne. However, most larger churches reflect in some degree the impact of the great abbey church of Cluny (now destroyed): its three-storied internal elevation with pointed arches in the nave arcade; the barrel-vaulted nave with transverse arches; the octagonal dome over the crossing; the complex choir plan with ambulatory and radiating chapels; and the wonderful sculptured ornament. A variation on the Cluniac theme, which we find first at Vézelay, has a two-storied internal elevation and a groin-vaulted nave. A crossing tower is universal, and sometimes there are twin towers at the west end. There are many Roman motifs in the architectural ornament of the churches, the Corinthian capital, pure or with variations, being very common. There is also some Moorish influence, e.g. the cusping of arches. Monumental sculpture is confined to the tympana of portals. Cistercian building, by contrast, is simple in design and without decoration.

The first Romanesque monument we find in Burgundy is **Bellenaves**, with a finely sculpted tympanum. The *Cathedral* of **Nevers** has lost its Romanesque character in Gothic rebuilding. In plan it is double-ended. The Cluniac priory of *St-Étienne*, on the other hand, is almost in its original state. Completed in 1097, it is an example of mature Romanesque at its best. One daring and unusual feature of the church is the clerestory window openings directly beneath the barrel vault. The capitals of the columns are very smooth and represent the extreme simplification of the Corinthian prototype.

The abbey church of **La Charité-sur-Loire** (11th–12th century) is called the 'eldest daughter of Cluny', and indeed, in design it closely resembles its mother. Unfortunately the religious wars of the 16th century, followed by long neglect have left it a partial ruin. Viewed from the Loire bridge the abbey's large ruined church and tall tower serve to extol even today the grandeur that met the pilgrim's eye as he approached La Charité. Freed of any roof or front wall, the ruins reveal the pilastered bays of the apse as external walls. Between the columns rising to the abbey's roof-line are windows usually occupied by cats. The animal sculpture is one of the first uses of the Bestiary for this purpose. The finely decorated walls of the tower and remaining enclosed bays suggest the sumptuous finish of this abbey. Unspoilt mediaeval alleyways around it give the modern visitor a few glimpses of how the tower must have looked to burghers and travellers centuries ago. Some distance to the east of La Charité is the Cluniac priory of **St-Révèrien**. The elegantly

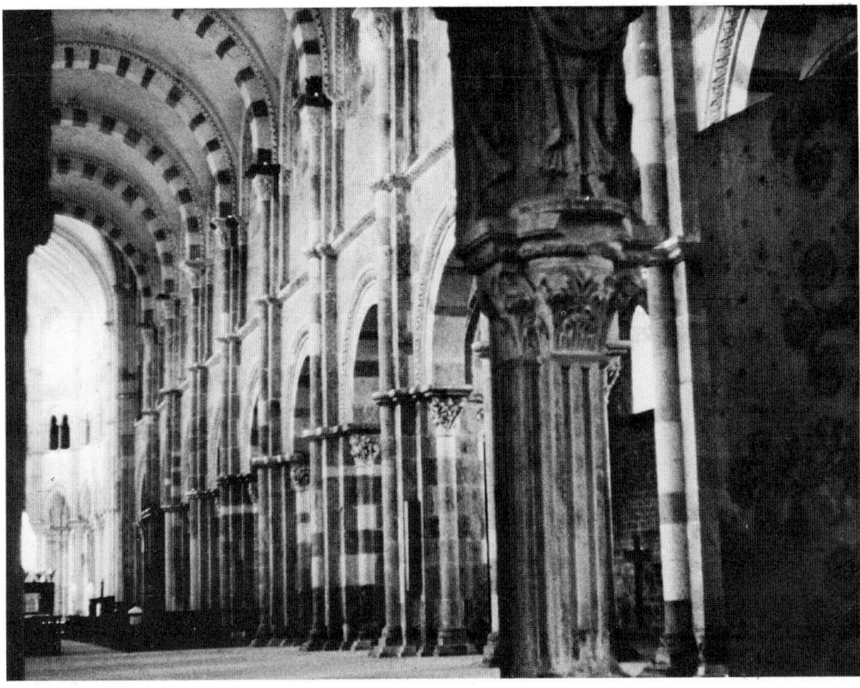

Interior of the abbey church of Vézelay.
12th century.

composed choir still stands, but the rest of the church was rebuilt in the 19th century.

The historical associations, splendid situation and beauty of the monument combine to make the abbey church of **Vézelay** (1096–1146) one of the high points of Romanesque art. It is situated on a ridge overlooking rolling cultivated lands. Its history dates from 860 when a nunnery was founded on the site. Less than fifteen years later, this was seized, despoiled and burned by the Normans, who raided deep into central France. Reorganized thereafter, Vézelay was founded at its present site as a monastery. It became famous (for reasons that are not clear) as the repository of the relics of Mary Magdalene, the sinner, and thus became the scene of great pilgrimages. Between 1100 and 1137, Vézelay was under the tutelage of Cluny. In 1120 a disastrous fire seriously damaged the church and killed many pilgrims.

The relations of the abbots of Vézelay and the local authority – the count of Nevers – were bad. Violence, kidnapping, sieges and flights marked the turbulent attempts of the counts to subject the abbey to their influence. Frequent appeals to the Pope and the kings of France must have made the abbey a terrible nuisance to both. The enormous popularity of the abbey as a pilgrimage centre, and its position on the route to Compostela, however, maintained its high prestige through these difficult times. Here in 1145, St

Above : Central portion of the tympanum inside the west entrance of the abbey church of Vézelay, *c.* 1125–35.
Left : Detail of the left-hand side of the tympanum of Vézelay.

Bernard preached the Second Crusade in the presence of King Louis VII of France and the nobles of many lands. Here in 1190 King Philip Augustus and Richard the Lion Heart met before departing on the Third Crusade.

The tympanum *inside* the entrance, in the narthex, is a masterpiece of Romanesque. 'Aquiver with emotion', as one writer put it, 'each figure and even that of the Lord himself is distorted by a blast of inspiration, literally evident in the swirling folds and ridges of drapery'.* The iconography, though not the style, reflects Byzantine influence. The figures in the archivolt and lintel are representations of distant peoples among whom the Gospels had been preached. The famous figured capitals of the columns are full of lively humour, deep feeling and naïve pictorial devices.† Their appeal is more popular than that of the tympanum.

* Charles E. Morey, *Mediaeval Art* (N.Y., 1942).

† Viollet-le-Duc restored Vézelay and removed some of the capitals, replacing them with copies or with capitals of his own creation. The following capitals are his: Worship of the Golden Calf, Judith with Holophernes' head, angel holding a demon by the arm – all in the nave; plus seven others in the narthex tribune. The outer western portal is all by Viollet-le-Duc.

Opposite above
Tympanum of St-Lazare, Avallon, *c.* 1150.
Opposite below
Portal of St-Lazare, Avallon, *c.* 1150.
Right
Detail of the portal of St-Lazare, Avallon, *c.* 1150.

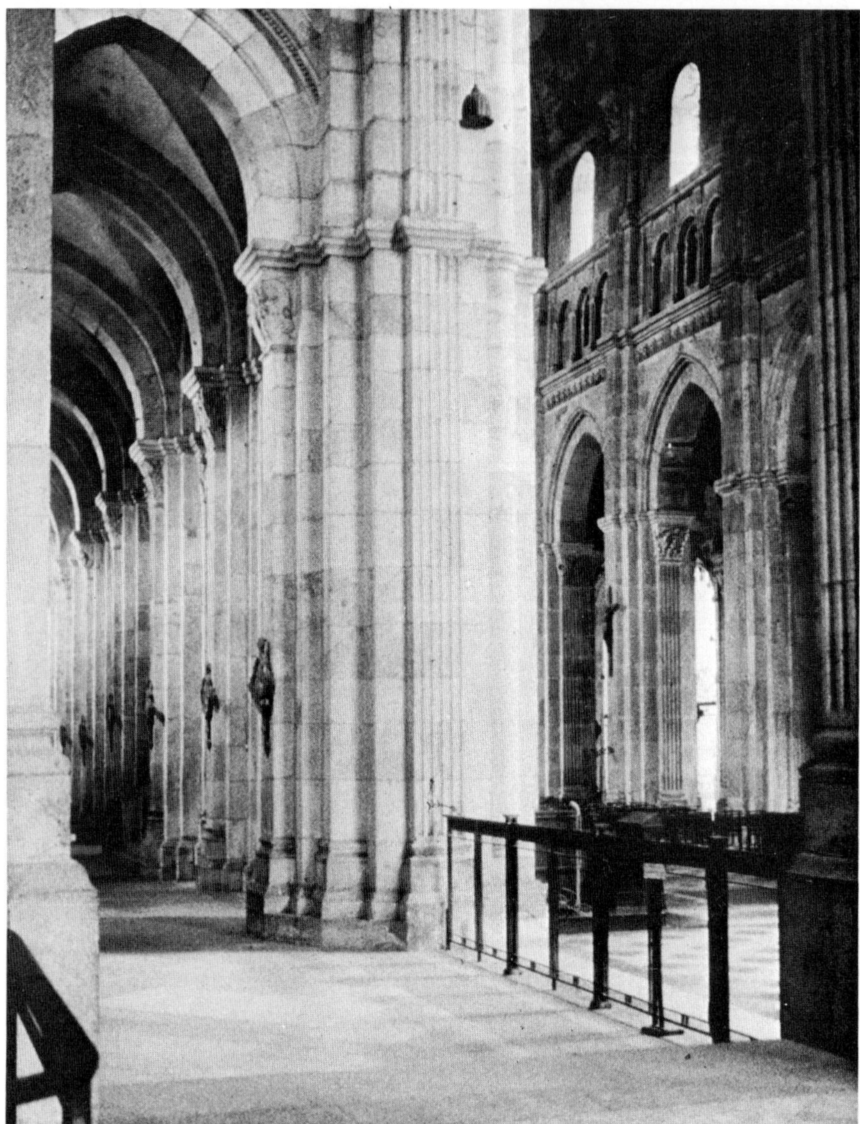

Interior of the Cathedral of Autun.
Begun *c.* 1120.

Near Vézelay is **Avallon** and the church of *St-Lazare*. It has a fine sculptured portal with varied and imaginative carved columns. The elongated statue is in the same style as the works of Vézelay and Autun, and is one of the treasures of 12th-century French Romanesque.

The *Cathedral* of **Auxerre** has a crypt of *c.* 1025–30 with beautifully composed grouped piers and fine vaulting. The fresco depicting a large cross with Christ in front, on horseback, is of northern inspiration. There are also frescoes of the mid-9th century in the crypt of *St-Germain*. The bell-tower of this church is 12th century. The former *Bishop's Palace*, now the Prefecture, is a good example of Romanesque secular building.

Twelve miles north of Auxerre is the church of **St-Cydroine** (11th–12th centuries), in the Middle Ages a priory of La Charité. To the east of Auxerre at **Châtillon-sur-Seine** is the early Romanesque church of *St-Vorles*, with later vaulting. Lombard bands decorate the east end of the church.

Fontenay is the oldest Cistercian ensemble in existence, the early foundations of Cîteaux and Clairvaux having been destroyed in the Revolution. It is in a lovely remote setting. The church dates from 1139–47; the cloister and monastic buildings adjoining are somewhat later. The façade is austere, the interior very simple, since in the 12th century any kind of embellishment was prohibited. Yet for all its bareness Fontenay has a dignity and quiet beauty which is unforgettable.

Gothic reconstruction and revolutionary vandalism have almost completely destroyed the important early Romanesque church of *St Bénigne*, **Dijon** (1001–18). The plan of the church reflected the strong early Christian influence which was prevalent at this time. The main church was a vaulted basilica. The east part derived from the Holy Sepulchre. *St-Andoche*, **Saulieu** is particularly notable for the beautiful colour of its stone and its sculptured capitals which show a great variety of biblical scenes, and which were probably influenced by Autun. The *Treasury* of the cathedral contains the 6th-century Byzantine ivory book-cover of the Missal of Charlemagne. The covers are set in an 8th and 12th-century metal decorative frame.

The cathedral town of **Autun** is an old Roman community. Parts of the amphitheatre, the Roman walls and the Roman gates are still extant. The *Cathedral of St-Lazare* has a portal of *c.* 1135 by Gislebertus, justly among the most famous in France. It depicts the Last Judgement. It was saved from destruction by having been walled over for many years. The fluted classical pilasters of the interior are inspired by local Roman remains. The capitals are of the first order of importance in French sculpture. Some of the original capitals are preserved in the *Musée Lapidaire* attached to the cathedral.

The extent to which the stories of the Bible were illustrated in 12th-century sculpture can be seen at Autun. In the tympanum and on the capitals, Jesus appears in twelve episodes, the Virgin Mary in seven. There are eighteen devils, thirty angels and numerous Apostles, saints and Old Testament personages. The figure of Eve, now in the Museum, is particularly famous. 'The Eve of Autun rests on elbow and knee and crawls in the attitude of swimming – a delightful figure, perhaps the most feminine and insidious of this great epoch', wrote the great historian Focillon.*

South from Vézelay is the church of **Perrecy-les-Forges**, with a fine 12th-century tower porch. The church itself is 12th century. **Paray-le-Monial** (early 12th century) is a 'pocket edition' of Cluny. In the choir are classical-inspired fluted pilasters, like those at Autun.

* H. Focillon, *The Art of the West, I: Romanesque Art*, new ed. (London, 1963), p. 109.

The 'Eve' of Autun, *c.* 1125–35.

The 12th-century church of *St-Martin*, **Anzy-le-Duc**, is of simple design with a handsome crossing tower. The exterior is decorated with Lombard arcading.

In the ruins of the abbey of **Charlieu** there is a collection of mediaeval sculptures. The Carolingian pieces were preserved by having long been immured inside a wall. The great door (reproduced in life-size plaster casts in museums in Chicago and Paris) contains two tympana. The inner one dates from *c.* 1088–90. It shows a low-relief Christ in Majesty between two angels. The static poses of the figures recall Byzantine art. The outer portal, which is later, depicts Christ enthroned with the four symbols of the Evangelists. In the lintel beneath the tympanum is the Virgin flanked by two angels and the Apostles. According to Mâle it follows the composition of the 6th-century apse painting of the church of Baouit in Egypt. Of this doorway Joan Evans, the great English scholar, writes that 'in its chiselled delicacy, restless composition and decorative over-elaboration there are marks of decay. It is a work of luxury, in which stone is treated as if it were gold and the façade of a church as if it were the side of a shrine'.*

A scalloped decorative motif commonly used here and in other Cluniac buildings has an interesting history. The ornament can be traced to altars of the 5th century. It has been found in Corinth and on a slab near Rome, and in a 10th-century altar slab in the south of France. The marble has been traced to a Cluniac house, which is regarded as the workshop whence this motif emerged to grace so many walls and entrances of Cluniac buildings.

All that remains of the once great and immense abbey of **Cluny**, destroyed in the French Revolution, are parts of the south arm of the greater transept and the central crossing tower. These give us the barest hint of the vast structure which was the finest creation of the Cluniac Order, and which probably represented the epitome of Romanesque architecture. In the *Musée Ochier* are preserved stone fragments and capitals from the church, the most interesting of which are the series representing the eight modes of the Gregorian chant. In the village of Cluny there are several rare and interesting 12th-century houses.

Seven miles from Cluny is the priory church of **Berzé-la-Ville** which was affiliated to Cluny. In the chapel are early to mid-12th-century frescoes of very high quality. They were probably inspired by the paintings decorating the great abbey church. Byzantine influence, probably coming from Italy, is clearly in evidence. In the same area is the late 11th-century church of *Notre-Dame*, **Gourdon** and the monastery church of **Chapaize** (*c.* 1050 and 12th century), with a very well preserved oblong tower.

At **Tournus** is the abbey-church of *St-Philibert*. St-Philibert was an early author of monastic rules at Jumièges, and later Noirmoutier. Noirmoutier, along with much of the Loire valley, suffered cruel raids from the Normans shortly after Charlemagne's death. The monks were forced to move away and

* Joan Evans, *Cluniac Art of the Romanesque Period* (Cambridge, 1950), p. 35.

Opposite above
Capital from Autun, showing the dream of the Magi. *c.* 1125–35.

Opposite below
Detail of the tympanum of the west portal of the Cathedral of Autun, showing the weighing of souls. *c.* 1125–35.

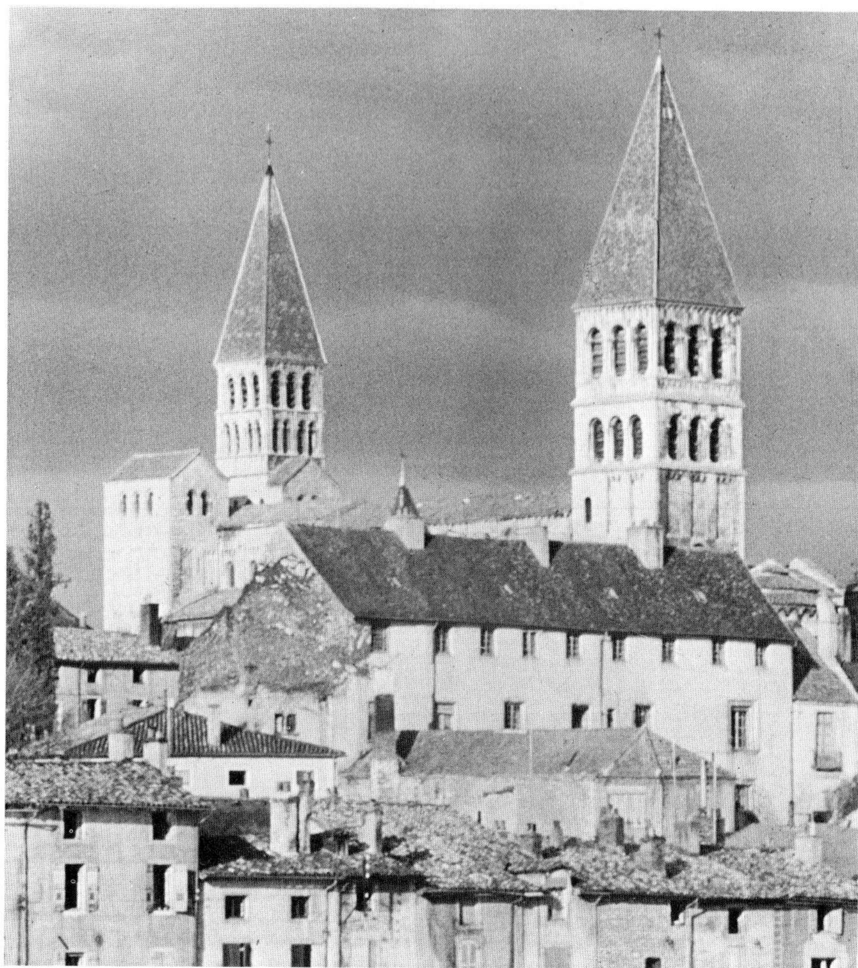

The abbey church of St-Philibert, Tournus.
Late 10th–12th centuries, and later.

took the relics of St Philibert with them. They moved from haven to haven for forty years, finally settling at Tournus in 875. This spot also proved vulnerable, and suffered pillage and fire from the Hungarians in the 10th century. The existing church was begun towards the end of the 10th or the beginning of the 11th century. This early date makes it one of the oldest abbey churches intact.

Provence

We now come down the Saône to the Rhône and Provence, where the numerous antique and early Christian remains serve to remind us that we are in the old Roman 'Provincia'. The Romanesque art of this region has a

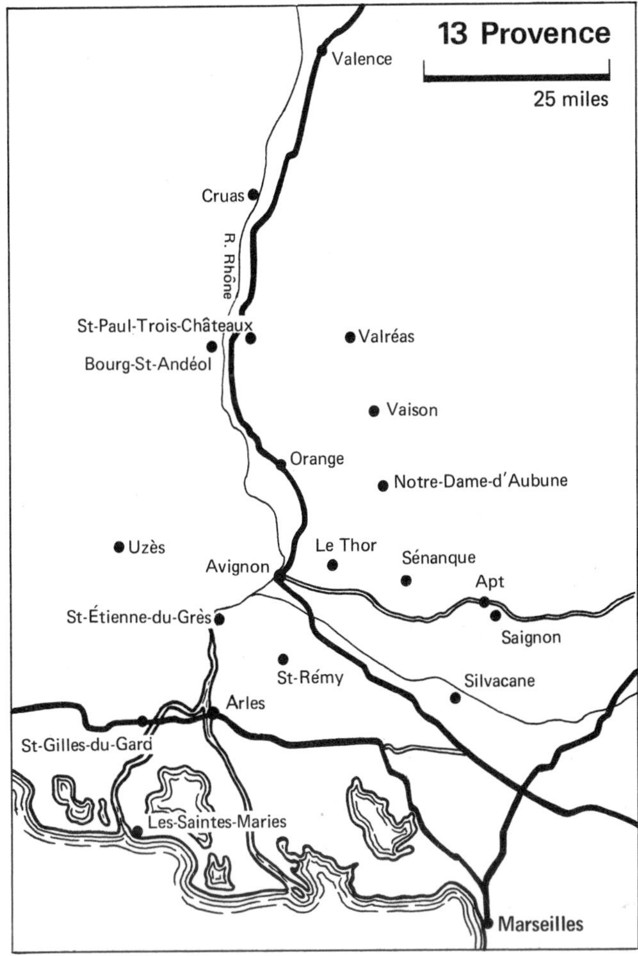

markedly Roman stamp. Its substantially built and conservative churches are on a fairly small scale and simple in plan. Invariably they are barrel-vaulted.

At **Vienne** is the basilica of *St-Pierre*, of the 5th or 6th centuries with 10th-century additions. It is the oldest extant early Christian basilica in France. It now houses an important museum. The abbey church of *St-André-le-Bas* has a fine mid-12th-century cloister, restored twenty years ago.

The *Cathedral* of **Valence** (1095) shows influences from neighbouring regions. The apse has an ambulatory with radiating chapels. The tower is like those common in the Limousin. At **Cruas** is the church of *Notre-Dame* (11th–12th centuries). The exterior of the apses and the lower stages of the circular tower are decorated with Lombard bands. Beneath the east end of the church is an interesting large groin-vaulted crypt.

The former *Cathedral* of **St-Paul-Trois-Châteaux** (mid-12th–13th centuries) resembles in some respects Cluny and Paray-le-Monial. The west front is obviously incomplete, e.g. the columns have no capitals. The interior of the choir carries a delicate carved frieze of classical inspiration. The late 12th-century south porch of *Notre-Dame-de-Nazareth*, **Valréas**, combines fine Romanesque work with earlier sculpture. **Bourg-St-Andéol** (12th century) has a handsome octagonal crossing tower.

Orange *Cathedral* (consecrated 1208) is a good example of the cave-like, dark, aisleless churches which abound in Provence. The *Cathedral* of **Vaison** has three apses of horseshoe plan, ascribed to the Merovingian period. In the early 11th and again in the 13th century, the church was rebuilt. It has the general character of late Romanesque buildings. The early 12th-century cloister adjoining the cathedral has been heavily restored. Near Orange is the picturesque shrine of *Notre-Dame-d'Aubune* with a lovely tower decorated with fluted pilasters.

The *Cathedral* of **Avignon** (*c.* 1140–60 and later), beside the 14th-century Papal Palace, is approached by a handsome Renaissance stairway. In plan it is very simple, with neither aisles nor transept. The famous *Bridge*, now broken, dates from the end of the 12th century. Near Avignon at **Le Thor** there is a 12th-century church with a richly decorated south portal. Charmingly placed in a grove of vines and olives is the chapel of *St-Gabriel* (12th century) at **St-Étienne-du-Grès**. It has an elegant classically-inspired portal. *St-Paul-de-Mausole*, **St-Rémy**, has a 12th century cloister with carved figure capitals of exceptional quality.

Arles was the capital of Roman Gaul in the 5th century, and later of a mediaeval kingdom. It contains the most important example of Provençal Romanesque art – the former *Cathedral of St-Trophîme*. It was founded in the Carolingian period, and parts of this earliest structure survive in the west front and nave side walls. The transept is late 10th or early 11th century; the nave was rebuilt in *c.* 1140. There are also some Gothic additions. The late Romanesque west portal appears to have been inspired by Roman triumphal gateways. The figures are 'romanized'. The crouching lions recall those of Italian portals. Over the crossing is a very fine tower. Next to the church is a magnificent cloister, begun in 1183 but not finished until two centuries later. *St-Honorat* is an unfinished late 12th-century building. It also has a fine tower, influenced in its design by the amphitheatre nearby.

The monastery group at **Montmajour** deserves to be better known, despite its remote situation. The abbey was affiliated with Cluny, and this, combined with the fact that it was situated on the route to Compostela, which began at Arles, probably accounts for the complex design of the choir with ambulatory and radiating chapels, and a spacious crypt beneath. The austere design of the main body of the church, which is aisleless, is more in keeping with the simplicity of Provençal building. Next to the church is a well-proportioned cloister, and nearby, a cruciform chapel almost classical in appearance.

Opposite
Cloister of St-Trophîme, Arles. Begun 1183.

The design of **St-Gilles-du-Gard** (12th century) was influenced by the same conditions, and it too is exceptional. The interior of the church has been much altered by 17th-century reconstructions, but the wonderful western portal is intact. Its three recessed doorways, each with a carved tympanum, are connected by a colonnade carrying a sculptured frieze, depicting scenes from Christ's life. The columns supporting the arches of the portals rest on lions, as in Italy.

All that remains of the *Cathedral* of **Uzès**, destroyed in the Wars of Religion, is the remarkable lofty circular bell-tower, known as the 'tour-fenestrelle'. South from St-Gilles-du-Gard on the coast is the fortified church of **Les-Saintes-Maries-de-la-Mer** (12th century).

Returning to Avignon and journeying to the east we come to **Apt**. The chief interest of its *Cathedral* (12th century and later) are two superimposed crypts, survivals from earlier buildings. **Saignon**, to the south-east, has a well-preserved, typically Provençal 12th-century church. There are also the remains of two Cistercian abbeys near Apt: **Silvacane** with a cloister which though late 13th century is still Romanesque; and **Sénanque** (*c.* 1148 and later).

Fréjus on the Mediterranean coast, to the west of Cannes, was once a Roman port situated on the Aurelian highway connecting the important Roman colonies of the south of France with Rome. The octagonal baptistery is a fine example of 5th-century architecture. The columns and capitals are, in the fashion of Italy, 'cannibalized' from antique monuments. The interior is an artful combination of alternating square and curved bays, which give it variety and interest. The connected church tower and cloister are 12th century. Though lacking decorative mosaics, paintings or sculptures, this harmonious group makes a monument of rare value. Also at Fréjus are *stele* of the early Christian period with horseshoe arches. Near Fréjus at **St-Raphael** is the 12th-century church of *St-Pierre*.

Languedoc and Roussillon

Travelling west from Arles we come to that area of southern France which in the Middle Ages was called Languedoc. Here we find two of the most important of the surviving pilgrimage churches, *St-Sernin* at **Toulouse** and *Ste-Foy* at **Conques**. A third church, **Moissac**, is related to these from the point of view of sculpture. The genius of Languedoc expressed itself more in sculpture than in architecture. As in other parts of southern France, most of the churches are fairly small, simple in plan – some basilican, some aisleless, and vaulted.

Picturesquely situated in a mountain valley above **Aniane** is the church of *St-Guilhem-le-Désert* (11th–12th centuries). It has the simplicity of 'first Romanesque' buildings. Next to the church was a very fine cloister, now partly re-created at The Cloisters, New York. Just south of Montpellier is the 12th-century *Cathedral* of **Maguelone**, the lone survivor of an ancient city.

Opposite
Statue of St Foy, Conques, *c.* 950.

Some distance farther along the coast is the *Cathedral* of **Agde** (late 12th century), fortified against sea-raiders. At **Quarante**, fifteen miles north-west of Béziers, is an early Romanesque church. **St-Pons-de-Thomières** has a handsome fortified church. (1151–81).

The *Cathedral* of **Carcassone** dates from the first half of the 12th century, except for the choir and transept, which are Gothic. The church of *St-Salvi* at **Albi** is of the same date. The tower, however, is earlier. There are a couple of examples of secular building in this area. In the little town of **Burlats** is the *Pavillon d'Adelaide*, a 12th-century manor protected by a fortified wall. **St-Antonin** has a *Town Hall* of the 12th century.

Ste-Foy, (*c.* 1050–1130) **Conques** is a fine example of the superb abbeys on the pilgrimage routes to Compostela. The narrow gorge, the terraced town and rugged country give this church an unique setting. The relics of St Foy, its patron saint, and its location on one of the routes to Compostela attracted a large number of pilgrims throughout the Middle Ages. It has a standard pilgrimage church plan, though it is the smallest and most rustic of the group. One curious feature inside the church is the grille surrounding the choir which is forged of shackles and chains presented to the church by freed prisoners.

The masterpiece of Conques is the tympanum on the west entrance representing the Last Judgement, in terms a pilgrim (mediaeval or modern) would have no difficulty in understanding. The appeal is more popular than the intellectual versions of apocalyptic visions of Cluniac churches. This tympanum is unique in French monumental sculpture in showing traces of its original colouring.

Parts of the church cloister also remain. The *Treasury* of Ste-Foy is the finest church treasure preserved in France. It was saved from destruction in the Revolution by the cunning of the monks. The central feature of an abbey's decoration was the gilt or golden image of its patron saint. A rare surviving example is that of St Foy (*c.* 950). The treasure of Conques also includes gold chalices, frequently gifts from kings or other rich patrons, Gospel book covers of precious metal adorned with jewels and enamels, gold crucifixes also adorned with gems, and decorated chests for the preservation of relics.

Not far from Conques at **Aubrac** is a church dating from the end of the 12th century; at **Espalion**, a church of the 11th–12th centuries, with a richly decorated apse.

Henry James wrote of *St-Sernin* (*c.* 1060–12th century and later) at **Toulouse**: 'this great structure, a masterpiece of 12th-century Romanesque, is, I think, alone worth a journey to Toulouse'.* Certainly, despite mediaeval additions and modern alterations, it is important as an accomplished example of pilgrimage building.

The sculpture of St-Sernin is entirely different from that of Burgundy. The style of the altar (around 1096) is derived from early Christian sarcophagi in

Opposite
Angel relief in the ambulatory of St-Sernin, Toulouse. *c.* 1096.

* Henry James, *A Little Tour in France* (London, 1900), p. 145.

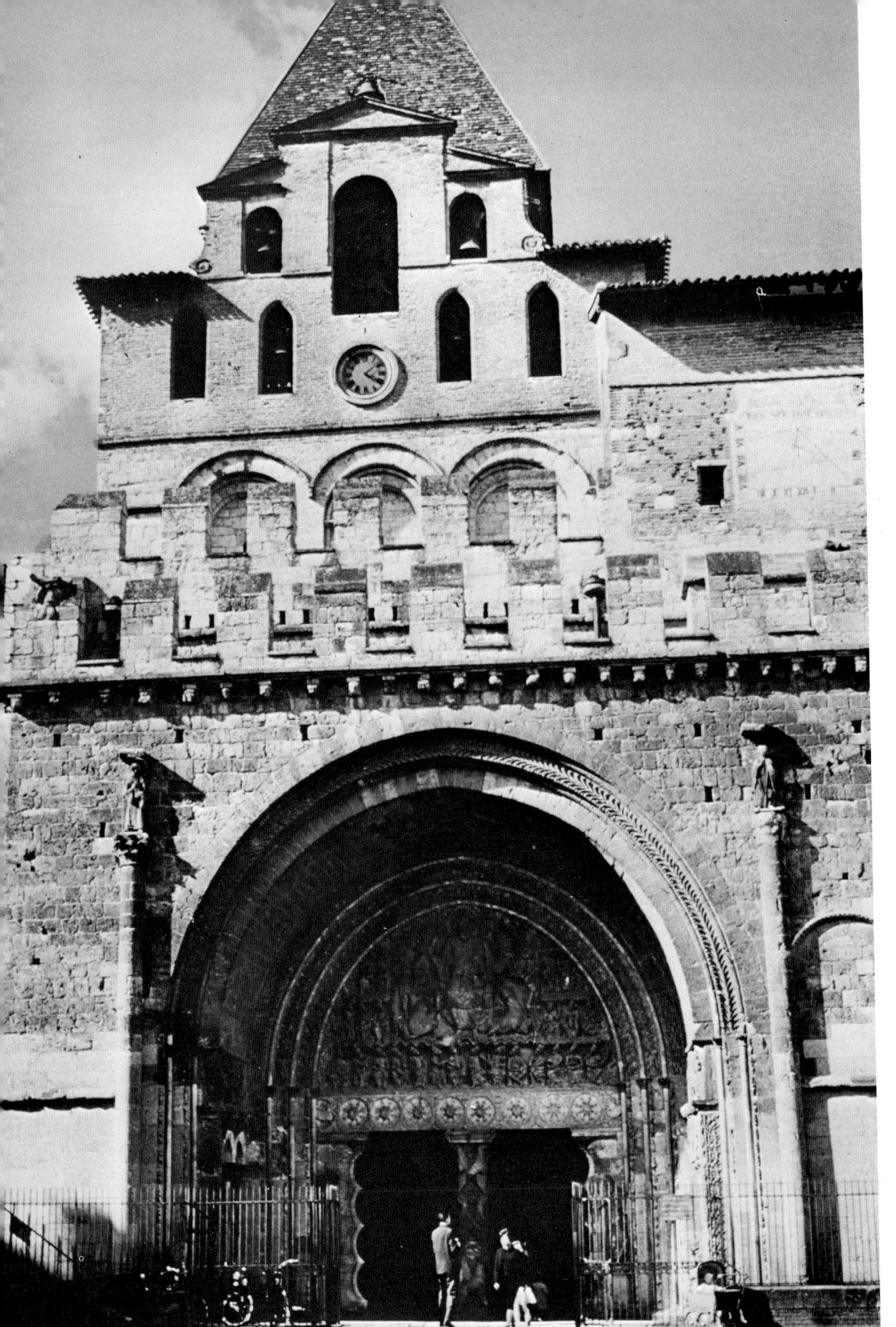

which southern France abounds. The marble plaques, built into the ambulatory, of which the 'Christ in Majesty' is the most famous, are of the same date. The sculpture of the Miègeville tympanum, which dates from the first or second decade of the 12th century, was also influenced by early Christian sarcophagi reliefs. Its subject is the Ascension, with a row of Apostles beneath. The tympanum dates from the beginning of the great revival of monumental sculpture. Within a generation every great cathedral and abbey of France was to be equipped with one or more of these great compositions, mingling architecture and life-size sculpture with smaller figures in elaborate story-telling ensembles.

The *Museum* contains a very interesting and important collection of sculpture, derived from destroyed monasteries.

The fortified abbey of **Moissac** was a chapter of Cluny. Its great fame rests on two outstanding sculptural groups: the portal and the cloister. The work here is regarded as the high-point of the Languedoc school of sculpture. The portal tympanum (first third of 12th century), containing twenty-eight figures, is a replica of a miniature in the manuscript *Apocalypse of St Sever*, an 11th-century copy of the 8th-century Beatus *Commentaries*. The elongated forms of the prophet Jeremiah and St Paul support the lintel. These portal sculptures inspired those of Souillac and Beaulieu. The fine cloister with its sculptured capitals is rivalled in the whole of France, only by the cloister of St Trophîme, Arles.

The capitals in the choir and transept of the *Cathedral* of **Agen**, now mostly Gothic, reflect the influence of Moissac. There are also fine capitals in the chapter-house. The church of **Aubiac**, six miles from Agen, has a trefoiled east end and an interesting tower (12th century). There is an 11th-century church at **Moirax**, also near Agen. North-west of Agen at **La Réole** is a 12th-century *Town Hall*.

In the far south of France below Toulouse and near the Spanish border are some interesting churches: *St-Just*, **Valcabrère** (11th–12th centuries), a basilican structure with the remains of earlier buildings within its walls and a north portal with column statues like those of Chartres; *St-Christophe*, **Montsaunés**, a large fortified church; and the church of **St-Lizier** (12th century and later), with recently uncovered frescoes in the apse and a cloister with fine Romanesque capitals, perhaps of Toulousan workmanship. The church of *St-Jean-Baptiste*, **St-Placard** is a double-ender, unique in the south of France. The apse of the southern wing is covered with mid-12th-century frescoes, archaic and crude in style and resembling Coptic paintings. The slightly earlier frescoes of the apsidiole are more refined.

Few regions are so permeated with Romanesque art as Roussillon and north Catalonia, the provinces of France and Spain bordering the Pyrenees as they descend to the Mediterranean sea. Here Charlemagne's warriors crossed the mountains and drove the Saracens out of 'the marches of Spain', now known as Catalonia. Recaptured only to be lost again, this frontier region offered a

Opposite
South portal of St-Pierre, Moissac. *c.* 1115.

200 *Above:* Detail of the trumeau of the south portal of Moissac, showing Jeremiah. *c.* 1115.
Opposite: Detail of the trumeau of the south portal of Moissac, showing St Paul. *c.* 1115.

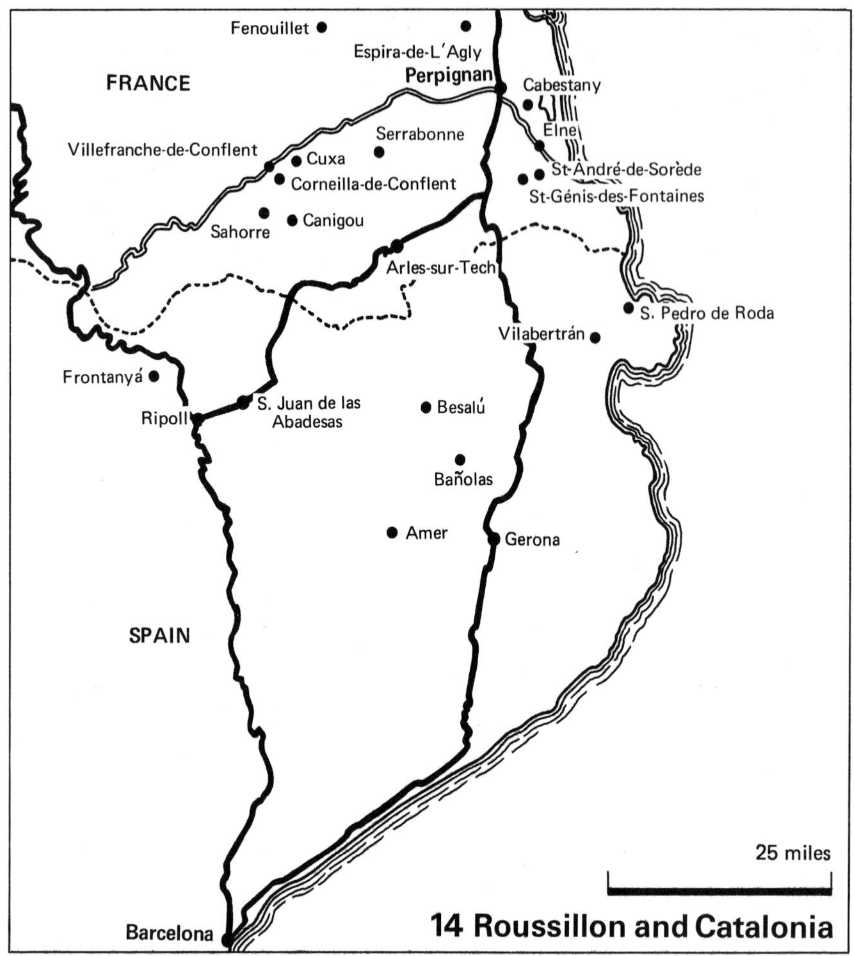

14 Roussillon and Catalonia

measure of protection to the abbeys in the mountains, near the great castles occupied by the warlike counts, engaged in conquering Spain. In such picturesque surroundings, one finds abbeys and churches dating from around 1000. Built out of the huge wealth that came from driving the Arabs out of Catalonia, these abbeys and castles fell into ruins with the passage of wars to other areas. However this poverty protected them from the later reconstructions which have obscured so much of Romanesque architecture in other parts of Europe.

There are two main points of interest in the art and architecture of this region. In the first place a considerable number of so-called 'first Romanesque' churches, which once spread across southern Europe from the Alps to the Pyrenees, have been preserved. These date from the late 10th and early 11th centuries. They are small in scale, simple in plan, and partially or wholly stone vaulted. Stone vaulting made churches more fire-proof, which was of particular relevance to this region, since it provided additional protection to the fortifications of monasteries beyond such features as windowless walls and high towers. A defensive network linked churches and castles through a system of oral and visual signalling posts in the towers, to warn of marauding raids, which in truth were conducted not only by Saracen bands, but also by rival counts and even rival abbeys. The other interest of these churches lies in the later sculpture and murals, representing a far more sophisticated period, when native art is modified by foreign elements. For the present we shall confine our description to those buildings on the French side of the Pyrenees.

The church at **Corneilla de Conflent** (11th–12th centuries) was situated in the centre of the private domains of the powerful counts of Cerdagne near their castle. There are excellent sculptured capitals inside the church and a fine tympanum outside. A short distance from Corneilla is the church at **Sahorre** with windows decorated with sculptured capitals of excellent quality, dating from the 12th century. The walled city of **Villefranche de Conflent** has a church, two doors of which are decorated with sculptures of the same period.

At **Fenouillet** there is a small church with fine 12th-century capitals. Here may be seen the Eastern 'Bird-Woman', so frequently mentioned in Russian folk-tales. Two of the capitals are believed to have come from the castle of Fenouillet, residence of the ruling counts, ruins of which may be seen at **St-Pierre**.

St-Martin du Canigou (*c.* 1000–26) is in the heart of the Pyrenees. The traveller has a climb of 1000 feet to reach it. For the first two centuries of its existence the abbey enjoyed the patronage of the family of the counts of Cerdagne who gave it lands, vineyards and villages, and contributed to the construction of the church. Its subsequent history was less happy. In the 16th century the church suffered grave damage in an earthquake, and it was thoroughly looted in the French Revolution. It was restored to its present condition in 1903.

The church is basilican in plan, roofed by three long tunnel vaults. There are two crypts beneath, one with groin vaulting. The capitals and columns of the interior are granite. The capitals have crude animal carvings and interlaced patterns. Their archaism contrasts strongly with the sophistication of the Languedoc influenced capitals of the 12th-century cloister. Next to the church is a handsome square tower of Lombardic inspiration.

The leading monastery of Roussillon was **St-Michel-de-Cuxa**, situated on the ancient road, the 'Strata Francisca', taken by Charlemagne to seize Catalonia from the Saracens. The beginnings of Cuxa are well documented and relate to transactions between 866 and 878. In the latter year, the ancient monastery of Exalada was completely destroyed by an inundation. The ruling family of the counts of Cerdagne turned over the vast possessions of Exalada

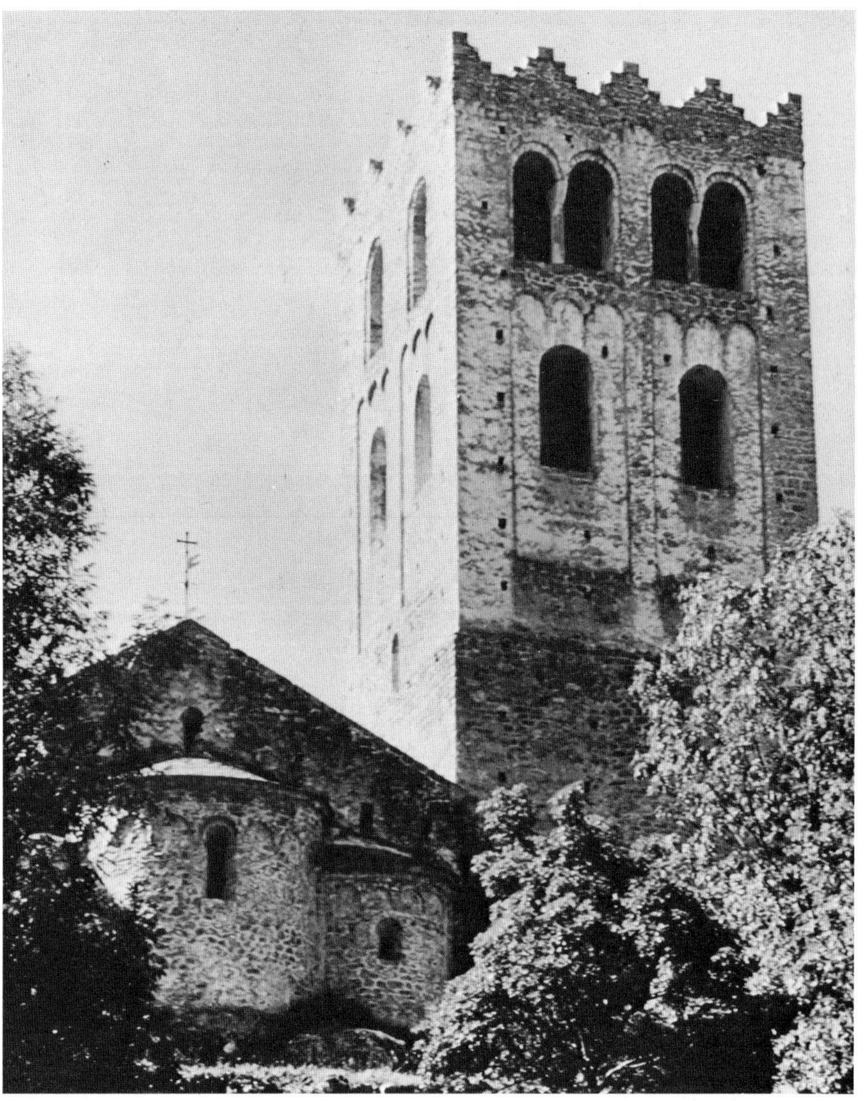

St-Martin-du-Canigou from the east.
c. 1000–1026.

to the newly founded Cuxa. By the 11th century, Cuxa was the dominant monastic power in the region and a score of small abbeys became tributary to it. It was a great landlord, owning a large proportion of the arable land. It had properties as far away as Barcelona. The monastery also worked mines and lent money to the nobility.

The present church was built between 955 and 974. From this period date the Moorish-influenced horseshoe arches. In the first half of the 11th century it was extended to the east and the west. The earlier crypt beneath the westward extension, a round structure with a single supporting column in the

Cloister capital from St-Michel-de-Cuxa. 12th century.

centre, has long been known. But the quatrefoil chapel of the Trinity above has only recently been excavated. Two large towers of Lombardic character were also added. This 11th-century building was the work of Oliba, abbot of Cuxa, of the great abbey of Ripoll and bishop of Vich.

The 12th-century sculpture of Cuxa is perhaps of greater interest than the architecture. No less than fifty-five of the capitals of this abbey are in the United States. Most of these are in The Cloisters, New York, but there are also some in the Museum of Fine Arts, Boston, and in the private collection of Mr Pitcairn of Philadelphia. Several may still be seen at the Restaurant Sicart at Olette. Capitals were recovered from a thermal bath, a tobacconist shop and private collections. The remaining ones are being re-erected on the original site, with marble for the supporting columns from the quarry used in the 12th century.

The most striking capitals belong to a series depicting lions in varied positions flanking oriental-looking faces or torsoes. There are at least a dozen of these at Cuxa. The variety of the poses and proportions of the lions, always within the framework of the capital and always symmetrically arranged, is like variations on a musical theme. The changing emphasis leaves the original theme intact.* The only sculptural example that readily comes to

* Artists like Picasso and Matisse have used the same technique of repetitive exercises with a stylized, theme to exploit the latent possibilities of the 'given' composition.

mind is the presumed original that inspired the series: the bronzes depicting Gilgamesh which show varying treatments of two lions and Gilgamesh the warrior. These date from the second millennium before Christ, but the bronzes were widely distributed in the Near East and might easily have come into the hands of Roussillon sculptors.

The common denominator of these and other Cuxa capitals is the total absence of biblical stories or even religious symbolism. The theme is boldly, though monotonously repeated, and does not bear comparison with the marvellous expression in the story-telling capitals of Burgundy. The sculpture of the 12th-century doorway of Cuxa is less rigid. It shows religious symbolic animals as well as large scale low reliefs of Sts Peter and Paul – an early example of monumental figure sculpture on a church portal.

The mountain abbey of **Serrabonne** (11th–12th centuries) was only made accessible by the construction of a road in 1945. It was founded in the 11th century, when a group of monks who settled there enlarged an older church. Like other churches in the region it is vaulted and virtually windowless. In the 12th century it was decorated with remarkable capitals, probably from the workshop of nearby Cuxa. An extraordinary feature of the abbey is the arched walk overlooking the mountains, decorated with double columns surmounted by finely carved capitals.

Seven miles north-west of Perpignan is the church of **Espira-de-l'Agly**, with an ornate doorway on the south side. South of Perpignan at **Cabestany** is a church with a very fine and expressive marble tympanum by the so-called 'Master of Cabestany', who worked in Toulouse and Tuscany as well as in Catalonia and Roussillon.

In the 11th-century church of **St-André-de-Sorède** there is a fine altar table. There are also some fragments, perhaps sculptured by the artist of St-Génis-des-Fontaines, and another lintel of similar design, though not by the same hand. The *Cathedral* of **Elne**, begun in the 11th century, has a pair of crenellated towers of Lombardic form at the west end. Next to the church is an excellent 12th-century cloister.

St-Génis-des-Fontaines marks the location of hot springs where pagan temples existed in dim antiquity. To exploit the fame of these springs, and to 'christianize' these 'holy spots', venerated in the past, abbeys were constructed, of which St-Génis is an example. It is windowless and barrel vaulted, and has a rare 11th-century door lintel of very early date (1020). The sculpture shows strong Mozarabic influence in the horseshoe arched niches of the six Apostles. Byzantine influences have also been discerned. The direct model for these low relief forms is supposed to have been found in altar fronts or reliquaries of precious metal which were generously bestowed by the patrons of many abbeys. An example of this art is the Arca Santa preserved in the cathedral of Oviedo.

At **Arles-sur-Tech** the Cluniac abbey church of the 11th–12th centuries, is simple but dignified.

12 Spain and Portugal

In the Spanish peninsula we find not only Romanesque, but also well-preserved examples of earlier national styles: Visigothic, Asturian and Mozarabic. The actual area of Christian art here is small because, it will be recalled, the Arabs conquered the Visigothic kingdom and overran the whole peninsula in the 8th century. At the end of this century there remained the small Asturian kingdom in the mountainous north-west, the only part of Spain to withstand successfully the Arab onslaught, and Navarre and Aragon, which had been reconquered. Gradually the Arabs were forced back, but even in the 12th century they held most of southern Spain.

In the first two centuries of their isolated existence these Christian states evolved a highly individual art which owed little to the Carolingian art of the north. Rather, it developed in its own way the early Christian inheritance, with the leavening influence of Visigothic and Arab art, and through Islam, the culture of Byzantium and the Near East. Churches were small but substantially built (proof of this is the comparatively large number which have survived to this day), with highly developed plans. The decorative arts are penetrated by Visigothic and Eastern motifs: rosettes, affronted animals, vine-scrolls, etc.

Two pre-Romanesque styles have been distinguished: Asturian, centred in Oviedo, the capital of the mountain kingdom; and Mozarabic, the art of the conquered Christians, brought with them when they emigrated to the north. It is distinguished by the use of horseshoe arches.

Romanesque came early to Catalonia, in the first decades of the 11th century, from Provence and Lombardy. The latter style was particularly influential. This was largely through the efforts of Abbot Oliba, who had spent a long period in Italy. French influence is predominant in other parts of Spain because of contacts with Cluny and the pilgrimage which ended at Santiago de Compostela.

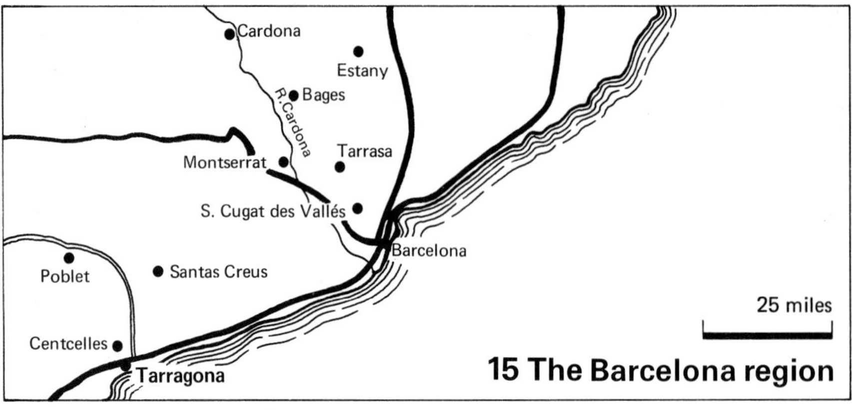

15 The Barcelona region

It is sometimes argued that the national art of Spain was swamped beneath these foreign influences, yet it was never wholly subservient. The preservation of an indigenous quality is most apparent in painting, but in architecture and sculpture, too, one finds a number of elements which have survived from earlier art, as well as a certain 'fastidious warmth'* which is peculiarly characteristic of Spanish art.

The first monument we come to in Spain is the monastery church of **S. Pedro de Roda**, (begun in 979 and consecrated in 1022). Although now a partial ruin, it is still an impressive building and important as one of the earliest Lombard-style churches in Catalonia. It has the typical barrel vault over the nave with transverse arches and striking T-shaped piers. An unusual feature is the ambulatory around the central apse, reflecting French influence. The church is richly ornamented. Most beautiful of all are the half-Moorish sculptured capitals in the nave. The bell-tower is one of the best Catalan examples of the time.

Sta María, **Vilabertrán** and *S. Pedro*, **Besalú** are both good examples of mature Catalan Romanesque. There are also Romanesque houses at Besalú. *St Stephen*, **Bañolas** and *Sta Maria d'Amer* are 10th-century 'first Romanesque' vaulted churches.

Gerona is rich in Romanesque art. The former abbey church of *S. Pedro de Galligans*, consecrated in 1150, is a museum today. On the west front is a fine portal and a rose window, perhaps of Lombard workmanship. The bell-tower is very impressive. Adjoining the church is a cloister of *c.* 1130. The parish church of *S. Nicolas de Galligans* is very simple. The exterior is decorated with Lombard bands.

The Romanesque cloister of the *Cathedral* of Gerona resembles that of S. Pedro. It contains some very fine carved capitals, some purely ornamental,

* K. J. Conant, *Carolingian and Romanesque Art, 800–1200*, p. 202.

Tympanum of the west portal of S. Pablo del Campo, Barcelona. 12th century.

others depicting religious scenes and stories of everyday life. Inside the cathedral is an altar table and marble bishop's throne, both of the 11th century. The cathedral's *Treasure* includes a 12th-century Beatus manuscript. The *Archbishop's Palace* is attached to the cathedral. It contains a most remarkable tapestry of the Creation with a central figure of Christ. There are pagan figures representing the seasons and a marvellous collection of beasts of the water, land and air. Numerous figures, brilliant colouring and oriental backgrounds characterize this needlework tapestry. After much debate it is now rather firmly attributed to the 10th century, which makes it an unique example of the elaborate needlework of that early period.

At **Ripoll** is the monastery of *Sta María*, founded in 874. The original church was enlarged in the 10th century and rebuilt in the 11th century, on a vast scale, by the Abbot Oliba. The church's later history was dismal, and in the 19th century it was completely restored. The foreign influences, mostly Lombardic and Italian, which permeated Catalan Romanesque are well illustrated here at Ripoll. The church is patterned after St Peter's in Rome. The sculptured screen applied to the west front in the 12th century is reminiscent of several north Italian churches, and the two *couchant* lions underline this connection. However the unusual iconography of the reliefs appears to derive from the Catalan Bible of Farfa, now in the Vatican Library. This portal is one of the supreme achievements of Spanish Romanesque sculpture. On the south side of the church is a magnificent two-storied cloister, also of the 12th century.

North of Ripoll are **S. Jaime de Frontanyá** (1070) and **S. Juan de las Abadesas** (*c.* 1114–*c.* 1150), the latter showing French influence in its plan (ambulatory with radiating chapels) and sculpture.

At **Barcelona** there are to be found the churches of *S. Paolo*, with an early Romanesque interior, and *S. Pablo del Campo*, a charming little late Lombardic church which has a tiny cloister of *c.* 1200 with cusped Moorish arches. The church of *Sta María de Barbará* is decorated with 12th–13th-century frescoes. The *Museum of Catalan Art* is one of the best museums for Romanesque art in Europe. It contains nearly all the Romanesque frescoes of the province, removed from churches early this century. In addition there are painted altar fronts and crucifixes. That intense spiritual fervour which is a feature of all Spanish religious art is here seen in the brilliant colours of the paintings and the highly expressionistic figures.

South of Barcelona is the Romanesque church of **S. Pons de Corbeira** (*c.* 1080). At **Centcelles** near Tarragona is a 4th-century mausoleum with poorly preserved mosaics in the dome. Also near Tarragona are two Cistercian monasteries, **Poblet** and **Santas Creus**.

About nine miles north-west of Barcelona is the church of **S. Cugat des Vallés** with a fine cloister whose carved capitals resemble those of the Romanesque cloisters in Gerona. At **Tarrasa** is the baptistery of *S. Miguel*, built between 450 and 720. It was originally the baptistery of the basilica of Egara, of which only a mosaic pavement survives. It is square in plan with a cupola and groin-vaulted ceiling. There is a baptismal basin. The church of *Sta María* has 12th-century fresco remains.

Sta Cecilia de Montserrat, rebuilt between 957 and the 11th century, is one of the oldest examples of early Romanesque in Catalonia. It is basilican in plan and has no transept. The cloister of **S. Benito de Bages**, built after 1150, probably incorporates carvings of an earlier period (972). At **Cardona** is the church of *S. Vicente* (*c.* 1020–40).

The little fortress-like town of **Seo de Urgel** is dominated by its *Cathedral*. The eastern portion, which replaced a Visigothic structure, was begun in 1010 and consecrated in 1040. Building continued throughout the 11th and 12th centuries. The church has a T-shaped plan, rather like that of Ripoll, though simpler. Over the crossing is a curious ribbed dome. Perhaps completed by Lombard masons, the cathedral is almost pure Lombard in style, particularly its exterior. This is apparent in the development of the west front, in the lions supporting the portal columns, in the decorative arcading, and the exterior apse gallery.

A few miles north of Seo de Urgel is the little church of *Santa Coloma*, of simple design with an unusual belfry resembling the campanile of S. Apollinare Nuovo at Ravenna.

The old *Cathedral* of **Lérida** dates from the 13th century and is half-Gothic in style, but the west portal, despite this late date, is pure Romanesque. The *Exchange* is also 13th century and Romanesque.

At **Tahull** are the churches of *Sta María* and *S. Clemente*, famous for their frescoes which are now in the museum at Barcelona. S. Clemente is a plain triapsidal wooden-roofed basilica without a clerestory, almost archaic for its date (*c.* 1132). It has a handsome square Lombard tower.

S. Pedro el Viejo at **Huesca** (1100–1241) is a basilican barrel-vaulted church

Opposite
Altar-front from Mosoll, Cerdagne. Scenes from the lives of Jesus and Mary. Detail: the Magus Melchior. 12th century. Barcelona, Museum of Catalan Art.

Overleaf left
St Paul and St John from the church of Sta María de Tahull. 12th century. Barcelona, Museum of Catalan Art.
Overleaf right
Altar-front from Gesera, dedicated to St John the Baptist. 13th century. Barcelona, Museum of Catalan Art.

of the Catalan type. On the north portal is a beautiful tympanum with the Byzantine XPESTOS (Christ) monogram. The cloister has elaborately carved capitals. The chapter-house of the monastery of **Sigena** is decorated with mid-13th-century frescoes which were appallingly damaged in a fire of 1937. Yet their exceptional quality can still be discerned. Strong Byzantine influence came here from two main sources – directly from Palermo or indirectly through late 12th-century manuscripts decorated in the Byzantine style in the south of England.

The castle of **Loarre** with its ruined walls and keep is one of the most romantic in Spain. It was famous for the relics which it guarded. The church belongs to the late 11th–12th centuries. Over the central bay is an oriental-type dome. The apse is very elegantly arcaded. The sculptured capitals resemble Provençal carvings.

S.Cruz de la Séros was built in the latter half of the 11th century. The most remarkable part of the building is the raised south arm, intended to serve as a refuge in times of danger. The tympanum is decorated with the XP monogram which we have already seen at Huesca and will find again at Jaca.

The remote abbey of **S.Juan de la Peña** (about fifteen minutes walk from the new monastery) is situated in an extraordinary position, under the edge of a cliff. The church was the Pantheon of the kings of Aragon. The present structure, which was consecrated in 1095, has preserved three earlier horse-shoe choirs carved out of the rock. The interior has 18th-century decorations. The cloister to the south of the church uses the overhanging cliff for a covering. The historiated capitals of the columns date from the second half of the 12th century. They are in the style of Toulouse.

The *Cathedral* of **Jaca**, begun in 1063, is a cruciform basilica with a fine Moorish type dome. The nave is perhaps the first Spanish example of the use of alternating piers and columns. Inside the church is a remarkable 11th-century sarcophagus from S.Cruz de la Séros. The west entrance is a porch with decorated capitals, in the style of St-Benoît-sur-Loire. Some of the capitals have well-proportioned nude figures reminiscent of Roman sculpture and anticipating Renaissance sculpture. The subject matter of the scenes is not biblical but appears to stem from Arab or Jewish writings. In the tympanum is an XP monogram. The south portal of the cathedral is later in date than the west portal.

S.Salvador, **Leyre** is the earliest Spanish Cluniac church still existing. It was dedicated in 1057. Not surprisingly it shows a good deal of French influence. The vaulted crypt belongs to an earlier period, perhaps Visigothic. The deeply projecting west portal is mid-12th century. Its carvings are reminiscent of Toulousan work.

At **Sanguësa** are the churches of *S.Pedro* and *Sta María la Real* with fine 12th-century sculpture. The portal of Sta María, which was incorporated into the south transept, is on a vast scale with columnar statues which were inspired by Chartres.

In the *Museum* of **Pamplona** are five capitals from the old cloister of the *Cathedral.* Two are ornamental; the remaining three tell the stories of Job and the Passion, Crucifixion and Resurrection. These carvings are an unsurpassed achievement and appear to be independent of any French model. The handling of all the subjects is perfectly mastered.

At **Eunate** is a Templar's church, of octagonal plan with an apse and surmounted dome. It is surrounded by a curious portico of forty arches which is detached from the church. The church of *Crucifijio*, **Puenta la Reina** has a decorated portal. That of **Santiago** also has a large carved doorway.

San Miguel, **Estella** is another church with a very fine portal of the 12th and 13th centuries on the north façade. *S. Pedro de la Rua* dates from the last quarter of the 12th century. The *Palace of the Dukes* (1200) conserves some excellent Romanesque windows. There are carvings depicting the battle between Roland and the Saracen giant Ferragat.

In **Torres del Río** is an octagonal church of the *Holy Sepulchre* (12th century). Its vault closely resembles that of the *mihrab* of the Mosque of Cordoba. The collegiate church of **Tudela** (late 12th–13th centuries) has some very fine sculpture. The west porch is one of the richest of late Romanesque examples with one hundred and sixteen groups of figures taking part in the Last Judgement. There is another less elaborate portal on the north transept. Adjoining the church is a cloister of *c.* 1150. Inside is a wonderful statue of the Virgin and Child.

The hermitage of *S. Baudelio de Berlanga* (11th century) near **Burgos** is almost inaccessible. Its design is extraordinary, consisting of a central cylindrical pier supporting eight radiating horseshoe diaphragm arches carrying a domical vault. It was formerly decorated with 12th-century frescoes, which are now in Cambridge, Mass., and New York. Also near Burgos are the impressive ruins of the abbey church of **Arlanza** (*c.* 1080–1100). In plan, it resembles Jaca.

A little way from Arlanza is the *Tower of Doña Urraca*, **Covarrubias** – a rare example of 10th-century civic architecture. Of the original 12th-century abbey church of *S. Domingo*, **Silos** nothing survives. A new church was built in the 19th century. However the 11th–12th-century cloister is perhaps the most important example of Spanish Romanesque sculpture. There are sixty-four pairs of columns, all with elaborately carved capitals, the majority ornamental with Eastern motifs. There are also reliefs on six stone pillars inlaid in the corners, depicting the main episodes after the Resurrection. These show a wonderful feeling for drama and narrative. According to Charles Morey the sculpture of Christ and the two disciples on the journey to Emmaus is basically of the Toulouse school, with Burgundian and English influences, the latter seen in the tiptoe stance. However an interpretation of this kind tends to underestimate the originality of the achievement here at Silos.

South of Burgos on the road to Palencia is the 7th–8th-century hermitage

of *Quintanellas de la Viñas*. The exterior of the apse is decorated with three parallel bands of richly decorated stylized foliage, alternating with carved animals – a typically Visigothic piece of work.

The *Crypt of S. Antonin* under the *Cathedral* of **Palencia** is difficult to date. Some ascribe it the 7th century, others to the 11th. It is decorated with horseshoe arches and capitals carved with Syrian motifs. The date of the church of *S. Juan de Baños de Cerrato*, is also disputed. It is a few miles south-west of Palencia, near Venta de Baños. Built by King Recceswinth in 661 the church is the finest example, not only of Spanish Visigothic, but of all architecture of the 7th century. It shares many characteristics with the churches of Syria of the 5th and 6th centuries. S. Juan has horseshoe windows and Visigothic decorations. Some authorities think this building is of later construction.

North of Palencia is *S. Martín*, **Frómista**, (late 11th–12th centuries), the only complete example of a pilgrimage style Cluniac church in Spain, without later additions. The church of *Carríon de los Condes* has a remarkable Christ Enthroned surrounded by the symbols of the four Evangelists in the carved frieze above the round arch.

There is a 12th-century church at **Santillana del Mar**, near Santander. Beautifully situated in a valley dominated by towering cliffs, is the church of *Sta María de Lebeña* (*c.* 924), an excellent example of the Mozarabic style. The carved capitals are considered the finest example of Mozarabic craftmanship.

Seven miles south-west of Villaviciosa is *Sta María de Valdediós* (893). It has many features which we shall find in the Oviedo churches. The church is a three-aisled basilica with a barrel-vaulted nave. Against the south aisle is an enclosed porch with capitals carved with Visigothic-Asturian motifs. They show a free treatment.

Oviedo is a centre of Asturian building. It was here that the kings of Asturia had their capital and the region contains a number of priceless architectural treasures. In the *Cathedral* of Oviedo is the *Cámara Santa* (*c.* 802) famous for the treasures preserved therein: two fine Asturian crosses – the Cross of the Angels and the Cross of Victory; a 10th-century gold reliquary; and the Arca Santa (1075), a reliquary box showing Byzantine, Germanic and Mozarabic influences. The Cámara Santa was partly rebuilt in the 12th century and embellished with sculptures of French type.

On the outskirts of Oviedo is the church of *S. Julián de los Prados*, built some time between 812 and 842. Generally known as 'Santullano' it is attributed to Tioda. S. Julián is the best preserved of the churches of the Oviedo region and contains recently uncovered mural decorations which are the finest of the epoch. Like some of the other churches, it has a feature which has mystified archaeologists. Above the santuary is a small chamber with no means of access other than a decorative window high up off the ground. It is not known whether this small chamber was a place of refuge from hostile

Opposite
Panel from cloister of S. Domingo, Silos, showing Christ and the two disciples on the way to Emmaus. 12th century.

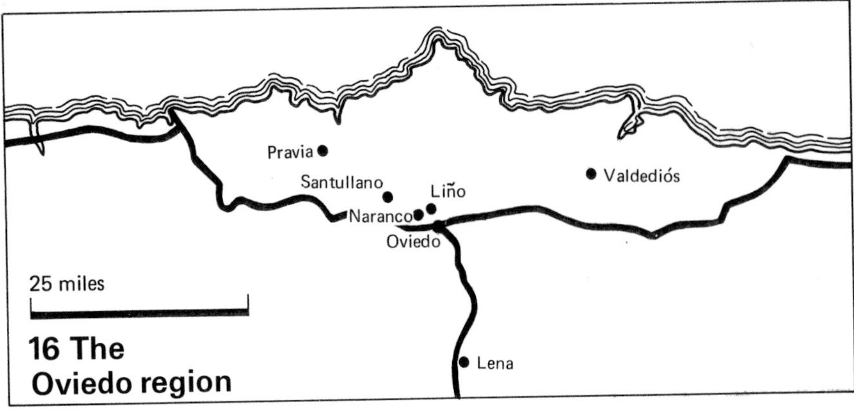

16 The Oviedo region

visitors or whether it had some religious significance as 'God's dwelling place' above the altar.

Two miles from Pravia is *S. Juan de Pravia Santianes*, founded in 774 and later completely rebuilt, though in the style of the original structure.

Sta María de Naranco (824–50) was built during the reign of Ramiro I. It is two-storied with a side entrance of two flights of stairs leading to the upper storey. The building is barrel vaulted with transverse arches. There is some speculation as to whether it was originally the palace of King Ramiro and only converted into a church in the 11th or 12th centuries. There is no doubt that the building could have been used as a royal residence and that Ramiro did build a palace and baths at this site. The reader is at liberty to make up his own mind on this issue.

To the west of Naranco is **S. Miguel de Liño** (848), a very fine structure though now incomplete. It is a columnar basilica. Some authorities have found a resemblance to Armenian churches, though this kind of influence would be indirect. The upper storey contains fresco remains. The church has decorations in the double cable pattern, rosettes, and other designs seen in Visigothic works of art. The low relief carvings on the jambs of the west doorway appear to be copies of early Byzantine ivory work.

At **Lena** is the charming little church of *Sta Cristina* (*c.* 905). Worth noting is the interesting chancel screen carved with barbaric motifs. These three churches we have just described are in a state of almost perfect preservation.

The city of **León** was founded in the late Roman period. Despite the protective wall built at this time it was captured by Goths and later destroyed by Arabs in 983. León's most glorious epoch was in the 11th to 13th centuries when many fine Romanesque buildings were erected. Few of these survive today. The *Royal Pantheon* (1054–67) now forms the narthex of the church of *S. Isidoro* (early 12th century). The capitals in the Royal Pantheon are

Opposite
The church of Sta María de Naranco from the west. 824–50.

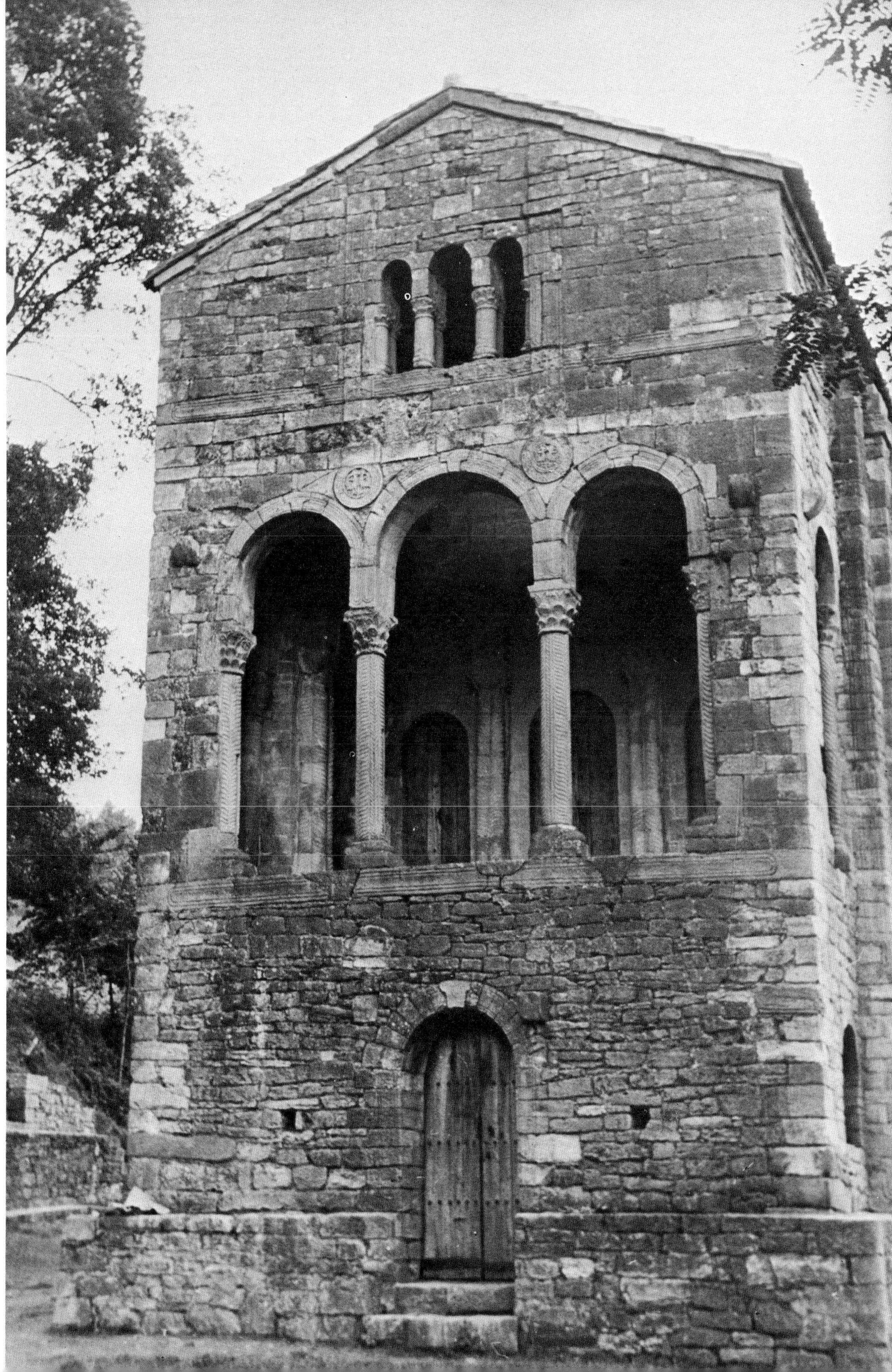

among the most interesting of their period and mark an important point for dating sculpture in France and Italy which resembles them. There are also late 12th-century sculptures and frescoes. The lateral apses of the main church have interesting sculptural decorations.

The *Convent of S. Marcos*, formerly a lodging for pilgrims on the Compostela route, contains a *Museum*. It has Roman-Spanish *stelae* with horseshoe arch decorations.

In the León region there are two good examples of Mozarabic building. *S. Miguel del Escalada* (913) incorporates Roman, Visigothic and Arab features. It is in an excellent state of preservation and has been carefully restored to its original state by the elimination of Baroque decoration. The church is basilican in plan and wooden-roofed, except for the apses, which are horseshoe in plan with horseshoe arches. The arches of the chancel screen are of the same form. Another good example is *Santiago de Penalba*, founded in 913. *Sta María de Bamba* (*c.*928) has many Visigothic and Mozarabic features. The nave is 12th century. There are no decorations of any importance.

Sahagún is the centre of Mudéjar art, i.e. the art of conquered Moors working for Christian masters in the Romanesque style. In the neighbourhood of Sahagún at the village of Quintana was a Mozarab colony settled in the 10th century. Many were workers in brick and the later influx of Moorish craftsmen strengthened this element. The Mudéjar churches of this region are made of brick.

Sahagún was also the seat of a great Clunaic monastery. The abbey church has been destroyed, but there is still the brick chapel of *S. Manco* (*c.* 1100). *S. Tirso* and *S. Lorenzo*, both 12th-century churches, have Mudéjar towers. These are decorated with ornamented arcading resembling Lombard work, except that the arches are set in Moorish-looking oblong panels.

The *Cathedral* of **Lugo** (1129–77) is essentially a copy of Santiago de Compostela, the one important difference being the use of a pointed barrel vault and pointed arches in the nave. Worth noting are the wooden panels of the door in the north transept, which have fine wrought-iron fittings.

The *Cathedral* of **Santiago de Compostela** is named after the Apostle James whose relics were believed to have been found here. Conflicting legends exist as to how these precious remains got to Compostela. One says that the Apostle came here in the flesh, another that the relics were brought here and discovered much later by Bishop Theodemir, who founded the cathedral at the burial spot. At all events the relics became the most famous in Europe, apart from the tomb of St Peter in Rome, and St James became the patron saint of the Crusaders who liberated Spain from the Moors. Santiago became a religious centre of great importance with the increase of pilgrimages to the tomb of the Apostle.

Opposite
Capital, showing Moses leading the Exodus, from the Royal Pantheon, S. Isidoro, León. 11th century.

Of the forty or more churches of the town, the cathedral is by far the most important. It is the grandest Romanesque monument in Spain. Started around 1078, its construction and decoration continued into the 12th century.

IN·NO
S·QVI
TER·DEVM·O
SVM

Interior of S. Miguel del Escalada. 913.

Opposite: Fresco showing the Massacre of the Innocents, Royal Pantheon, S. Isidoro, León. 12th century.

Baroque additions have marred much of its original beauty and dignity. It is sometimes argued that Santiago was the earliest of the whole line of pilgrimage churches, being of the age of St-Martin, Tours and roughly contemporaneous with St-Sernin, Toulouse. Be that as it may, it has all the standard features of a pilgrimage church: it is very large, with a three-storied internal elevation, a barrel-vaulted nave reinforced by transverse arches, a dome over the crossing of transepts and nave, and a complex apse system with ambulatory and radiating chapels. Below the west portal is an interesting crypt.

There are a few Romanesque carvings on the façade, which is mostly Baroque. Beyond this façade is the famous west portal, the *Pórtico de la Gloria*. Its sculpture, which dates to 1188, is the work of Master Matheus, believed to be French or at least trained in France. Chartres was the prototype, and like the prototype, the sculpture of the portal is distinguished for its naturalism and close integration with its architectural setting. The best example of this is the statue of St James himself.

Earlier Romanesque sculpture is to be found on the south portal. This does not have the unity of the Pórtico de la Gloria, partly because it had to be repaired after damage during a fire in 1117, partly because it acquired bits and pieces from other parts of the building. In the structure of the interior columns, aisles and vaults, and in the *Chapel of Corticela* in the lower church further work can be seen.

Sta María de Sar has a cloister sometimes attributed to Master Matheus, builder of the cathedral.

The *Cathedral* of **Orense** (1132–94) has many of the features of Compostela, but the vaulting is Gothic. The narthex decorative sculpture is a rather sterile imitation of Compostela. In the *Cathedral Treasure* there is a 12th-century seated statue of the Virgin and Child, one of the rare Romanesque statues in the round. *S. Combe de Bande* has retained part of its 7th-century Visigothic building.

The church of **Aguas Santas** near Taboadela has a number of Burgundian features. The *Cathedral* of **Tuy**, built in the last quarter of the 12th century, was another church inspired by Santiago de Compostela. It was radically altered in the Gothic period.

We now turn south-east to examine some of the churches of Castile. *Sta Marta de Tera* some miles north of Salamanca is dated 1129 but it shows a number of Visigothic features. The half-Gothic *Cathedral* of **Zamora** has a remarkable cupola of most elaborate design. Thirteen miles west of Zamora is *S. Pedro de la Nave*, 700, which is difficult of access. Its origin is clouded in mystery and its date is in dispute. In plan the church is cruciform within a square. Of particular value is the rich sculpture of the capitals and in the friezes along the walls of the chancel. They show Visigothic motifs: wheels, stars, rosettes and six curved rays. There are also human figures and horses.

The collegiate church of *Sta María la Mayor*, **Toro**, has a great lantern tower like that of Zamora, as does the *Old Cathedral* of **Salamanca**. The

Opposite
Interior of Santiago de Compostela, *c.* 1078–1150.

latter has an elegant spire, known as the 'Torre del gallo' after the weathercock on top. West of Salamanca is **Ciudad Rodrigo** with its *Cathedral* (1165–1230). The interior has domed-up rib vaults like those of Anjou, yet another example of the strong French influence on the architecture of the western half of Spain.

S. Vicente (1100–1241), **Avila** is a church of the pilgrimage type resembling Compostela. The high quality of the statues of the west portal is still evident, despite the damage they have suffered. There is also expressive sculpture on the south entrance. Parallel to the south aisle of the church is an elegant portico. French masons worked on the *City walls* which date from about 1090.

The Romanesque *Cathedral* of **Segovia** has been destroyed but there remain a number of interesting parish churches, with unusual colonnaded porches enclosing the exterior. The function of these porticoes is not known, but it has been suggested that they were used for meetings of the town populace. The sculpture of the capitals is not dependent on French influences. In style and form it is more purely 'Spanish'. *S. Estéban*, *S. Martin* and *S. Millán* are all good examples of the type.

Just out of Segovia is the *Sanctuary of the Vera Cruz* (1206), one of the strangest of the Templar's churches. It is dodecagon in plan and surmounted by a dome. The middle of the sanctuary is encircled by an ambulatory.

The *Archaeological Museum* in **Madrid** is richly endowed with early mediaeval treasures. Among these are: the 7th-century Visigothic Crowns of Guarrazar; a large ivory crucifix presented to the church of S. Isidoro, León, in 1063; and a remarkable sculptured Virgin and the Mausoleum of Alphonso VI (1093) from Sahagún. In the *Prado* is a fresco from the Sanctuary of the Vera Cruz. The *Royal Armoury* contains Visigothic works of art.

The church of *Santo Cristo de la Luz*, **Toledo** has columns of Visigothic origin. *S. Eulalia* and *S. Sebastian* also contain Visigothic capitals. South of Toledo at **Melque** is the Mozarabic church of *Sta María* (*c.* 950).

Naturally one cannot expect to find any Romanesque churches in the south of Spain, which was still under Arab domination in the 12th century, but there are a few early Christian and Visigothic remains, and the most important of the early Arab monuments should be considered, since influence of their art extended as far north as Burgundy.

At **Elche** near Alicante on the south-east coast is a church with Visigothic capitals. In **Manacor** on the island of Majorca there is the early Christian basilica of *S. Pereto*. **Granada** has an early Christian baptistery, *Gabia la Grande*, with a Byzantine-type dome. It contains a winding staircase, probably the earliest in Europe.

The *Great Mosque*, **Cordoba** (786–976) is the second largest mosque in the world and larger than any Christian church. It was begun during the great age of Mohammedan building by the Caliphs of Cordoba. The Mosque was built on the foundations of a Visigothic church and has 1200 columns with Roman, Visigothic and Mohammedan capitals. It was expanded and improved

Opposite 'Torre del Gallo', Old Cathedral, Salamanca. Late 12th century.

over a period of 200 years, during which time it acquired brilliant decorations of mosaics, marbles and Arabic carvings. The horseshoe arch, geometric decoration and the design of the ribs of the domes are all features that almost immediately found their way into the Mozarabic style of Christian architecture, and from there into Spanish and French Romanesque.

The *Giralda* at **Seville** is a Moorish tower of 1159, capped by a Renaissance belfry. It is beautifully decorated with geometric designs and is regarded by experts as one of the finest towers in the world.

At **Mérida**, are the remains of a late Roman house-basilica with mosaic pavements and an open pillared court. Two rooms terminate in apses, one containing Christian frescoes. *El Conventual Castle* was at first a Roman fortress. It was turned into an Alcázar by the Arabs and after the Reconquest it became a convent. It now contains a museum. Of particular interest are two light windows from the Roman period with two horseshoe arches which considerably pre-date their appearance in Moorish architecture.

Portugal

There are only a handful of Romanesque churches in Portugal worth seeing, since most have suffered from later rebuilding and decoration and from earthquakes. The *Cathedral* of **Lisbon** was begun in 1150, three years after the city had been captured from the Arabs. It has been well restored to something like its original form. Between the two western towers is a deep portico with an open arched gallery above. The eastern portion of the interior is of Gothic construction. The cathedral preserves a Visigothic fragment with Eastern decoration – confronted beasts, foliage and horseshoe arches.

At **Tomar** is the church of *Convento do Cristo* one of the finest Templar buildings in existence. It was begun some time after the middle of the 12th century. The exterior is sixteen-sided, enveloping a small octagonal central sanctuary, pierced by an arcade. A nave was added in the 16th century.

The *Old Cathedral* of **Coimbra** (*Sé Velha*) was begun in 1162. The church is a variation on the Santiago de Compostela theme. The main doorway of the severe west façade is surmounted by a deeply recessed window. The interior is very elegant and in no way spoiled by the early 16th-century decoration.

The *Castle of Guimarães* goes back to 927, but was rebuilt in about 1100. It is the finest Romanesque castle in Portugal, and very picturesque. The church of *S. Miguel do Castelo* was built in about 1100 but is archaic in style and shows many Asturian features. The *Council Hall*, **Bragança** (*c.* 1200) is a fine example of secular building. Around all its five sides, below the roof line, there runs a sturdy arcaded gallery.

Opposite: Interior of the Great Mosque, Cordoba. 786–976.

13 The British Isles

The rise of the Norman dukes from local overlords in Normandy to the rulers of England had as its by-product the rapid spread of their law and social system throughout England. They also brought their ecclesiastical and military architecture. Great edifices were erected, distinguished by their solidity, simplicity and clean perfection. Norman architecture stands at the foundation of all English mediaeval building. At the same time it is rather unfortunate that Romanesque building in England, church building at any rate, should be called 'Norman'. It implies that native traditions and methods were totally submerged, which was not the case. The conquerors were energetic, but they were also *parvenus*, while the conquered had centuries of culture behind them.

Early Anglo-Saxon churches and monasteries were built of wood 'after the manner of the Scots* ... of hewn oak, and covered with reeds.' Such was the first Lindisfarne church built by Bishop Finan. Later churches were rebuilt of stone, after the manner of the Romans, a fact which the author of the foregoing quotation, the Venerable Bede (673–735) notes in his *Ecclesiastical History*. They were small and simple in plan, those in the south-east being slightly more complex, with a cruciform plan and triple arcade separating chancel and nave. Carolingian and Ottonian influences entered in the 9th and 10th centuries, as seen in the west tower and cushion capitals. In fact cushion capitals were adopted in England earlier than in Normandy.

After the Conquest, the scale of churches increased and the more complex continental plans were adopted, as well as Norman alternating simple and compound piers, and three-storied internal elevation and crossing tower. However in the 12th century, older English traditions and tastes reasserted themselves. The Anglo-Saxon preference for tall, narrow proportions is apparent in the lengthening of the nave. There was a return to the simple

* i.e. the Irish.

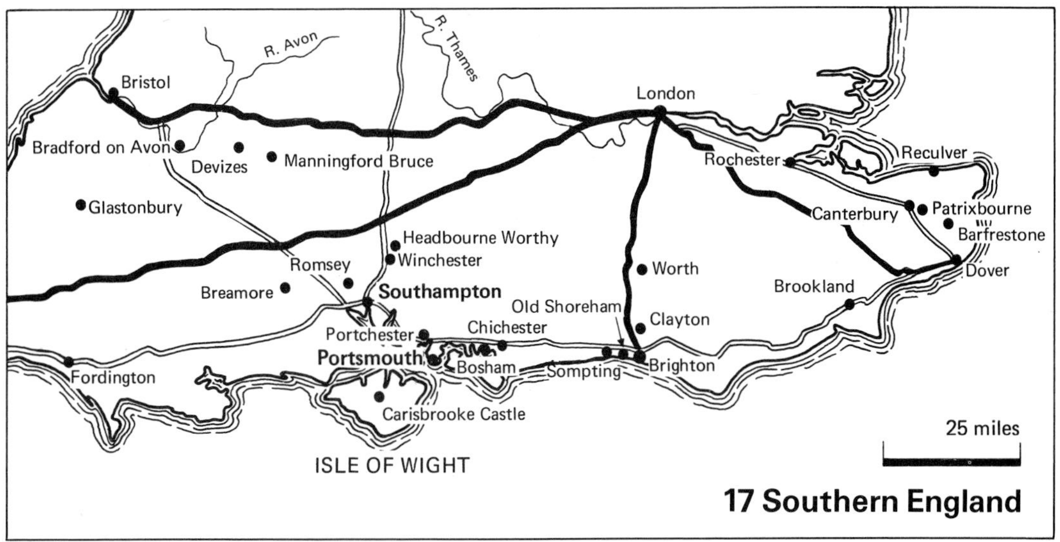

17 Southern England

square east end. Anglo-Saxon and Scandinavian decorative motifs were revived and two ornaments of doubtful provenance became very popular – the zig-zag (or chevron) and the beak-head.

The Normans were architects before artists. The clumsiness of the capitals in Durham Castle chapel is illustrative of their weakness as sculptors. The English, on the other hand, had early reached a high level of sculptural achievement, e.g. the Ruthwell Cross, though sculpture on buildings tended to be applied haphazardly with regard to its architectural setting. Both the style and use of sculpture in the 12th century were influenced by France. At the same time native tastes persisted, particularly for linear pattern making. This taste invaded architecture, where walls dissolved behind a web of trellis work, interlaced arcades, and tiers of arches. A separate and important branch of sculpture are baptismal fonts in stone and lead. Some of these were imported, but there were also flourishing local workshops. In remote Cornwall and Devon a fierce, barbaric style persisted.

We know from manuscript paintings the skill of English artists, and we know too that frescoes were an important branch of their art. Only a handful have survived, and from these it is clear that continental and Byzantine influences were important.

Virtually nothing remains of pre-Romanesque art in Scotland. Romanesque reached this part of Britain in the 12th century. Building here is generally dependent on Anglo-Saxon and Norman prototypes.

The magnificently situated *castle* of **Dover** dates from the 12th century. Over the centuries it was England's defence against invasion across the shortest

Channel crossing. It is concentric in form, reflecting the influence of Near Eastern fortifications, particularly those of the Crusaders. This influence became increasingly important in the 12th century and led to the replacement of the older, less effective, square-shaped castle. The 11th-century Saxon church of *St Mary* stands on a knoll within the castle walls. It stands close to the ruin of a Roman lighthouse or *pharos*, believed to have been originally eight stories high. The church is cruciform with a central tower. Some Roman brick was re-used in its construction. The lighthouse was used as a west tower.

At *St Augustine's*, **Brookland**, is a fine 12th-century font, possibly imported from the Continent. It is cylindrical in shape and decorated with reliefs depicting the signs of the Zodiac, with scenes of the Labours of the Months, beneath. *St Nicholas*, **Barfrestone**, is one of the treasures of English Romanesque. It probably dates from the end of the 11th century and in layout is typical of the Kentish Anglo-Saxon churches, i.e., nave and chancel, with a screen dividing the two parts. The rich decorations were added a century later. On the exterior of the east end is a rose window and a string course supported by carved heads. The elaborate south doorway has a recessed door and a tympanum with a Christ in Majesty. In style and subject matter it is close to those of Charente in France. The church of *St Mary*, **Patrixbourne** (late 12th century) has a massive central tower and a sculptured south door.

Of the great abbey at **Canterbury** founded by St Augustine and sumptuously furnished by Pope Gregory, virtually nothing has remained. It was destroyed by fire a year after the Conquest. The English cathedral for the most part has a monastic origin. It had elaborate service buildings: refectories, cloisters, libraries, infirmaries, workshops, guest houses, etc., some of which are intact. This is the case at Canterbury *Cathedral*, begun in 1070 by the Lombard Lanfranco, who was brought over to England from Normandy. The Norman portions include the tower on the south side with four-storied tiers of arched decorations, and the lower arcades. There is a Norman infirmary and the walls of the adjoining structures are also Norman. In the groin-vaulted crypt are carved capitals and Byzantine-influenced fresco fragments, both of the 12th century.

The guest house for pilgrims, now part of Canterbury School, has a late Romanesque stairway of exceptional beauty. In the cathedral there is stained glass (1174) of very high quality.

The chancel and nave of *St Martin's*, Canterbury, date from the first half of the 7th century. The church contains a fine Romanesque font, with both Norman (intersecting arches) and pre-Norman (interlacing strap-work) decorative features.

St Mary's, **Reculver** was destroyed in 1805. The surviving fragment consists of a 7th-century west wall flanked by two late Romanesque towers.

Rochester was an important sea-port in mediaeval times. The *Cathedral*

Fresco showing St Paul being bitten by a viper, in
St Anselm's chapel, Canterbury Cathedral. Late 12th century.

has a fine west portal, whose strong French character is attributed to the influence of Eleanor of Aquitaine. It dates from about the middle of the 12th century. The badly damaged tympanum, with a Christ in Majesty surrounded by the symbols of the four Evangelists and seated Apostles in the lintel, resembles the tympana of southern French churches. The column statues, which are like the Chartres figures, are the first of this kind in England. The grim-looking castle was completed in the first third of the 12th century.

Virtually nothing remains of Edward the Confessor's building at **Westminster** *Abbey*, London, which, before it was altered, was a pre-Conquest typical Norman structure. *St Bartholomew the Great* (1123) at **Smithfield** is London's oldest church still intact. It was founded by Rahere, a worldly canon of St Paul's who, upon falling sick while visiting Rome, was cured, and inspired to found a hospital for men and women outside the London wall. This ensured its preservation from the Great Fire of London which destroyed all the contemporary churches inside the wall. The sturdy circular columns, solid cushion capitals and noble proportions make the Norman choir of St Bartholomew unique.

The *White Tower* in the Tower of London was built for William the Conqueror by Gundolph, bishop of Rochester, between 1070 and 1097, and used as his main castle in London. It is a keep which was surrounded by walls and a moat. The grim building, void of any decoration, is typical of the castles of this early age. The interior is gloomy, for the purpose of the building was defence, not comfort. The huge walls housed retainers and supplies. The king's abode was in the upper chambers. Here we find *St John's Chapel*, one of the finest examples of early Norman architecture in England.

It is hard to imagine the 'way of life' in such a structure. One is struck by the lack of both privacy and elementary comforts for the king and his family. The rugged conditions for the residents appear only slightly better than those of the prisoners, kept in dark cells in the same building.

The *British Museum* and the *Victoria and Albert Museum* are both indispensable to those interested in learning about Romanesque and its forerunners. Most important perhaps, at the British Museum, is the manuscript collection which includes the Lindisfarne Gospel, and the Saxon Treasure of Sutton Hoo. In the Victoria and Albert are works of great beauty of the early Christian and Byzantine periods as well as Romanesque. One of the greatest treasures is the 12th-century Eltenburg Reliquary from Cologne.

North of London, in Essex, is the church of *St Andrew*, **Greenstead-juxta-Ongar**, famous for its wooden nave built some time between 950 and 1100. It teaches us something about Anglo-Saxon timber construction methods. The church was restored in the mid-19th century. Nearby are the magnificent remnants of the once important Benedictine **Waltham** *Abbey*. The nave and aisles of the church are Norman. The alternating support scheme of simple piers and piers with engaged shafts is reminiscent of Durham. Also in Essex, at **Ongar** and **Pleshey**, are two good examples of earthen mottes.

On the outskirts of London is the mediaeval monastery of **St Albans** built around the shrine of St Alban, the first English martyr. The present church was begun *c.* 1077. Of the Norman period there remain sections of the nave and transept, and the huge crossing tower built of red brick taken from the ancient Roman town of Verulamium nearby. The nave and chancel of the church of *St Michael* belong to the 10th century. **Berkhamsted** near Hemel Hempstead has an earthern motte in good condition. About five miles south-west of Aylesbury at **Dinton** is the church of *St Peter and St Paul*, with an elaborate Norman south doorway. The sculpture shows Scandinavian influence.

Opposite
The White Tower, Tower of London. 1070–97.

If we travel south from London, we come to the church of *St Nicholas*,

Worth, two miles east of Crawley in Sussex. It is a cruciform building of the late 11th century, or possibly a little earlier. It has survived complete apart from some rather heavy 19th-century restoration, when it acquired a rather inappropriate tower.

The church of *St John the Baptist* at **Clayton** (six miles out of Brighton) was built shortly after 1000. The chancel was extended in the 12th century. The importance of the church lies in its frescoes, which betray a strong Byzantine influence. Their date is disputed. Some authorities think they are contemporary with the building of the church; others prefer to ascribe them to the mid-12th century.

St Nicholas, **Brighton**, has an admirable 12th-century cylindrical stone font with relief carvings. The church at **Old Shoreham**, near Brighton, is also dedicated to St Nicholas. The Normans lengthened its late Anglo-Saxon nave and added the central tower and chancel. The chancel and crossing arches are richly decorated with zig-zag ornament and other motifs. The effect is somewhat bulky.

St Mary the Virgin, at **Sompting** near Worthing, is unique in having an 11th-century Anglo-Saxon tower with a 'Rhenish helm' spire. The massive entrance arch inside has carved capitals which are among the best preserved sculpture of the Anglo-Saxon period in England. In *St Botolph's*, **Hardham**, are the remains of frescoes which once covered the whole interior of the church. They are of the first third of the 12th century. Continental influences are very strong, though the linear technique is reminiscent of Anglo-Saxon art.

Chichester *Cathedral* was begun in 1090 and rebuilt after a fire in 1187. It is largely Norman, however. In the south aisle of the choir are two panels, one depicting the meeting of Christ with Mary and Martha and the other, the raising of Lazarus. They date from about the second quarter of the 12th century and were probably originally part of a choir-screen. They are works of extraordinary power and expression. *St Mary's Hospital* was built in the 13th century.

About four miles west of Chichester, beside one of the channels of the harbour, is the church of the *Holy Trinity*, **Bosham**. It dates mostly to about 1050–1100 with early Gothic additions. One interesting fact is that a stylized representation of the church appears in the Bayeux Tapestry. **Portchester** *Castle* was built in the 12th century on the site of a Roman fort. The Great Tower was built between 1160 and 1173. In the south-east corner of the castle is the well-preserved 12th-century church of *St Mary*, with a handsome west front. **Carisbrooke** *Castle* on the Isle of Wight has an 11th-century keep.

At **Romsey** is a magnificent parish church, mostly 12th century except for the early Gothic west end. The interior is richly decorated, e.g. the string-course around the chancel and transept and the elaborately worked transept arches. The glory of the church is the large crucifix immediately outside the south door. Its exact date is not agreed upon – some time in the 11th century.

The *Cathedral* of **Winchester**, begun in *c.* 1079, is the longest in Europe.

Detail of the 'Raising of Lazarus' panel in Chichester Cathedral. Second quarter of 12th century.

The Norman church has been extensively rebuilt and only a few isolated parts are visibly Romanesque today: the crypt, transept and crossing tower. The crypt is very large, which was usual for great English Romanesque churches and most unusual for churches on the Continent, with the notable exception of Rouen. The groin vaults show great skill on the part of the builders. There are cushion capitals, which became popular in England sooner than in Normandy. In the north aisle of the church is a black marble font of *c.* 1160 which was imported from Flanders. The *Hospital of St Cross* was founded in 1136.

A mile and a half north of Winchester is the church of *St Swithun*, **Headbourne Worthy** with an Anglo-Saxon Crucifixion group, now mutilated. The former priory church of **Christchurch**, begun in 1099, has

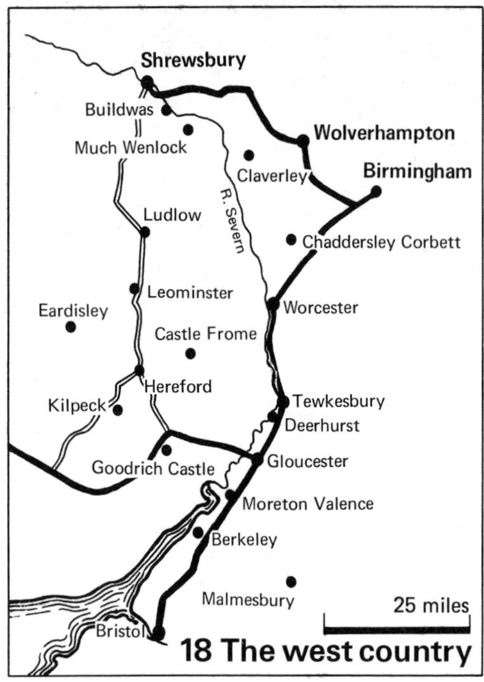

18 The west country

kept its Norman nave. The interlacing blind arcades on the exterior walls of the north transept once ran around the entire church. The turret of the north transept is also Norman. Within the castle walls is a ruined mid-12th-century mansion.

St Mary's at **Breamore**, eight miles south of Salisbury, is an unusually complete survival of a large Anglo-Saxon church, consisting of nave, low central tower, side-chapels and chancel. It was built in the last half of the 10th century. Over the south door of the nave, and now inside a 12th-century porch, is a late Saxon Crucifixion.

Further around the coast, past Dorchester, is the church of **Fordington** with a 12th-century Scandinavian-influenced tympanum. Continuing around the coast into Devon we come to **Bishopsteignton**, which is four miles north of Teignmouth. Its Romanesque tympanum, with an Adoration of the Magi, is very stylized and has a certain 'barbarous' quality. The decoration of the font has been much re-worked. The font of *St Mary's* **Luppitt**, is similarly 'barbarous'.

At **Glastonbury** in Somerset are the picturesque ruins of the abbey of *St Peter and St Paul*, which was founded in the 8th century. The only Norman remains are of the *Lady Chapel*, consecrated in 1186 – a splendid example of the luxuriance of late Romanesque in England.

Left-hand tympanum in the south porch of the abbey church of St Mary, Malmesbury. 1170–75.

Just east of Bath is **Bradford-on-Avon** with the important Anglo-Saxon church of *St Lawrence*. It was built in the late 7th century and remodelled a couple of centuries later, though it is now believed that part of the original building has survived. It is cruciform in plan and very lofty. The decorations on the exterior walls, which include blank arcading, date from the 10th century. Built into the east wall of the nave inside, and high above the chancel arch, are two angels, also of the 10th century. They show Byzantine influence which came to Anglo-Saxon England via Ottonian Germany.

St John, **Devizes** has an impressive 12th-century Norman chancel with elaborate decorations. Over the crossing is a mighty tower with a round stair turret. *St Mary* has a chancel of about the same date. The church of *St Peter* at **Manningford Bruce** is a completely preserved small early Norman building, well-restored in the 19th century.

In the south transept of the *Cathedral* of **Bristol** is a carved stone slab (incomplete) of the mid-11th century, depicting Christ's Descent into Limbo. It is a work of great artistic merit. The splendid chapter-house of the cathedral is an excellent example of late Romanesque and of the English taste for linear design. The walls are decorated with blind arcading surmounted by interlace with zig-zag and continuous trellis work in the lunettes above.

St Mary's at **Malmesbury** is the small part that remains of the abbey church, built in the 12th century. The nave arches are pointed, as in Burgundian churches, and rest on squat round piers. The elaborately worked south porch is unique in England and resembles the churches of the south of France like Moissac or Souillac, particularly in the use of the side walls of the porch for sculpture. The use of continuous mouldings for the doors and the large rosettes, however, are typical of the work of this part of England. Within the porch are two huge tympana with seated Apostles, a flying angel and a smaller tympanum with a Christ in Majesty. Stylistically these figures resemble the Autun sculptures. The ensemble dates from the second half of the 12th century.

Berkeley *Castle*, which was begun in 1155, is perfectly preserved. *St Stephen* at **Moreton Valence** has an early 12th-century tympanum with a St Michael and the Dragon relief. **Gloucester** *Cathedral* was begun in about 1089. The nave is Norman, except for the vaulting which is 13th century. Particularly striking are the exaggerated cylindrical columns which are a feature of Norman churches in the west of England. The huge crypt extends beneath the entire east end of the church. It has an apse, ambulatory and radiating chapels, thus repeating the eastern arrangement of the cathedral above it. Large sections of the chapter-house are Romanesque, with blind arcading.

This part of the country is particularly rich in early mediaeval monuments. North of Gloucester at **Deerhurst** is the Anglo-Saxon church of *St Mary*. It was built some time between 600 and 800, with later alterations. It has interesting windows set in the high blank west wall of the interior. The font is the best-preserved Anglo-Saxon example in existence. On the outside of one of the walls of the ruined apse is a carved angel-panel. *Odda's Chapel* (second half of 11th century) is incorporated into a later mediaeval house. It was restored in the 19th century.

Tewkesbury *Abbey* was begun in the last years of the 11th century. Its plan and nave elevation, with colossal round columns, resemble Gloucester. The crossing tower was built in the second half of the 12th century. The west front has been much altered, but the dominating theme of the recessed arches, extending practically the full height of the façade, is Romanesque.

Worcester *Cathedral*, founded in 1084, was transformed into a Gothic building in the 13th–15th centuries. However the transepts and great crypt (which resembles Winchester and Gloucester) are Norman, as is the circular chapter-house, the first to be constructed around a central column. The church of **Chaddersley Corbett** has a 12th-century font featuring Scandinavian-type dragons.

At *All Saints*, **Claverley**, near Wolverhampton, is one of the rare examples of English Romanesque fresco decoration. It consists of a frieze of fifteen horsemen, crude in execution and reminiscent of the Bayeux Tapestry. The church of the *Holy Trinity* at **Much Wenlock** is mostly Norman. The present *Priory* dates from 1080 and is now in well-kept ruins. Of particular interest

Font in the church of
Chaddersley Corbett. 12th century.

are the chapter-house with ornamental capitals and wall decoration more lavish than Bristol, and the octagonal lavatorium which contains fine relief carvings. Both buildings date from the late 12th century.

At **Buildwas**, to the south of Shrewsbury, are the immense remains of a Cistercian abbey, founded in 1157. The best preserved part is the church. The early castle walls of **Ludlow**, which were built between 1086 and 1095, are the most complete in England.

Only part of the abbey church of *St Peter and St Paul*, **Leominster** has survived. The most important feature of the church is its distinctive carvings, examples of a regional school of sculpture which made a brief appearance in Herefordshire towards the middle of the 12th century.

More examples of this sculpture may be seen at *St Mary Magdalene*, **Eardisley** and *St Michael*, **Castle Frome** which have wonderful carved fonts, both the work of one man.

The nave at **Hereford** *Cathedral* has the large round piers which we have already found at Gloucester and Tewkesbury. They are characteristic of the West Country. Perhaps it was because the Anglo-Saxon Church remained in a strong position here and the traditional links with Carolingian and Ottonian Germany may not have been severed. Further evidence of the continuation of contact is the chapel at Hereford (now destroyed) built after the style of Aachen. The cathedral has a typical Anglo-Saxon square apse (1115).

St Mary and St David, **Kilpeck**, is an excellently preserved 12th-century late Romanesque church which has suffered few alterations. Its plan and method of construction show a number of Anglo-Saxon features. The glory of the church is the rich sculptural decoration, the best surviving work of the 'school' referred to above, and the best illustration of the variety of influences – Celtic, Scandinavian, and western French – which formed it. Around the top of the church there runs a corbel table with imaginatively and vigorously

Sculpture above the south doorway of the church of St Mary and St David, Kilpeck. 12th century.

carved figured supports. More naturalistic and sculptural in conception are the Apostles on either side of the chancel arch.

At **Goodrich** are the ruins of a castle, which consists of a Norman keep of the second half of the 12th century, surrounded by late 13th-century walls. There is another Norman keep at **Ogmore** which is three miles south-west of Bridgend in Wales.

In and around Oxford there are a few churches with interesting sculpture. *St Matthew* at **Langford** has a handsome early Norman tower and a sun-dial. On the walls of the south porch are two large stone Crucifixions, of the 11th century. *St John the Baptist*, **Inglesham** has an unusual late Anglo-Saxon Virgin and Child with the Hand of God above. At the former abbey church of **Dorchester** is a cylindrical lead font with figured reliefs resembling the font at Brooklands. It dates from 1170–80.

The magnificent *Cathedral* of **Oxford** is mostly Norman. It was begun *c.* 1170–80. The Norman central tower is capped by a Gothic spire. Two features of particular interest are the carved capitals in the presbytery, nave

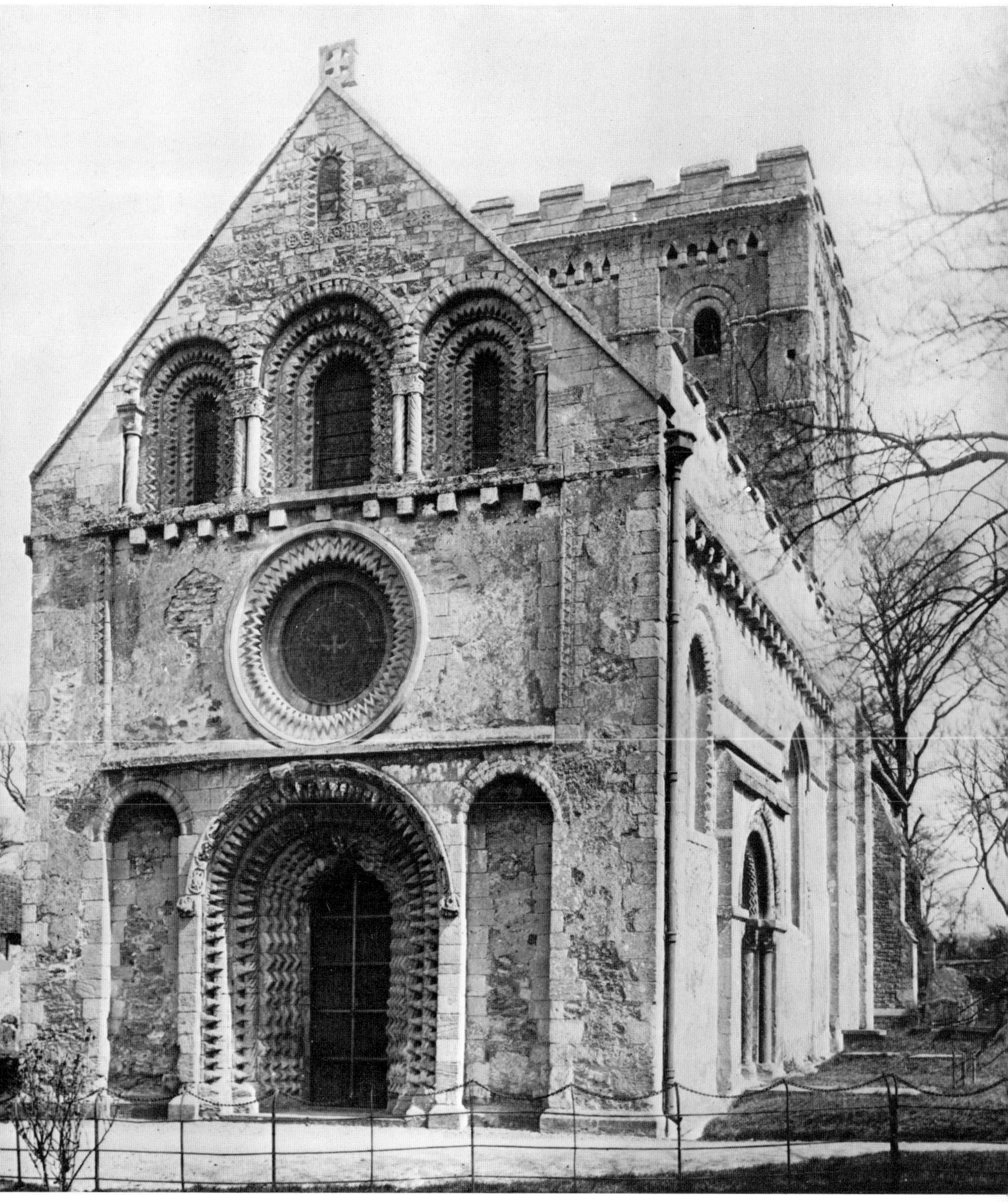

Church of St Mary the Virgin, Iffley, from the south-west. *c.* 1160–80.

and choir, where we find a number of revived Anglo-Saxon motifs, and the classically-proportioned columns in the choir and north transept. *St Peter's-in-the-East* (1140–*c.* 1150) has a fine south porch with two decorative motifs very characteristic of English late Romanesque, the zig-zag and beak-head. In the early Norman crypt are cushion capitals, some figured, some plain.

St Mary the Virgin (*c.* 1160–80) at **Iffley**, on the outskirts of Oxford, is a wonderful late Norman example, although it was extensively restored in the 19th century. The imposing façade is richly worked and shows beak-head and zig-zag ornament. The south porch, which has been accurately restored, is also decorated. Inside we find more rich decoration on the chancel and apsidal arches.

North of Oxford at **Hook Norton** is the church of *St Peter* with a Norman font, and north again at **Little Barrington** there is another church dedicated to *St Peter* with a Christ in Majesty tympanum of the second half of the 12th century. In the ruins of **Kenilworth** *Castle* there is a Norman keep begun in *c.* 1122.

All Saints, **Earl's Barton** features a 10th-century tower with the characteristic Anglo-Saxon strip work, i.e., slightly projecting strips of stone thought to be imitative of wood stripping. The entrance door to the church is Norman. Not far distant is **Barton Seagrave** with its impressive Norman parish church. It has an interesting tympanum.

Near Northampton is the church of *All Saints*, **Brixworth**, an Anglo-Saxon church of unusual size and outstanding interest. Most of the surviving structure dates from the second half of the 7th century. After the Danish raids of the early 9th century, the church was largely reconstructed towards the end of the 10th century. A tower was added over the west porch and an apsidal chancel was built.

At **Cambridge** is a round church of the *Holy Sepulchre*, freely restored in the last century. Around the shrine is an ambulatory with eight arches supported on eight piers.

A good deal of the Norman building has survived at **Ely** *Cathedral* which was begun in 1083 – in the nave, chancel, transepts and towers. There are alternating pier and compound pier supports in the nave, as at Durham, but, as they are set closer together, the effect is more decorative. The timber roof was repainted in the 19th century. On the south side of the church are richly decorated portals of *c.* 1140 which originally led to the cloister (now destroyed). Continental influences are very much apparent in the carvings of the *Prior's Portal.* The projecting lion is reminiscent of north Italian sculpture, while the tympanum relief of Christ in a mandorla flanked by two angels appears to derive from Burgundy. The *Monk's Portal*, on the other hand, is more English in feeling.

At **Bury St Edmunds** are the ruins of one of the largest Benedictine monasteries in England. The most impressive Norman feature is the gate tower, built between 1120 and 1150. *St Nicholas*, **Ipswich**, has a St Michael

Tower of All Saints, Earl's Barton. 10th century.

Exterior and interior of the church of the Holy Sepulchre, Cambridge, *c.* 1130.

and the Dragon tympanum of *c.* 1100. In *St Peter's* there is a 12th-century font decorated with reliefs of lions.

St Botolph's Priory (*c.* 1100) **Colchester** is now in a ruined state. Brick was used from the Roman town which preceded modern Colchester. The recessed entrance door, though partly destroyed, is yet impressive. The castle, which was built on a former Roman temple, is now a museum. The keep is a Norman construction of *c.* 1085 and resembles the White Tower, London.

North-east of Ipswich, on the coast, is **Orford** *Castle* built by Henry II between 1165 and 1173. Only the keep survives. **Framlingham** *Castle* (1190–1200) has an early and complete example of the high curtain wall with towers type of defence system. On Castle Hill in **Thetford** is the highest surviving motte in England. This, with its bailey, was demolished in 1173.

Norwich *Cathedral*, begun in 1096, is a homogeneous Norman building with the exception of the Gothic east chapel, chancel clerestory and nave vaulting. Its plan is based on Norman prototypes and also the great church at Cluny. However, it differed from these in the lengthening of the nave, a characteristic tendency in English mediaeval building. The mid-12th-century crossing tower is highly decorated, reflecting the taste of the time for rich surface ornamentation. This same taste may be seen in the arcades of the interior.

At **Castle Acre** are the ruins of a motte and bailey fortress built in the 11th century. Also in ruins is the *Cluniac priory* founded in *c.* 1090. The richly decorated mid-12th-century façade is very impressive. **Castle Rising** (*c.* 1150) is one of the last in the long line of rectangular fortresses which were replaced by centrally-planned constructions. It is very well preserved. Within the keep is a late Romanesque church. The castle stands upon some of the largest earth-works in England. The church of *St Martin*, **Fincham**, has an interesting Norman font.

The façade of the *Cathedral* of **Peterborough**, originally a Benedictine abbey church, is Gothic. The nave inside, however, is a wonderful example of mature Romanesque. Alternating cylindrical and octagonal piers carry elaborately moulded arches with soffit rolls. The double arches of the galleries are decorated with zig-zags, and above these is a clerestory wall passage with triple arches. The total effect is of rhythmical movement which quickens as the eye moves upward. The original wooden ceiling has survived with its paintings (carefully restored) dating back to *c.* 1220.

West of Peterborough is **Castor** and the church of *St Kyneburga*, dedicated in *c.* 1124. It has a magnificent, elaborately worked crossing tower. Inside the church are lively figured cushion capitals and a very fine example of Anglo-Saxon sculpture on the south wall of the choir. *All Saints*, **Wittering** is a well-preserved Anglo-Saxon church, with chancel and nave. The massive 10th-century chancel arch has roll-moulded soffits and zig-zag ornament.

Just south of Stamford is *St John the Baptist*, **Barnack**, with a west tower of the second half of the 10th century, decorated with birds, vines and

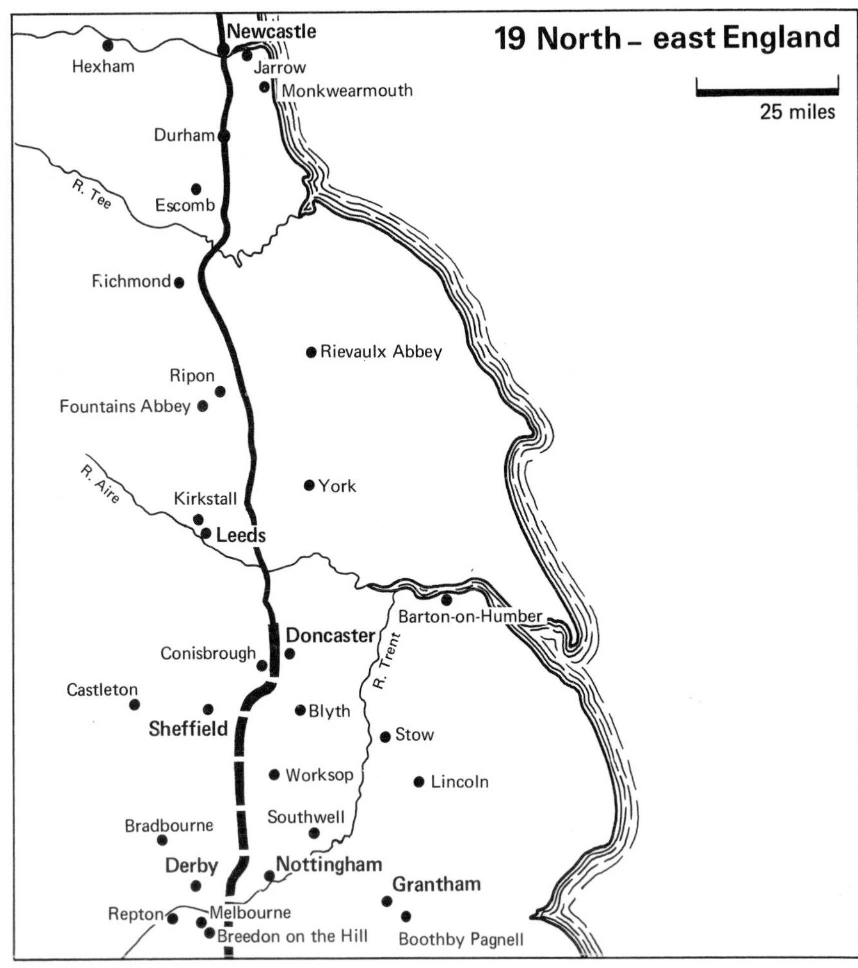

acanthus leaves. A little north of Stamford at **Oakham** is a mediaeval castle with a splendid 12th-century banqueting hall. At **Boothby Pagnell** near Grantham is a Norman house of *c.* 1200 in the grounds of Boothby Hall.

There are three interesting churches south-east of Derby: *St Mary and St Hardulph*, **Breedon-on-the-Hill**, which has many sculptural relics of the 8th century; *St Wystan*, **Repton** with an early to late Anglo-Saxon interior except for the nave; and the large and elaborate church of *St Michael and St Mary*, **Melbourne**, mostly 12th–13th centuries. It is cruciform in plan and has a two-towered front flanking a portal of five orders. One very unusual feature is that the church has a narthex with a gallery, as in many central European buildings.

The church at **Bradbourne**, north of Derby, has a 12th-century portal with fine jamb carvings of writhing animals and human figures showing Scandinavian influence. Above the village of **Castleton** stands the ruined Norman keep of **Peveril** (1176) surrounded by the remains of a stone curtain wall of the 11th century.

North-east of Derby is **Southwell** *Minster* begun before 1114. The rectangular treatment of the apse was a new development of this period. The remaining Norman portions are the nave, transepts and crossing tower. The capitals on the piers in the crossing are decorated with scenes from the life of Christ. The tympanum, which is earlier than the church, about the third quarter of the 11th century, is now in the north transept. It has a St Michael and the Dragon (or Samson and the Lion) in Scandinavian style.

The Norman *Cathedral* of **Lincoln** was begun in 1072. Parts of this building survive at the west front, in the three doorways surmounted by a large scale frieze containing elaborate scenes from the Bible with finely chiselled figures. This magnificent work dates from *c.* 1140. The castle was built by William the Conqueror in 1068. There are the remains of a Norman gateway. Lincoln has two rare examples of 12th-century domestic architecture, the *Jew's House* and the *House of Aaron the Jew*, both traditionally associated with a famous Jewish money-lender of the city.

North of Lincoln at **Stow** is a late 10th-century church, cruciform in plan, with splendid crossing arches. **Worksop** *Priory* has an interesting late Norman nave of *c.* 1180, with alternately octagonal and round piers and elaborately worked arches. This may be contrasted with the stern simplicity of the early Norman nave of the priory church at **Blyth**. It was founded in 1087 and the nave design was derived from Ste-Trinité, Caen. The church is now much reduced in size. At **Conisbrough** there is a late 12th-century circular keep.

St Peter's at **Barton-on-Humber** is famous for its Anglo-Saxon part – the west annex and lower two stages of the axial tower. The treatment of the wall reveals the most authentic ensemble of Anglo-Saxon decorative motifs. There is pointed blank arcading, a double window with a pointed lintel, and another double window with a round arch and round central column.

At **Kirkstall**, near Leeds, are the ruins of a Cistercian monastery founded in the 12th century. In the 12th-century crypt of **York** *Minster* there are some fine late Romanesque carved capitals. The crypt also contains a Virgin and Child relief of the 11th or 12th century (its dating is much disputed). Byzantine influence has been seen here, probably deriving from the Near East via Germany. **Fountains** *Abbey* and **Rievaulx** *Abbey* are two more Cistercian ruins. **Richmond** *Castle* is one of the few surviving English castles to have kept its 11th-century walls. Equally rare are the remains of the original hall in the south corner.

St John at **Escomb**, a few miles north-west of Bishop Auckland, is the most perfect example of a 7th-century church in north England. It has suffered only minor alterations. An impressive tall, narrow chancel arch

Sculpture above the west portal,
Lincoln Cathedral. *c.* 1140.

divides the long nave from the small square chancel. High up on the south wall of the nave is an Anglo-Saxon sun-dial with a projecting animal's head.

Durham *Cathedral* is the foremost Norman monument of England and one of the masterpieces of the Romanesque period. It was founded in 1093 and the Norman work, which included the outer wall of the cloister and dependent buildings, was completed forty years later. Gothic alterations and additions mainly affected the east end. Durham was probably the first church in Europe designed from the outset to carry ribbed vaults. The chancel is much longer than in churches in Normandy. However the cathedral follows Jumièges in its three-storied nave elevation with alternating cylindrical and compound piers. Spiral mouldings and zig-zag ornament decorate the piers. The zig-zag motif also appears on the ribs of the vault and arches. The elegant narthex, completed in 1175, contains the tomb of the Venerable Bede, the historian of Saxon England. Interesting minor features of Durham are: the bronze knocker on the north-west door; the Prior's Portal (1104), and the damaged stone panels with scenes from the Resurrection dating from the third quarter of the 12th century.

The *Cathedral Library* has a remarkable collection of 7th-century Northumbrian art which includes the Easby Cross. Among works of art of a later date are a 10th-century stole and the 11th-century Carilef Bible.

South of the cathedral lies Durham *Castle*. The earliest surviving buildings date back to *c.* 1070. Elaborate decorative work of the late 12th century may be seen in the main entrance door to the lower hall and in the arcaded wall and windows of the Constable's Hall. In the castle chapel (1072) are crude figure-carved capitals, very rare for such an early date.

St Peter's at **Monkwearmouth** was founded by the great Northumbrian ecclesiastic, Benedict Biscop, and was consecrated in 674. This very early stone church was a wonder in its day. All that has remained of the original

building is the west porch and this was altered and heightened at later dates to become a tower. The porch contains the only extant Saxon vault above ground in England. The wall is decorated with beasts, now almost indecipherable. Another foundation of Benedict Biscop is *St Paul's*, **Jarrow** (685). Of this church there remains the present chancel, originally the nave. The lower part of the tower dates from *c.*800, the upper stage is much later. The Venerable Bede lived and died in Jarrow.

The 7th-century foundations and barrel-vaulted crypt of St Wilfrid's church at **Hexham** survive. St Wilfrid had been to Italy and the church was built under Roman influence. Contemporaries were amazed by its size and splendid fittings and decorations, remnants of which are preserved in the cathedral library. They believed that at Hexham they could see the glories and splendour of Rome.

Alnwick *Castle* was established in the 12th century. Part of the keep and curtain walls dating from this period still stand.

The *Abbey of Lindisfarne* on **Holy Island** off the Northumberland coast, was founded by monks from Iona in the 7th century and destroyed by Viking raiders. The existing ruins dated from the 11th century. We see the influence of Durham in the alternating cylindrical and compound piers of the nave.

Scotland

On either side of the Scottish border are the two famous carved crosses – the *Bewcastle Cross* in Cumberland and the *Ruthwell Cross* on the north side of Solway Firth just south of Dumfries. These standing crosses are of a purely native monumental type. The carvings which date from the second half of the 8th century, are superior to any contemporary Continental work.* They follow on the great Northumbrian cultural revival, a period of intense artistic and building activity. This too was the time of the victory of Rome over Ireland at the Synod of Whitby. The inspiration is Mediterranean, which is not surprising when one remembers the close contacts maintained with that distant region. Bishop Hadrian, an African skilled in Greek and Latin, and Bishop Theodore of Tarsus, in Asia Minor, were sent to Britain in the middle of the 7th century and there led a rejuvenation of the church. Benedict Biscop had visited Rome frequently and had also brought craftsmen from Gaul. Because of these contacts it has been argued that the crosses are the work of skilled sculptors imported from the Near East. However, in view of the Irish nature of the subject matter, which concentrates on asceticism and the native interpretation of Mediterranean decorative motifs, the argument in favour of local craftsmen cannot be dismissed.

Jedburgh *Abbey* in Roxburghshire was founded in 1138 and work began soon after on the church. The magnificent recessed west doorway is a fine

Opposite
Interior of Durham Cathedral, showing the south aisle and nave. Founded in 1093.

* At first the disposition of scholars was to date the crosses to the 12th century, thus relating them to the full development of Romanesque art.

example of late Romanesque geometric carving. The door on the south transept has been heavily restored. The interior elevation of the choir is unusual as the cylindrical pier is carried up through the main arcade to support the triforium arch.

Kelso *Abbey*, which must have been the most splendid Romanesque building in Scotland, now lies in ruins. Fragments of the west crossing, the transepts and two bays of the west nave remain from this 12th-century foundation. On the north face of the west transept is a gable with criss-cross trellis work. At **Dalmeny**, near Edinburgh, is a well-preserved mid-12th-century church, consisting of a western tower, oblong nave and square chancel. There is fine decorative work, especially on the south portal of the nave and interior arches.

Dunfermline *Abbey* was founded in 1074 by monks from Canterbury. The abbey buildings are in ruins and the church, begun in 1128, is only a fragment of the original. Only the nave still stands, deprived of its east bay. The design is monumental and the effect stern and subdued. The cylindrical piers are enriched with zig-zag or spiral fluting, as at Durham. However, unlike Durham, there is no vertical articulation and the emphasis is horizontal.

Beside the *Cathedral* of **St Andrew's** is the church and tower of *St Rule* dating from shortly before the mid-12th century – all now in ruins. The construction is massive and the proportions are very narrow. Just north of St Andrew's at **Leuchars** is a church with a magnificent Romanesque chancel and apse of the 12th century. The round, beautifully decorated tower shows strong Lombardic influence.

Restenneth *Priory*, near Forfar in Angus, is built on a site sometimes associated with the early history of the Scottish Church. The most striking feature of this church is the tall square tower capped by a spire, which includes work of several different periods. It is possible that the lower stages date from the 8th century.

The influence of Durham penetrated up to **Kirkwall** *Cathedral* in the Orkneys, evident in the treatment of the nave piers. The church was founded in 1137, and though it underwent many alterations, the transepts and parts of the nave and choir date from this earliest period of construction.

Ireland

Two important facts should be kept in mind when discussing Irish art. The first is that Roman soldiers never set foot there; the second, that the island remained untouched by the Great Migrations until the 9th century. Thus, largely unaffected by classical art and comparatively undisturbed, Ireland was able to develop to its ultimate point of refinement her prehistoric culture. There were some Mediterranean influences, particularly from Coptic Egypt, but these should not be exaggerated. We have seen how Celtic art, allied to Anglo-Saxon, had a decisive influence over the evolution of European culture in the Middle Ages. Its greatest achievement lay in the illumination of manuscripts. Church building, on the other hand, was humble and remained so.

The earliest examples of Irish architecture are the undatable stone huts or 'clochans' inhabited by hermits and usually located in the most inhospitable spots. These reveal the intensity of Irish religious zeal, inspired by the austerity of the Coptic monks who withdrew into the solitude of the Egyptian desert, and by the similar excesses of Syrian monks. The 'desert' in Ireland was found in lonely islands, in the bogs and other remote places. The hermits would not touch meat, milk or butter and lived on wild herbs, green vegetables, dry cereals and water. Dozens of communities of such cells with small oratories and tiny churches were established.

The simplicity and holiness of these solitary men of God, like that of St Francis, became legendary. When St Molus died it was said that the birds wept, as he had never harmed a single one of them. And of St Columba it was written that a bear let him share his cave and did his bidding.

Great monasteries of a more conventional type were established at Bangor, Armagh, Clonmacnoise, which, like all the foundations in Northumbria and on the Continent, were subsequently destroyed. Irish builders were conservative. The persistence of the small rectangular church, with merely a chancel added in the 11th century, when the Rhineland cathedrals were built, gives a misleading appearance of antiquity to Irish churches.

Even the Romanesque churches of Ireland are typically small and rectangular, with square chancels, small windows and single-storied interiors. The round apse is not used, nor are interior columns. There was some influence from the Continent, most obvious in King Cormac's Chapel at Cashel. The heavily sculptured doorways of the 12th century were also the result of closer contacts with Europe, but both design and decorative motifs are predominantly Celtic.

Of great fame as a specialized form of religious art are the large sculptured crosses found in both Ireland and England. The tradition of raising crosses is described by Bede: 'The place is shown to this day, where Oswald, being about to engage (in battle), erected the sign of the holy cross . . .'

The custom of erecting large stone crosses near the entrance to churches to stand like sentinels warding off evil spirits may well have its origin in paganism. The earliest crosses in Ireland are contemporary with Ruthwell and Bewcastle. The practice continued here until the 12th century, long after it had fallen into disuse in England. By this time the crosses were covered in biblical reliefs and their function was more didactic than commemorative or superstitious.

Another type peculiar to Ireland was the detached Round Tower. It resembles the *campanile* of Ravenna, though if this was the prototype, the means by which it was transmitted has yet to be discovered. These towers had a dual purpose, as a bell-tower and as a refuge against Viking marauders.

The entrance was high above the ground. The earliest tower dates from the 10th century, the latest from the 12th.

In the library of *Trinity College*, **Dublin** are the Book of Kells (8th century) and the Book of Durrow (7th century), wonderful examples of Anglo-Celtic manuscript illumination. The *National Museum* is rich in Celtic art, and contains the Ardagh Chalice (750) and the Tara Brooch (700–50), both illustrating very well the intricate interlace so characteristic of this style.

South-west of the cathedral of **Kildare** is a fine *Round Tower* (1061) with a Romanesque porch. Nearby are the remains of a tall granite cross.

Glendalough lies in a narrow valley of the Wicklow mountains. St Kevin, a contemporary of St Columba, founded a hermitage near the upper lake towards the end of the 6th century. There are two fragments which probably represent this original settlement, *St Kevin's Cell* and a small cave known as *St Kevin's Bed*. The saint attracted disciples, and a monastery was founded, which in the following centuries spread along the valley. Glendalough became a great pilgrimage centre claiming for itself the title of 'Rome of the West'.

The best preserved remains are the group of buildings around the old 12th-century *Cathedral*, now a ruin. In the north wall are the remains of a late Romanesque doorway. Nearby is a *Round Tower*, of the 10th–11th centuries, one of the first of its kind in Ireland. The so-called *Priest's House* dates from *c.* 1170; the *Lady Church* is a much older foundation, but it has a Romanesque chancel and north door. The *Oratory of St Kevin* is the only church here to have survived intact. It is a stone-roofed fortress-like structure of the 10th or 11th century, and its modest dimensions and simplicity illustrate the conservatism of Irish church building. Scattered elsewhere in the valley are the ruins of small churches: *St Saviour's Priory* with an interesting doorway of *c.* 1162, *St Ciaran* and *Reefert*.

Fragments of the church and cloister are all that we find today of the Cistercian abbey at **Baltinglass**. In layout it was typically Cistercian, but the ornament shows Irish motifs. At **Moone**, near Ballitore is an important *Tall Cross* of the 8th or 9th century. It was discovered buried in the ground in the last century and was re-erected. The proportions are unusually narrow. The sculptured reliefs depict subjects from the Old and New Testament. One interesting feature is that the iconography of the crucifixion follows a Near Eastern prototype, not western European.

Three miles north-west of Carlow at **Killeshin** are the remains of a 12th-century church with a very fine triangular-headed west door decorated with animal sculpture reminiscent of the art of the Steppes. Just out of Callan is the *Tall Cross* of **Killamery** (8th century). In contrast with later crosses, abstract ornament predominates over figured scenes. To the south-east at **Jerpoint** are the most interesting of the Cistercian remains in Ireland. And a little further south at **Kililispeen** are two excellent *Crosses* and the base of a third.

One of the best preserved buildings of the time is the *Chapel of King*

Opposite
Cross of the Scriptures, Clonmacnoise. 10th century.

Cormac, **Cashel**, accurately dated to 1134. It was founded by the prince-bishop Cormac MacCarthy, king of Desmond. It is believed that the unusual twin towers and blank arcading show Rhineland influence. The ribbed vaults could derive from France and on the chancel arch is a sort of zig-zag motif reminiscent of England. Such foreign influences would not be difficult to establish through the close connection Irish monasteries maintained with their sister houses in Europe. But the massive stone roof of the nave is wholly Irish. The south and north doorways have carved tympana. The north doorway, which was the main entrance, now opens straight onto the wall of the 13th-century *Cathedral*. On the north transept of the cathedral is a *Round Tower* of the early 10th century. There is also a *Tall Cross* of *c*. 1150.

At **Ardmore** is a late *Round Tower*, perhaps the finest in Ireland. The west front of the ruins of the former *Cathedral* is decorated with reliefs of figures in arcades, which is unusual.

The most spectacular of existing architecture dating from pre-Romanesque times is **Skellig Michael** off the Kerry coast, which consists of six little beehive cells of unmortared stone, two tiny oratories and a miniature church, all perched on a lonely rock ledge 500 feet above the sea. This monastery was reached by stone stairs carved in the face of the rock.

North of Ballyferriter is the small oratory of **Gallarus** (9th–10th century). There are remains of an early monastery at **Illauntannig** off the Kerry coast, and of another early monastery on **Scattery Island** which also has a *Round Tower*.

An incomplete *Round Tower* and a ruined church mark the site of **Disert Aengus**, the hermitage of the monk Aonghus. It lies a little to the north-west of Croom in Co. Limerick. At **Disert O Dea** in Co. Clare there was another hermitage. Today we find a fine 12th-century *Tall Cross*. More *Tall Crosses* can be seen at **Kilfenora** which is not far to the north-west. The most interesting of the four is in the graveyard.

On **Inishmore**, one of the Aran Islands, is the tiny *Teampull Benen*, a typical example of early Irish architecture. It is only 11 feet long and 7 feet wide.

On the shores of Lough Derg is **Killaloe**. *St Flannan's Cathedral* has a rich Romanesque doorway, a survival from an earlier church. Nearby is a *Tall Cross* of the 12th century. **Holy Island**, which is in the Lough, has some interesting early monastic remains, as well as a *Round Tower*, a *Tall Cross*, and Romanesque doorways in the rebuilt churches of *St Caimín* and *St Brigid*.

At **Roscrea**, Tipperary, are the ruins of *St Cronan's Abbey*. The west door of the old church now forms the entrance to the grounds of a modern Protestant church. The most attractively situated Romanesque church in Ireland is **Mona Incha**, near Roscrea. Its important artistic feature is a pair of sculptured doorways. The church itself is very tiny.

The *Cathedral* of **Clonfert** in Galway was built in the 10th century. There have been a number of alterations since, the most important being the addition

Opposite
Round Tower, Glendalough. 10th–11th centuries.

of a porch in the 12th century. Here we find the finest Romanesque sculpture in Ireland. The sides and arches of the doorway and a tall gable over it are a mass of highly varied and most interesting carved decoration. A score of abstract designs have been used and they include interlace patterns similar to those found on 7th-century manuscripts. There are animal heads of great variety and a dozen human heads of varied expression. The work shows a mixture of Irish and Continental features.

A little way to the north-east in **Clonmacnoise** are three 12th-century churches. The *Nun's Church* was completed in 1167. The west doorway and chancel arch were re-erected in the last century. The *Cathedral* has kept fragments of a fine Romanesque west portal. *St Finghin's* has a strong round tower ingeniously growing out of its side. There are also stone crosses, the finest being the *Cross of the Scriptures* (10th century). The Last Judgement scene, though common enough in Ireland, is most unusual in comparison with the normal European iconography. Christ looks like the Egyptian god Osiris. The iconography of the crucifixion is also Near Eastern.

At **Rahan** is a pre-Romanesque church with a lovely Romanesque west doorway. The Protestant parish church has a stone-roofed chancel, probably of *c.* 1100. There is an unusual chancel arch, carved capitals, and a very rare round window heavily sculptured. Some authorities have sought the origin of the decorative motifs here in Armenian churches of the 7th century and would date the structure accordingly.

The 19th-century Protestant *Cathedral* of **Tuam** incorporates the barrel-vaulted chancel of a small cathedral of *c.* 1170–80. The six order arch and triple east window are elaborately enriched. In the centre of the town is a *Market Cross*, assembled from scattered pieces.

On the island of **Duvillaun** off the coast of Mayo are the remains of a small, ancient hermit settlement. More significant and more accessible is the early monastery of **Inishmurray** on an island of the same name, this time off the coast of Sligo. Here a small area of less than an acre is surrounded by a thick wall enclosing several small 'clochan' cells and a restored oratory.

The *Round Tower* of **Antrim** in the north of Ireland survives almost complete. At **Monasterboice** near Drogheda in Co. Meath there is another example. There are also some fine *Tall Crosses* in the churchyard. The best known of these is the *Cross of Muiredach* which is over seventeen feet high. It is dated at about 920. At one time, scholars claimed that the superb craftmanship it displays was utterly impossible in the 10th century and they attributed the work to the following century. As well as interlacing patterns and cable patterns there are biblical scenes, including an Irish-type Last Judgement.

Just south of Monasterboice are the fragmentary remains of **Mellifont** *Abbey*, the first Cistercian monastery in Ireland. At **Kells**, once the site of an important monastery, there are five 10th-century *Tall Crosses*, a *Round Tower*, and *St Columb's House*, which has a typical stone roof built layer upon layer until the walls meet.

Opposite
West porch of the Cathedral of Clonfert. 12th century.

14 Scandinavia

Christianity came to Scandinavia in the 10th and 11th centuries. The first churches were of wood and their design was based on Viking pagan temples. The most famous of these are the stave churches of Norway of which a few later examples have survived. The introduction of Romanesque brought masonry building. Romanesque in Scandinavia reflects the inspiration of Anglo-Saxon and Norman England and Germany. The former influences were predominant in the west and north of Norway and in parts of Sweden, the latter in Denmark. However the heavy walls, steep roofs and simple forms which the rigorous climate dictated, gave to Scandinavian churches their particular character.

Murals in churches also show English and German connections, apart from Gotland, the centre of trade with Novgorod in Russia, where painting is Byzantine rather than Romanesque. Foreign elements are present in sculptural decoration, but quite a few Viking motifs also survived. Most Viking art is preserved in museums but there are a few examples to be seen *in situ*.

Denmark

In Jutland we come first to **Ribe** with its *Cathedral*, begun *c.*1130. The three-storied interior design resembles the churches of Cologne. There are echoes of old pagan art on the portal carvings. South of Vejle at **Skibet** is a church with a mid-12th-century fresco of horsemen, one of the masterpieces of Romanesque painting anywhere.

The village of **Jelling** is very close to Vejle. It was once the seat of the Viking kings who ruled Jutland, and two round burial mounds have survived. In the church-yard are two famous rune stones, the larger of which is decorated with a relief of Christ, an entwined serpent and dragon, and other Viking ornamentation. It was erected by Harald Bluetooth in 988. Much of the

Fresco of horsemen, Church of Skibet. 12th century.

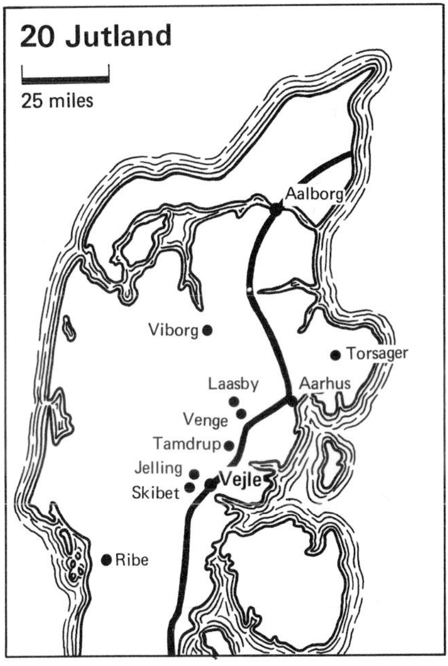

Romanesque church has been preserved. In the chancel are interesting 12th-century frescoes (restored). There are some more frescoes of *c.* 1125 in the 12th-century church of **Tamdrup**, a little to the north-west of Horsens. They are rather stiff and archaic.

The *Vor Frue Kirke*, **Aarhus**, was begun *c.* 1100. There were later extensions and alterations. Under the chancel is a remarkable Romanesque crypt, opened up when the church was restored in 1957. There is a good collection of Viking art in the *City Museum*.

South-west of Aarhus at **Venge** is a Benedictine church of 1125. English inspiration is obvious – the church might even have been built by an English mason. West of Aarhus at **Laasby** is an early 12th-century 'lion' font, many examples of which still survive in Jutland.

Brick building was introduced into Denmark in the second half of the 12th century. At **Torsager** there is a round brick church. Round churches were a notable feature of Danish Romanesque. The granite *Cathedral* of **Viborg** follows the general lines of Lund, which is now in Sweden. Remnants of the earlier Romanesque church survive in the nave of the late Gothic *Cathedral* of **Aalborg**.

Kalundborg in Zealand has the most monumental example of the Danish round church. The plan is a Greek cross and there are four octagonal towers and a central square tower. The church was rebuilt in the 14th and 19th centuries. At **Trelleborg** there are Viking camps and houses (reconstructed), dating from *c.* 1000.

At **Fjennesley**, near Sorø, is a church of *c.* 1120–30. Twin towers were added at the end of the 12th century. Inside there are 12th-century frescoes. The figures are rather stiff and stylized. **Bjernede** has a round church of *c.* 1150. At **Sorø** is the very beautiful late Romanesque church of a Cistercian monastery founded in *c.* 1160. It is built of brick.

The church of *St Bendt*, **Ringsted** is perhaps the oldest brick church in Denmark. It was founded in *c.* 1082, and rebuilt a century later. The choir, apse and transepts of the Romanesque structure still stand, and they show north Italian influences. The rest of the church is Gothic.

Store Heddinge has an octagonal centrally-planned church of *c.* 1200, with later rebuilding. The *National Museum*, **Copenhagen**, has a rich collection of pre-Christian and mediaeval Danish art. There is a fine selection of rune stones. Also of interest are two 'lion' fonts from Jutland, a wooden crucifix of *c.* 1050, and the 'Golden' Altar of Odder.

The *Cathedral* of **Roskilde** was begun in 1170–80 in the Romanesque style and finished in the 14th century in the Gothic style. The church of *Tveje Merløse*, **Holbaek**, was built in the early 12th century. The frescoes date from *c.* 1200.

On the island of **Bornholm** there are many examples of mediaeval round churches. The most characteristic are at **Ny, Nylar, St Olaf** and **Østerlars**. The ancient church of **Aakirkeby** has a massive tower which was obviously used for defence. Inside the church is a remarkable granite font of *c.* 1170 with scenes from the life of Christ, and runic explanations.

Sweden

Cathedral of Lund from the north. Consecrated 1146.

The present *Cathedral* of **Lund** is a 12th-century enlargement of an earlier building of *c.* 1080. Its architect was Donatus, presumably a Lombard. Its architecture and decoration have many of the features which appear in

Lombard and Rhineland building, e.g., the arcaded gallery around the main apse. The church has a remarkable Lombard-style crypt and the west doorway, with a projecting outer order on columns, is of Italian origin.

The *Cathedral* of **Dalby** dates from *c.* 1060. The west-work was built in the third decade of the 12th century. In the churches of **Finja** and **Vinslöv** there are interesting 12th-century frescoes.

Visby *Cathedral* on the island of **Gotland** was founded in the 12th century and rebuilt and dedicated in the early 13th century. The influence of the German church of Schwarzheindorf is apparent in the church of the *Holy Spirit*. In *Visby Museum* are some fine examples of Viking art. At **Lojsta** is a Viking *palace* rebuilt on its original foundations.

Back on the mainland at **Vreta** is a little basilican church begun after 1100. Later in the century a small royal burial chapel and a new cruciform east end was built. **Stockholm** *Museum* contains an important collection of Viking art.

At **Sigtuna** on Lake Mälar are the ruins of two Romanesque churches. The earlier, *St Peter's*, was in the Anglo-Saxon tradition. Norman influences were dominant in the church of *St Olaf* (*c.* 1100–34). The former *Cathedral of* **Gamla Uppsala** was built on the site of a pagan wooden temple in the first half of the 12th century. This was burnt down in 1245 and rebuilt. Only the choir still stands.

At **Sädra Röda** is a barn-like nave and chancel church of *c.* 1300, with solid log walls. The church of **Husaby** (*c.* 1150) has a Saxon-influenced façade, very massive and sombre-looking.

Norway

The 12th-century *Cathedral* of **Oslo** is now in ruins. In the *Universitets Oldsaksamling* is the *Osberg Ship-Tomb*, discovered in 1904. It dates from the mid-9th century. This great find has greatly enriched our knowledge of Norse art.

North of Oslo at **Hamar** are the ruins of the *Cathedral* (begun in 1152). It was built under the influence of Hirsau. The *Cathedral* of **Trondheim**, in the far north of Norway, began as a small church built over the tomb of St Olaf in the latter part of the 11th century. It became a cathedral in the mid-12th century, from which period dates the Romanesque transept. The nave is Gothic. In the *Trondheim Museum* is the re-erected *Holtålen* church (*c.* 1050–1100). It is the oldest extant example of a nave and chancel wooden church.

The 12th-century wooden church of **Urnes** has incorporated the beautiful door and façade carvings of the 11th-century structure into the north side. At **Borgund** is the oldest surviving example of a stave church. It dates to *c.* 1150. *St Mary's*, **Bergen** has the most elaborate Romanesque doorway in Norway. The *Cathedral* of **Stavanger**, which is very well preserved, resembles an Anglo-Norman aisled church.

Index

References in italics are to maps and illustrations

Index

Index

Index

Index